# Artificial Consciousness

# Artificial Consciousness

Edited by

Antonio Chella and Riccardo Manzotti

imprint-academic.com

Published in the UK by
Imprint Academic, PO Box 200, Exeter EX5 5YX, UK

Published in the USA by
Imprint Academic, Philosophy Documentation Center
PO Box 7147, Charlottesville, VA 22906-7147, USA

ISBN 9781845400705

A CIP catalogue record for this book is available from the
British Library and US Library of Congress

# Contents

**Part III: Artificial and Natural Consciousness**

# Foreword

## Do Engineers Dream of Conscious Robots?

*Quam multa fieri non posse, priusquam sint facta, judicantur!*
(How many things, that were held to be impossible,
have been accomplished!)
*Plinius the Elder, 70 CE.*

A slight change in the title of Phil K. Dick's famous novel might help us in understanding the dream pursued by some engineers. Our answer to such a question is yes. As far as we know, natural selection developed conscious agents — human beings for sure, almost certainly most mammals, perhaps other species. Engineers have always tried to mimic nature: helicopters and aeroplanes for mimicking birds, steam engines for challenging the power of horses, computers for imitating the logical capability of humans, submarines to ape fishes. Can engineers succeed in replicating what seems to be one of the most intimate and private features of human beings, namely consciousness?

At the beginning of the twenty-first century, some engineers are dreaming of conscious robots, not just intelligent robots. For the first time in the history of engineering, a term so vague as consciousness is taken into consideration in the technical world (Steels, 1995; Schlagel, 1999; Jennings, 2000; Aleksander, 2001; Buttazzo, 2001; Holland, 2003). What do they mean exactly by 'conscious robots', 'artificial consciousness' or 'machine consciousness'? This book[1] gathers

[1]    This book is possible thanks to the precious support offered by the 'Accademia di Studi Mediterranei', lovingly and passionately directed by Prof. Assunta Gallo Afflitto, in Agrigento that supported the 1st International Conference on Artificial Consciousness, November, 2005. The

state of the art work of researchers engaged worldwide in the seemingly oxymoronic field of artificial consciousness. It follows up the previous effort made by Owen Holland four years ago (Holland, 2003).

In English we have two related terms: consciousness and conscience. The former refers to phenomenal experience. The latter refers to ethical and moral issues. Engineers don't talk about conscience: they talk about consciousness. Some authors held that if nature has been capable of producing conscious beings, through natural selection, there is no reason why the same should not be done in artefacts, through design and craft.

The nature and mechanism of consciousness are still far from being understood. There is no consensus on what consciousness is and how it must be studied. This situation is at the same time an opportunity and a curse for the engineers engaged in such an endeavour. It is an opportunity because very often, in the history of engineering, engineers built artefacts even if they were unaware of the underlying scientific principles. It is a curse because engineers prefer to apply formalized and well-established techniques.

The former position is well expressed by Gerard Edelman and Giulio Tononi's words (Edelman and Tononi, 2000):

> To understand the mental we may have to invent further ways of looking at brains. We may even have to synthesize artefacts resembling brains connected to bodily functions in order fully to understand those processes. Although the day when we shall be able to create such conscious artefacts is far off we may have to make them before we deeply understand the processes of thought itself.

The latter position is succinctly expressed by Ron Arkin (Arkin, 1999), p. 427: 'Most roboticists are more than happy to leave these debates on consciousness to those with more philosophical leanings.' All those gathered in the present book think otherwise.

Although we are aware that there is no commonly accepted crystal clear definition of consciousness, we do not think that this lack ought to hinder the scientific research of consciousness. We agree with the standpoint adopted by Christof Koch (Koch, 2004), p. 12:

> Historically, significant scientific progress has commonly been achieved in the absence of formal definitions. For instance, the phenomenological laws of electrical current flow were formulated by Ohm , Ampère, and Volta well before the discovery of

support of Prof. Roberto Lagalla, president of the 'Polo Universitario della Provincia di Agrigento' is also greatly acknowledged.

the electron in 1892 by Thompson. For the time being, therefore, I adopt a working definition of consciousness and will see how far I can get with it.

Engineers are trained in a reductionist cultural environment. Consciousness seems unfit to such reductionist standpoint. Nevertheless consciousness beings are a fact. Current science developed an objectivistic ontology of nature that seems incapable of dealing with subjectivity. The recent upsurge of interest in the scientific study of consciousness has raised methodological and empirical problems. At the intersection between engineering and current scientific approaches to consciousness lies the seminal field of artificial consciousness. As Igor Aleksander puts the matter (Aleksander, 2000): 'This was the moment when the seemingly incongruous idea of an artificial consciousness came into being. Did the concept make sense?'

Artificial consciousness is apparently an oxymoron since the artificial is the domain of human artefacts, thus of objects, and the quintessential feature of consciousness is subjectivity. Subjects and objects are an uneasy match. Designing and implementing an artificial conscious machine appears an impossible task. However, it is possible that in the course of attempting it we shall develop new concepts and reformulate old categories.

It is worthwhile to stress that, since mid-eighties, in the field of engineering, the issue of consciousness has come out in many different contexts. The crisis of artificial intelligence, the new perception of artificial physical bodies, the relevant progress in brain sciences have shifted the attention of many researchers from the study of intelligent behaviour to the study of consciousness: how agents develop the capability of having experience, of being aware of what happens to them and around them.

The distinction between subjects and objects once seemed clear. Subjects have the capability of having experiences, of being aware of what happens to them and around them — that is, they are conscious. Objects are unconscious. But things are changing. As the novelist David Lodge wrote in one of his tales (Lodge, 2001), p. 36: 'Once upon a time nobody was interested in the problem of consciousness except a few philosophers. Now it's the biggest game in town.' In this cultural framework, engineers try to participate. Inside this group, Igor Aleksander was the first one in 1992 to mention the term 'artificial consciousness' in a scientific paper (Aleksander, 1992).

Even if the boundaries, methods and goals of this field are still rather unclear, even if we have not yet outlined measurement methods for the appearance of consciousness in artefacts, many researchers are trying to develop models of consciousness that can be implemented in machines.

Nevertheless, it seems that there is some kind of ontological mistake that thwarts any attempt to deal explicitly with consciousness. The aim of this book is to understand why it is so difficult to approach the problem of subjectivity from an engineering viewpoint and, then, to propose alternative frameworks that could cope with the design and implementation of a conscious subject. Any proposal for ontological revision must not remain a sterile metaphysical project but must be tested empirically. That is where engineers might provide a unique opportunity to advance our understanding of consciousness. Robotics is a field in which experiments might be carried out. If there were a theory of consciousness, which sets the conditions by which an object could let a subject emerge, such conditions could be replicated. Hitherto, there have been only a few sparse attempts to understand and propose an architecture capable of producing a conscious machine.

The book collects many different authors whose views and methods are rather different. A rule of thumb to compare them is based on their opinion about the nature of subjectivity. For a few of them subjectivity must be reduced to objective or functional processes. For a few others, subjectivity will require a conceptual change in our fundamental categories.

The book is organized in three parts: the race for artificial consciousness, design and implementation of an artificial machine, and artificial and natural consciousness.

In the first part the authors introduce the reader to the current situation of the field, highlighting the relation between artificial consciousness and previous approaches like artificial intelligence, cognitive science, neuroscience, and philosophy of mind.

**Vincenzo Tagliasco** introduces the reader to the undoubted roots of artificial consciousness, tracing its origins in first years of cybernetics and artificial intelligence. Sketching a brief history of the theme of 'artificial consciousness' in the scientific and technological panorama, he explores the relation between different cultural traditions in dealing with the issue of an artificial subject. Finally, he highlights the implicit legacy between this new field and other areas such as cinema and literature.

In the second chapter, **John Taylor** analyzes the principles on which machine consciousness should be based, as arising from crucial features of human consciousness. Employing present knowledge of attention as a control system, an engineering control model is developed in neural network terms to provide suitable control over the movement of attention. This is then extended, guided by notions of the inner or pre-reflective self of continental phenomenology, to the CODAM model of consciousness. This model regards the inner self as arising as the echo of attention movement. It is suggested that thereby consciousness is used to speed up attention processing, so providing consciousness with a powerful function.

The third author, **Tom Ziemke**, focuses on the link between embodiment and consciousness. Much research in embodied AI and cognitive science emphasizes the fact that robots, unlike purely computational models of cognition and consciousness, are 'embodied'. Contrary to the current majority opinion in machine consciousness research, he argues that the biological autonomy of living bodies is likely to be a necessary condition for many forms of self and consciousness. Combining the theory of autopoiesis with somatic theories of emotion, self and consciousness are placed in the context of homeostatic bioregulation of bodily activity in living organisms, and the implications for computational/robotic models of consciousness are discussed.

In the fourth chapter, **Igor Aleksander** and **Helen Morton** analyze whether synthetic phenomenology is a valid concept. In approaching consciousness from a computational point of view, the question of phenomenology is not often explicitly addressed. They review the use of phenomenology as a philosophical and a cognitive construct in order to have a meaningful transfer of the concept into the computational domain. Then they lay down some architectural ground rules that establish when phenomenology is addressed in an architecture and when it is not. They submit that 'depiction' is the key property of such architectures. Two architectures are discussed with respect to these rules: our 'kernel, axiomatic' structure and the widely quoted 'Global Workspace' scheme. The conclusion suggests that architectures with phenomenal properties clarify the way that phenomenal consciousness may be synthesised in a machine.

**Andrea Lavazza** deals with the phenomenological foundation of artificial consciousness, especially focusing on the notion of sense. 'Sense' is defined as an internal non-sensory experience of coherence (or rightness) and/or a feeling of affective resonance linked to the assessment of something, to an experience of fitting something, a strong experience of unity between the object and the subject. Despite the fact that sense might appear to be a vague concept, it is risky to deny its role. By modelling sense in terms of 'mind-content translation', a machine might be able to 'reproduce' sense inside.

The second part of the book, 'Design and implementation of an artificial machine' focuses on a series of possible architectures for machine consciousness.

**Salvatore Gaglio** begins by wondering whether human-level intelligence can be captured by a computable model, a theme analysed under different perspectives. After an historical introduction to the field of artificial intelligence (AI), the basic notions of computability are considered in connection with the two fundamental theses of symbolic AI: the physical symbol hypothesis and the knowledge representation hypothesis. The limits of the symbolic approach are discussed with reference to the grounding problem, which can be solved only by means of a subsymbolic device interacting with the outside world through sensors and actuators. But this is not enough, since in the case of vision, the construction of perceptions starting from the signals coming from the sensors in the interaction with the outside world requires an opportune reorganization and aggregation of information in significant entities; therefore intermediate levels are also needed.

In the following chapter, **Maurizio Cardaci, Antonella D'Amico** and **Barbara Caci** shed additional light on the social context of consciousness focusing their attention on the use of conscious processes in the regulation of motivated behaviours. In the Social Cognition perspective, consciousness is a function that involves purposive accessing to information, and deliberative processing of information for selecting, constructing, regulating and evaluating courses of action. The above-mentioned theoretical notes allowed them to depict an artificial agent that uses conscious processes in the regulation of its own motivated behaviours.

**Antonio Chella** pursues the design and implementation of a generalized loop for conscious perception in autonomous robots. The chapter takes into account the externalist point of view about artificial consciousness by hypothesizing that the conscious perception process is based on a generalized loop between the brain, body and environment. In particular, the proposed perception loop is in part internal and in part external to the robot, and it comprises the interactions among the proprioceptive and perceptive sensory data, the anticipations about the perceived scene according to the robot movements, and the scene itself by means of a suitable focus of attention mechanism implemented by means of neural networks. The perception model has been tested on an effective robot architecture implemented on an operating autonomous robot RWI B21 offering guided tours at the Archaeological Museum of Agrigento.

Ricardo Sanz, Ignacio López and Julita Bermejo-Alonso address the role of consciousness in controlling a complex system. They even go further by implying that consciousness could be nothing but a higher level capability of control. The science and technology of computer-based control is facing an enormous challenge when increased levels of autonomy and resilience are required from the machines that are supporting our ambient environment. Control systems complexity is rising. In some sense, software intensive controllers are becoming too complex to be built by traditional software engineering methods, this complexity appearing as an increase in size and a decrease of system dependability; this last being the most frightening one. Systems must be more aware and more responsible of themselves than they are today. A question emerges: Can artificial consciousness be a solution to the performance/dependability problem?

In the last chapter of the second part, Owen Holland, Rob Knight and Richard Newcombe address the role of the self process in embodied machine consciousness. Although embodiment is becoming a key issue in the fields of cognition and consciousness studies, its possible use in achieving machine consciousness has received relatively little consideration to date. However, the use of an embodied agent for the study of machine consciousness can lead to the neglect of what may be another key factor: the self process (or self structure), which is also an important element in many modern approaches to consciousness. The reason for this is clear: an embodied agent is a clearly defined and delimited structural and functional entity, with all of its elements bound by the common fate of the body, and this physical self seems to require no further elaboration — the system as a whole is already more complete than the self-free non-embodied information processing architectures at the heart of many machine consciousness studies. This paper sets out a theory of consciousness in which both embodiment and a self process play fundamental roles, and describes an ongoing robot-based machine consciousness project in which the key element is the development and use of such a self process. The nature, rather than the mere fact, of embodiment is thought to be important for the understanding of the structure of the self process, and this has led to the construction of a new type of robot—an anthropomimetic robot.

Part III, 'Artificial and natural consciousness', presents articles that address the fundamental issue lurking under the hood of consciousness modelling.

**Riccardo Manzotti** addresses the issue of the relation between phenomenal consciousness and the fundamental ontology of the world trying to highlight its implications for the field of artificial consciousness. In recent years, several researchers took in consideration the hypothesis of designing and implementing models for artificial consciousness—on one hand there is hope of being able to design a model for consciousness, on the other hand the actual implementations of such models are helpful for understanding consciousness. The traditional field of Artificial Intelligence is now flanked by the field of artificial or machine consciousness. In this chapter he analyses the current state of the art of models of consciousness and then presents a possible solution for the thorny issue of phenomenal experience in an artefact. For the purposes of robotics, this problem might be solved leaving aside the dualist framework of traditional Cartesian substance metaphysics and adopting a process-metaphysical stance. He begins sketching the outline of a process-ontological scheme whose basic entities are situated processes. Eventually he exploits these processes as an explanation of direct perception and other variants, such as illusions, memory, dreams and mental imagery. From within this scheme, he formulates a series of constraints on an architecture for consciousness.

**Domenico Parisi** questions the soundness of traditional approaches that start by asking, What is consciousness? From the point of view of science, this is the wrong question. If we ask what is consciousness we are led to think that there is some entity called consciousness which has the following properties: it is one single entity, it is an entity with well defined boundaries that separate it from other related entities, it is something that either an organism can have or not have, it is an entity with fixed characteristics. Real entities have the opposite properties: there is always a plurality and variety of them, they are never entirely different from other related entities, they have degrees, they change all the time, they evolve, develop, and disappear. It is language, i.e., the sheer existence of a word 'consciousness', which induces us to ask the wrong question 'What is consciousness?' This is a philosophical question, not a scientific one. Philosophers are restricted to working with language but scientists need to go beyond language and observe, measure, and analyze reality itself. Instead of asking 'What is consciousness?' what we should do is look at the variety of phenomena denoted, rather confusedly, by the word 'consciousness', and try to separately describe and explain these phenomena.

**Alberto Faro** and **Daniela Giordano** introduce an unusual approach to consciousness, namely an account of consciousness from the synergetics and quantum field theory perspectives. The starting position of the authors is that the symbolic theories of cognition, such as the Re-Representation theory proposed by Karmiloff-Smith, imply the existence of some entity in the brain that re-represents symbolically the world starting from the perceptual networks. On the other hand the non representational accounts of cognition, such as the one proposed by Dreyfus, are not rich enough to explain how the brain is able to carry out activities in complex, possibly rapidly changing, contexts. The theory of synergetics developed by Haken, which is at the core of the accounts of cognition based on dynamic systems, such as the ones proposed by Thelen and Kelso, is an important step to explain flexible behaviors. According to this theory different behaviors, or order states, can be activated in a given context. The prevailing order state is determined by the values of the control variables (or affordances in Gibson's terms) offered by the context and it is influenced by how many times the subject has experienced the current situation.

What is the role of the interaction between brain, body and environment in shaping consciousness? This is the question posed and answered by **Piero Morasso** who considers the analysis of haptic perception. Quoting Chiel & Beer (1997), consciousness cannot be a purely mental phenomenon because 'the Brain has a Body'. In this view, adaptive behavior is an emergent property of the bi-directional interactions of the nervous system with the body and the environment, which implies a continuous exchange of signals/energy between the nervous system, the body and the environment. This means that the motor neuronal input is shaped by the biophysics of the sensory organs and the motor neuronal output is transformed by the biomechanics of the body creating, at the same time, a large set of constraints & affordances. In this framework a musical metaphor illustrates the concept in vivid terms: the brain is not the director of a symphonic orchestra but rather a player in a jazz jam session. On the other hand, adaptive behavior is an emergent property but it cannot emerge without neural plasticity. Is consciousness an emergent property of the same sensory-motor-cognitive process? Can consciousness be equated with the ability to exhibit adaptive behaviour? The last paper, not wholly surprisingly, is presented by a firm critic of artificial consciousness, **Peter Farleigh**, whose view is not entirely sympathetic to the goal of artificial consciousness. In his controversial chapter, he addresses the limits of mechanism and functionalism in catching the essential features of consciousness. Functionalism, he claims, has fared badly with any attempt at the explanation of the phenomenal qualities which are regarded as a (or the) basic character of consciousness. By taking advantage of a series of thought experiments, he shows the conceptual limitations of functionalism in referring to mental and neural processes.

By the end of this book, we feel that we are just at the beginning of a long process of refinement and discovery of concepts. Old categories would need to be reorganized. Innovative experiments will have to be conceived and carried on. And yet, in the mist of doubt and uncertainties, we stress the importance and the potential benefit of the artificial consciousness quest — nothing less than the design of an artificial subject.

A few years ago, Antonio Damasio, in his chapter of the *Scientific American Book of the Brain* wrote that (AA.VV., 1999):

> At the simultaneous finish of the millennium, the century, and the Decade of the Brain, this volume lets the reader take stock of where neuroscience stands, for a fleeting moment, before the start of the next thousand years. The volume closes, quite appropriately, with three chapters on the matter of consciousness — the very last topic to be added to the agenda of neuroscience and one about which, not surprisingly, little consensus has developed so far. The next *Scientific American Book of the Brain* will probably begin with three chapters on consciousness and will summarize the agreements that will have been reached over the phenomena of consciousness. In fact, if another ten years go by, the entire book may be entirely about the biology of consciousness.

We hope that a substantial part of that future book will be the result of our efforts to replicate a conscious subject — by designing models of consciousness, by suggesting experiments, by proposing new conceptual framework that could fit the limitations of a robot, and, of course, by making mistakes.

The capability of designing a conscious machine, the Holy Grail of the field of artificial consciousness, will change forever the scope of engineering. Engineering will step from the mere design of complex artefacts to the design of subjects. And yet, we feel that the roots of this transformation were already contained inside cybernetics and artificial intelligence. A few years ago, didn't the expert of AI, John Haugeland, wonder in these terms (Haugeland, 1985/1997), p. 247: 'Could consciousness be a theoretical time bomb ticking away in the belly of AI?'

## References

AA.VV. (1999). *The Scientific American Book of the Brain*. New York, Lyon Press.

Aleksander, I. (1992). Capturing Consciousness in Neural Systems. *Artificial Neural Networks, 2, Proc. of. 1992 International Conference on Artificial Neural Networks (ICANN-92)*. I. Aleksander and J. G. Taylor, Elsevier Science: 17–22.

Aleksander, I. (2000). *How to Build a Mind*. London, Weidenfeld & Nicolson.

Aleksander, I. (2001). 'The Self "out there".' *Nature* 413: 23.

Arkin, R. C. (1999). *Behavior–Based Robotics*. Cambridge (Mass), MIT Press.

Buttazzo, G. (2001). 'Artificial Consciousness: Utopia or Real Possibility.' *Spectrum IEEE Computer* 18: 24–30.

Edelman, G. M. and G. Tononi (2000). *A Universe of Consciousness. How Matter Becomes Imagination*. London, Allen Lane.

Haugeland, J. (1985/1997). Artificial Intelligence: The very Idea. *Mind Design II*. Cambridge (Mass), MIT Press.

Holland, O., Ed. (2003). *Machine consciousness*. New York, Imprint Academic.

Jennings, C. (2000). 'In Search of Consciousness.' *Nature Neuroscience* 3(8): 1.

Koch, C. (2004). *The Quest for Consciousness: A Neurobiological Approach*. Englewood (Colorado), Roberts & Company Publishers.

Lodge, D. (2001). *Thinks*. London, Secker & Warburg.

Schlagel, R. H. (1999). 'Why not Artificial Consciousness or Thought?' *Minds and Machines* 9: 3–28.

Steels, L. (1995). Is artificial consciousness possible? *Consciousness: Distinction and Reflection*. G. Trautteur. Napoli, Bibliopolis.

Vincenzo Tagliasco

# Artificial Consciousness

## A Technological Discipline

When a new discipline springs up on the scientific scenario, the researchers who are involved—especially the oldest ones—try to find out when and where the new name had first appeared in their personal history. As relates to the term 'artificial consciousness' I also have my personal story. When I graduated in 1965, one of my dearest colleagues, whose wife was Hungarian, gave me, as a gift a book about cybernetics, *Kibernetikai gépek* (Nemes, 1962). Unfortunately, the book was written in Hungarian and the wife of my friend translated into Italian only the titles of chapters and paragraphs and not the whole text. One of the titles sounded very impressive, 'artificial consciousness', and my Hungarian friend told me that, in the small paragraph named 'artificial consciousness', there were a lot of 'I's'. Two years before, in 1963, I had the opportunity to read the translation into Italian of the novel *I, robot* by Isaac Asimov (published in English in 1950). The novel *I, robot* and the essay *Kibernetikai gépek* joined together in my mind and since then for me the robots, in science fiction, are conscious robots. A few years later, in 1970, while I was a research fellow at the Psychology Department of MIT, all of a sudden the book in Hungarian, that I had been unable to read, materialized in my hands thanks to a wonderful translation into English (Nemes, 1969). A part of that paragraph is given below (Nemes, 1969):

> Suppose that a walking machine receives information that this mechanism is active (in living beings, the proprioceptive [muscular, articular, and tactile] sensations accompanying the process of walking correspond to this information), this should be sufficient for it to construct the proposition 'I go'. The concept 'go' is evoked by markedly different 'sensations' in the two cases. A child learns by lengthy experience that the verb 'go' covers both

groups of sensations, in spite of their different character (it learns, on the one hand, from the fact that other people call its own walking 'going' and, on the other, that in the mirror it sees itself executing the same movements as other walking people). The machine can, of course, be programmed to reach, and profit by, both types of conclusions. As a next example, let us consider '*I think*'. Man can utter this proposition e.g. on receipt of proprioceptive information about the increased blood supply to his own brain; but the proposition 'he thinks' will be inferred from the behaviour and gestures of his fellowmen, e.g. from the Rodin posture. Propositions like 'I am in pain' and 'I feel ill' are mostly triggered by enteroceptive [sic!] information. We see that the word 'I' is called up by certain internal signals which in the model can be realized by units reporting to the central control of the machine. Even these superficial considerations reveal that speech and society are indispensable for the formation of the 'I' concept. Of course, even machines programmed in the most sophisticated way will imitate only some external manifestations of consciousness.

In these words there are many ingenuous aspects; however these concepts are still vivid and alive in common sense and in many technological fields. In 2003 M.R. Bennett and P.M.S. Hacker (Bennett and Hacker, 2003) deeply criticized the confused use of terms as 'I', consciousness and mental states in scientific literature and denounced the confusion stemming out from the works of Sherrington, Crick, Edelman, Damasio, Gregory, Marr, Johnson-Laird, Zeki, Libet, Humphrey, Damasio, Gazzaniga, Searle, James, Glynn, LeDoux, Shepard, Luria, Chalmers, Dennett, Nagel, Penrose, P.M. and P.S. Churchland, Dawkins, Sperry, Tononi, Albright, and many others.

Bennett and Hacker do not explicitly mention the words 'artificial consciousness', but their opinion can be inferred from some of their observations (Bennett and Hacker 2003):

> The question of how the brain can be conscious is misconceived and the question of how the brain ('this grey and white gook inside my skull') can be conscious is misplaced. For, as we have argued, it cannot. It is the living being whose brain it is that can be said to be conscious or unconscious. So, it is not hard to see 'how mere physical systems could be conscious'; it is altogether logically impossible. For a 'mere physical system' is precisely that of which it makes no sense to say 'it is conscious or unconscious'. ... We may safety leave speculation about androids to writers of science fiction. Our concepts are not tailored to deal with such imaginary cases, and there is no reason to suppose that reflection on such flights of fancy will shed any useful light on our current

concepts, any more than reflections on Mickey Mouse can shed light on our concept of a mouse.

We, as engineers, are deeply grateful to Descartes because thanks to him we worked on human beings as if they were machines. We left to other specialists the problems concerning mind, thought and consciousness. Thanks to Descartes, technology succeeded in avoiding any involvement in managing ambiguous entities such as consciousness. Even after the advent of computers, Descartes continued to be a guide for engineers in an updated version: hardware as *res extensa*, software as *res cogitans*.

Recently, consciousness has acquired the right to be regarded as a hard scientific discipline by the leading scientific journals, such as *Nature* and *Science*. On the contrary, artificial consciousness has a very long and difficult future.

### 'Artificial Consciousness' in Italy

I will briefly review the birth of 'artificial consciousness' in the Italian technological panorama. Obviously in other disciplines, such as history of philosophy and psychology, consciousness has had and continues to have a long and well assessed history.

In engineering the first who was brave enough to talk explicitly about consciousness was Giuseppe Trautteur (Trautteur, 1995) as reported on the website on machine consciousness (http://www.machineconsciousness.org) by Owen Holland:

> What was probably the first meeting took place in Venice in 1991; the proceedings appeared in book form in Trautteur, G. (Ed.) (1995) Consciousness: Distinction and reflection, Bibliopolis, Napoli.

The Symposium in Venice was sponsored by the Italian CNR Research Project on Robotics. The book 'Consciousness', edited by Trautteur, represented an important step of a very long path towards the understanding of the mystery of mind, which began with cybernetics. In 1991, many symposia were held in Italy about the mind-body problems (Giorello and Strata, 1991) but only Trautteur talked explicitly of consciousness in robotics. He introduced the issue of consciousness into a community whose goal is to build artificial beings.

Between the Eighties and the Nineties, in the Italian national Project on Robotics, three scientific communities had the opportunity to meet: cybernetics, bioengineering and artificial intelligence.

Trautteur belongs to the Italian second generation of cybernet-icians together with Giuseppe Longo and Giuseppe Gambardella. The first generation was represented by Antonio Borsellino, Silvio Ceccato, Edoardo Caianiello, Augusto Gamba. They addressed the problem of mind in men and machines. Riccardo Manzotti, Pietro Morasso, and I are bioengineers. Antonio Chella, Salvatore Gaglio, Giuseppe Spinelli, and Marcello Frixione are scholars in the field of artificial intelligence.

These three communities, in Italy, are involved in the brand new discipline of artificial consciousness. They are not converging — they have different ideas. This is not the time to choose the best approach towards artificial consciousness. It is still too early to predict whether there will be any chance to build a human-like robot with artificial consciousness.

Antonio Chella and Riccardo Manzotti, organizers of the *International Workshop on Artificial Consciousness*, held in Agrigento (November 2005), gathered scholars and researchers with different ideas and perspectives. They did not want to use the workshop to establish common definitions, approaches and methodologies. On the contrary they think that artificial consciousness is more an exigency than a fact, especially in these first years — it is rather a need of a new discipline than the existence of a clear and widely accepted field. In the history of engineering, very often engineers have not wanted to have a replica of something that they can define precisely, but they built artificial replicas which imitate some features of something, real or virtual, that elicited their imagination or needs.

At this stage of development, we have to stress diversities rather than look for a unique thought and perspective. We need to understand each other. It will be very difficult because the required background very often spans many different disciplines.

On the other hand, we cannot miss the opportunity to exploit the enormous efforts of neurosciences in order to shed some light on the biological foundations of consciousness.

### Confusion and Ambiguity of Artificial Consciousness

In artificial consciousness, researchers try to exploit features of human beings to define the blue-print of future man-made conscious beings. This is scientifically confusing because very often language used by researchers comes from the psychological terminology, which is strictly related to the human being as a whole. Therefore, it is very difficult to cope with the design of a robot, which is able to make experience, because the expression 'to make experience' derives from examining the behavior of an entire human being with all his history and his capacity to communicate. On the contrary, artificial consciousness is a sort of hope or, better, a technological path which will last decades — how is it possible to build a robot capable of having experience if 'having experience' is the final result of a long evolutionary path that living organisms reached in several millions of years? Nonetheless, even if definitions are confused and concepts are misleading, it is necessary to use ambiguous terms to give an insight of what the next step should be. Fortunately, technology does not require terminological precision unlike scientific endeavor. Technology overcomes ambiguity when it goes beyond a pure design to the construction of a physical prototype which has to work properly in the real world.

The ambiguous word 'artificial' is one of the first things that must be clarified. This adjective can be used in two meanings, and it is important to determine which one applies to the term 'artificial consciousness'. For example, we can use the expression 'artificial light' to refer to the fact that there are sources of light which have been man made. But artificial light is light and it does illuminate. It is fabricated as a substitute for natural light, but once fabricated it is what it seems to be. On the other hand, an artificial flower is not a real flower. In which sense do we use the word 'artificial' when we speak of artificial consciousness?

Some supporters of the idea of artificial consciousness, who claim that the term names something genuine and not merely apparent, would say that the word artificial is used with the first of the meanings outlined above (artificial light). They would say that although thinking machines are artifacts run by human beings, once made and set in motion, the machines do think. Their thinking may be different from that of human beings in some ways, just as the movement of a car is different from that of a rabbit and the flight of an airplane is different from that of a bird, but it is a kind of genuine thinking, just as there is genuine motion in the car and genuine flight in the plane.

Before proceeding to practical constraints, I remark that conscious artifacts have to be possible unless Cartesian dualism or some similar philosophical position is true — a dualist standpoint would put *res cogitans* forever out of reach.

However, even if dualism is rejected, there are other objections to the construction of conscious artifacts that are independent of any particular model of the brain.

Closely related to dualism is the argument (generally known as biological chauvinism) that only biological structures can achieve consciousness, either because only they have some requisite level of complexity, or only they embed some requisite collection of historical experience as a result of evolution, or only they are able to interact in some necessary way with the world by virtue of being part of autonomous living organism.

A second model-independent objection is that it is just not possible to construct an artifact with enough components or reliable enough to function like a brain.

Finally, the construction of such devices — whether with or without animal-like capabilities for self-assembly, self-repaired, and possibly even self-reproduction — would raise serious ethical questions.

In this sense, Bennet and Hacker are rather drastic:

> (*Sentient creatures do not 'contain' consciousness*): It is confused to query how physical bodies in a physical world can contain consciousness, or how mere physical systems could have consciousness.
>
> For, first, sentient creatures who are conscious beings do not contain consciousness, they are conscious (or unconscious), and conscious of various things ... (*Sentient creatures are not 'mere physical systems'*): Second, sentient beings are not mere physical systems. The atmosphere (weather system) might be said to be a 'mere physical system', a volcano can be said to be a mere physical system, and so too might a pocket calculator or a computer. But animals and human beings are not mere physical systems, but living, sentient 'systems'. Sentient beings are precisely what we contrast with mere physical systems.

### Towards Artificial Consciousness:
### The Concept of Minimal Man-Made Conscious Machine

A minimal human-like conscious being is a sort of man-made machine in which, as in biological androids devised by Karel Capek in his drama R.U.R. (1920), all the 'useless elements' which constitute a human being are eliminated. The concept of 'useless elements' introduced by Capek refers to all the potentialities and features of human beings which are not strictly coherent with the role of a hard and efficient worker. According to the same line of thought, a minimal human-like conscious being could be defined for a specific area of competence.

When a human being sees, it is not his/her brain that sees. It is the human being as a whole—with all his/her subsystems (endocrine, immune, digestive, respiratory) and with all his/her history of interactions with outside and inside worlds—that sees.

Artificial intelligence, fifty years ago, suggested isolating the main features which characterize human beings with respect to other animals. Artificial intelligence provided clearance, in the technological arena, to the concept of mind (Dreyfus and Dreyfus, 1988) created by philosophers and theater writers (three thousands years ago, writers tried to cope with the mystery of passions and emotions analyzing themselves and others).

No one has ever demonstrated that a mind is identical to brain activity—a mereological fallacy (Bennett and Hacker, 2003). We have experienced consciousness only in a human being, not in some of his/her parts, even in a very sophisticated one like the brain.

The concept of a minimal human-like conscious being is a confused and misplaced assumption in the scientific field of neurosciences, but not in the technological arena where we build artifacts.

I introduce here the concept of 'minimal human-like being', i.e. a man-made artifact which acts as a human being. Artificial consciousness springs up from this goal. It is an updated version of artificial intelligence. On this issue Rockwell writes that (Rockwell, 2005):

> Dreyfus claimed that one of the biggest mistakes of symbolic systems AI was to substitute the propositions that are caused by experience for the experience itself—a strategy that should have worked if all awareness was a linguistic affair. These AI researchers saw common sense as a particular set of concepts ... AI researchers tried to translate common sense into a set of propositions and store all the propositions in their machines' memories. But it became clear to almost everyone after a while that this was a doomed project. It was necessary to program in even statements as obvious as 'when you put an object on top of another object, and move the bottom object, both objects move', one of many statements that never has to be verbalized by anyone who has a body and has used it to move things in the world.

An artificial conscious human-like being is an artifact which behaves as a human being. Also in the study of artificial cell in synthetic biology the concept of minimal artificial cell was introduced to stress the role of those components strictly related to the minimal performance of the cell.

What are the minimal requirements for an artificial conscious human-like being?

We do not take into account beliefs and emotions, which are deeply related to the characteristics of the body of human beings: flesh and blood, neuropeptides and hormones, drive to sexual desire and reproduction.

A minimal set of aspects of 'being conscious' is retrievable in phenomenal consciousness. The core of phenomenal consciousness is the concept of experience which unfolds in several cases:

- to make experience about a set of minimal of goals which push subjects to make experiences;
- to keep trace of the experiences;
- to unify the experiences;
- to define new motivations which have the same role of the hard-wired pre-defined- goals set a priori in the design phase.

Conscious beings appeared during the evolution. Up to now, there is widely accepted evidence for the presence of consciousness only in human beings. The fact that a bird 'remembers' where it has put some food does not imply that it makes an experience in order to elaborate or acquire or define new motivations. This behavior could correspond only to the execution of a quite elaborate pattern of events.

### What Does it Mean 'to Make an Experience'?

I suggest that 'to make a new experience' means having the ability to derive from a present experience some hints in order to single out a new goal (Manzotti and Tagliasco 2005). According to this view, a reactive robot moving in an unstructured environment does not make new experiences whenever the environment changes, but it learns new behavioral strategies in order to achieve a pre-assigned goal.

The experience is open to gather facts able to generate new goals and motivations. It is not limited to the contents of the imposed goals which must be achieved autonomously. An experience closed in itself, which is the mere repetition of events which implement pre-assigned goals singles out a world in which autonomy is identical to the capability of coping with ever-modifying environments.

A system can be autonomous and intelligent in the context of pre-assigned goals. A conscious artificial agent must develop new goals. In the ordinary language 'to make experience' means to acquire new facts related with new parts of the environment and new stimuli. A newborn baby gains from making new experiences, from living in an environment rich in stimuli. Newborn babies are constantly pressed by parents and relatives who try to get their attention and their involvement. In mammals, games and plays have an important role in the constitution of animals as subjects of experience.

In the movie *2001: A Space Odyssey* by Stanley Kubrick, the computer HAL is a champion of classic artificial intelligence (it is intelligent even if it has not a body). On the contrary, Pinocchio is the best champion of artificial consciousness, much more than David, the child robot of the movie *A.I.* (Artificial Intelligence) by Steven Spielberg. In the latter, a company in New Jersey has the brilliant idea of producing a child robot capable of loving. The prototype, named David, is assigned to a couple whose only son has recently become fatally ill. According to the plot, the company inserts a pre-assigned module for love. On the contrary, Pinocchio has not any built-in pre-assigned emotional or experiential module. Pinocchio has only a few innate features (it cries when Geppetto hits him when it is yet in the wood trunk). The life of Pinocchio is a series of attempts to get new experiences: new colors, new objects, and new relationships. Pinocchio increases and unifies its experiences which give rise to its subject status. When the number of experiences is comparable to that of a human being it acquires the status of a human being.

It is reasonable to suggest some examples of features for a minimal conscious man-made being. A minimal conscious man-made being must be curious and able to define new goals.

A child in a toy shop explores the objects exposed (he/she is curious), decides for a Winnie-the Pooh (he/she defines a new goal) and adopts appropriate strategies in order to get one small soft bear even in the case the parents try to propose a different goal. This process is different from learning and it is loosely related to the concept of motivations and emotions studied in psychology.

In a preliminary study, an experiment was carried on in which a robot (Manzotti and Tagliasco, 2004) embodies a motivation-based architecture which develops a new motivation on the basis of its own experiences. In the experiment, an incoming class of visual stimuli (a series of colored shapes not coded inside the architecture) produces a modification that changes not only *how* (learning) but also *what* (goals) the system does. Something, which happens in the environment (the appearance of a class of colored shapes) becomes part of the agent's motivational structure. A series of different shapes associated with colors are shown to the robot. The system is equipped with a pre-assigned motivation aimed at colored objects – a colorless stimulus, independently of the shape, does not elicit any response. After a period of interaction with the visual environment (constituted by a series of elementary colored shapes), the robot develops autonomously a new goal aimed at colorless shapes also. A new goal became part of the agent motivational structure. The system shows the capability to develop a goal that was not envisaged at design time. This kind of artifact could be a very preliminary step towards the implementation of a minimal man-made conscious being.

Artificial consciousness researchers have to trace up a sort of evolutionary path from intelligent robots to conscious robots. In other words we have to start form the scratch: a minimal conscious artifact. A conscious artifact must not necessarily mimic the evolution of conscious living beings. At the beginning of the third millennium, artificial consciousness has those vague characteristics that a bunch of visionaries at the beginning of 50s gave to the term of 'artificial intelligence'.

Consciousness in the field of engineering is not 'something' which must be emulated artificially. Consciousness is not a thing which must be put in a machine. Consciousness in not an emergent property stemming out from complexity. An artificial conscious being would be a being which appears to be conscious because acts and behaves as a conscious human being.

### Artificial Consciousness: A Technological Discipline

Artificial consciousness is not a scientific discipline – it is a technological area nearer to robotics than to psychology or neurosciences. Nevertheless, in the future, artificial consciousness could give unexpected contributions to the understanding of the study of the human mind because it could be a reliable test bed for checking theories and hypotheses. In this perspective, artificial consciousness presents some common milestones with epigenetic robotics – both disciplines stress the role of development. However, artificial consciousness leaves to epigenetic robotics the implementation of the sensory-motor-cognitive system. Artificial consciousness stresses the role of establishing relations between the robot and the external world.

Artificial consciousness, just because it can see the future from the shoulders of two giants (neurosciences and artificial intelligence) does not want to make a confused use of linguistic terms by enthusiastic researchers, as denounced by Rockwell and by Bennett and Hacker (Bennett and Hacker, 2003; Rockwell, 2005). The term artificial consciousness must be read in a pure technological perspective; it uses the interpretation of consciousness and the linguistic content of the term consciousness — typical of folk psychology and of the common use. Making an artificial counterpart of the human consciousness is not among the objectives.

The researchers in the field of artificial consciousness know well that the study of natural consciousness is very far from conclusion (Koch, 2004). They adopt a typical engineering attitude — they build from the scratch artifacts which evoke some features and characteristics of a human being. However, they do not want to build a module (named 'consciousness module') to be inserted in a pre-assembled robot. They want to build a conscious-like robot, i.e. a robot which behaves as a conscious being.

A mind-like conscious robot may result mysterious as some important achievements have been mysterious in the history of engineering. Very often, engineers build artifacts before knowing exactly the laws which are at the basis of the processes and methods used in the construction of the artifact itself (engineers design and build proteins even if they do not know the laws governing the protein folding in 3-D).

Ray Kurzweil writes (Kurzweil, 2005):

> So how will we come to terms with the consciousness that will be claimed by non-biological intelligence? From a practical perspective such claims will be accepted. For one thing, 'they' will be us, so there won't be any clear distinction between biological and non-biological intelligence. Furthermore, these non-biological entities will be extremely intelligent, so they'll be able to convince other humans (biological, non-biological, or somewhere in between) that they are conscious: They'll have the delicate emotional cues that convince us today that humans are conscious. They will be able to make other humans laugh and cry. And they'll get mad if others don't accept their claims. But this is fundamentally a political and psychological prediction, not a philosophical argument.

# References

Bennett, M.R. and P.M.S. Hacker (2003). *Philosophical Foundations of Neuroscience*. Malden (MA), Blackwell.

Dreyfus, H.L. and S.E. Dreyfus (1988). 'Making a Mind Versus Modeling the Brain: Artificial Intelligence Back at a Branchpoint.' *Daedalus, Proceedings of the American Academy of Arts and Sciences* 117(1): 15–43.

Giorello, G. and P. Strata, Eds. (1991). *L'automa spirituale*. Bari, Laterza.

Koch, C. (2004). *The Quest for Consciousness: A Neurobiological Approach*. Englewood (Colorado), Roberts & Company Publishers.

Kurzweil, R. (2005). *The Singularity Is Near. When Humans Transcend Biology*. New York, Viking Penguin.

Manzotti, R. and V. Tagliasco (2004). 'Costruire oggetti o costruire soggetti?' *Technology review* XVI(5): 70–71.

Manzotti, R. and V. Tagliasco (2005). 'From "behaviour-based" robots to "motivations-based" robots.' *Robotics and Autonomous Systems* 51(2–3): 175–190.

Nemes, T. (1962). *Kibernetikai Gépek*, Akadémiai Kiadò.

Nemes, T. (1969). *Cybernetic machines*. Budapest, Iliffe Books and Akademiai Kiadò.

Rockwell, T. (2005). *Neither ghost nor brain*. Cambridge (Mass), MIT Press.

Trautteur, G., Ed. (1995). *Consciousness: Distinction and Reflection*. Napoli, Bibliopolis.

J.G. Taylor

# Through Machine Attention to Machine Consciousness

Machine consciousness is as yet an ill-defined concept, since so far we have no machines that posses it, only billions of humans who are known to be conscious. This does not help us implement similar consciousness in machines, even if that were possible, since the item to be implemented, human consciousness, is not itself yet suitably well understood to able to allow us to take such a step. Due to this difficulty it has been suggested that the details of human consciousness are not needed in the attempt to create machine consciousness: provided suitable basic principles deduced from human consciousness are implemented in the machine then it will possess qualities allowing us to claim it possesses 'machine consciousness'.

The problem with this approach is that the principles at the basis of human consciousness are themselves not universally agreed upon. Thus it is still very debatable whether or not the epithet 'conscious' can be applied to any such machines until this problem is sorted out. The problem of which principles may be most crucial for granting consciousness to any machine will be discussed in the next section, and a small set of crucial candidates will be presented.

There is overwhelming experimental support for the thesis that consciousness of a stimulus is attained only when attention is paid to the stimulus. Thus if machine consciousness is assumed to possess similar properties to those of human consciousness it would need to possess the ability of attention. However attention is not a sufficient but only a necessary condition: attention can be dragged by subliminal stimuli to speed-up response, but without awareness of the stimuli occurring. What more must be added to attention to boost it to a state of consciousness? This is a question at the basis of any attack on discovering the essential principles of consciousness. To answer it we will have to probe any model of attention to hopefully gain a glimpse of consciousness. At the same time we need to explore the experiential side of consciousness in order to obtain guidance as to what to look for in the upgraded model of attention. This will be done by considering the nature of consciousness seen through the eyes of Western phenomenology (Zahavi, 1999). Both strands: of attention and of continental phenomenology as well as aspects of meditation will be taken into account in framing the requisite principles.

I will start with a section on the principles that presently seem to be needed to attain human consciousness. Here will be taken into account both the attention basis of consciousness and the most important results of Western phenomenology. In the following section the nature of attention as seen by behaviour and brain imaging is discussed. We continue with the development of an engineering control framework for attention. This is shown to have validity in its ability to explain specific visual and visuo-motor attention tasks already in the literature. The CODAM model, extending our previously simple ballistic approach to attention, is then described in section 4. CODAM allows a brief glance through the gateway of attention into the heavenly garden of consciousness. The activity in CODAM is shown in particular to give a possible neural underpinning for the Pre-Reflective Self (PRS) introduced in section 1. It also possesses the ability to be extended to a specific and difficult task, that of the Attention Blink (AB). How a CODAM-style of attention control system could be implemented in a machine system to provide it with a modicum of consciousness is outlined briefly in the following section.

## 1. Essential Principles for Consciousness.

As noted above, it is essential to clear away some of the confusion surrounding consciousness and its nature. This proves very difficult in the present atmosphere of controversy over the subject. To achieve some progress, I will call on various features available from Continental Phenomenology, which analyse aspects of phenomenal experience. There is also evidence from meditation, using the tools of brain imaging, which can be related to the continental phenomenological discussions.

In order to cross the mind/ brain gap, help is needed beyond the control framework for attention. This is partly because there are many models of control that could be used, as is seen from the fact that there are numerous models of attention that have been created by computational neuroscientists. But in any case an important aspect to consider in probing deeper into attention, from an experi ential point of view, is that the Inner self is not part of mainstream consciousness studies. It has been rejected by Western Cognitive science, possibly due to the influential British philosopher David Hume stating categorically that there were only perceptions when he looked into his own mind. He could not see any 'self', only 'bundles of perceptions'.

What was caught by Hume was correct, in that there is no self to be observed as an object. But Hume's 'bundles of sense impressions' have no 'I' experiencing them; they are incoherent. There must instead be an inner pre-object self. This was delineated carefully later by Immanuel Kant, when he wrote: It must be possible for the 'I think' to accompany all my representations: for otherwise something would be represented in me which could not be thought at all, and that is equivalent to saying that the representation would be impossible, or at least would be nothing to me.' (Kant, 1933, pp. 131–2). He termed this essential a priori 'I', which unifies my experience and allows it to belong to 'me', as the transcendental unity of apperception. According to Kant, this was 'a pure original unchangeable consciousness of self' (Kant, 1933, p. 133).

From this description of the inner 'I' sprang more detailed analyses by continental phenomenologists. What emerged was a consensus as to the nature of the inner self: its experience as of a gappy character, as if it were composed of 'beads on a string', also mentioned in Eastern writings on meditation. More detailed analysis has come from the works of Husserl, Sartre, Merleau-Ponty, Frank, Zahavi, Parnas and others (Zahavi & Parnas, 1999; Zahavi, 1999). This has led to the acceptance of there being two parts to conscious experience:

a.    A purely intrinsic, non-relational, so-called Pre-Reflective Self (PRS)

b.    A relational consciousness, with content that of the external world.

The pre-reflective self gives us the sense of 'being there', of 'what it is like to be'. The component of self with content of the world is the one we experience when we are in close interaction with the world.

However we know during this interaction that 'we are there', as experiencing, conscious, persons, as Kant pointed out in his transcendental unity of apperception. We do not need to reflect on that fact, by saying to ourselves 'Ah, yes, here I am, after all'. You just are.

Such a division of conscious experience into two such components leads to a difficulty over how these two parts can interact. The first component — the pre-reflective self — is supposedly with no internal structure whatsoever. It is difficult to see how such an empty component of the self can ever get its teeth (especially since it cannot have any such items) into the external world. That is a problem not resolved in any satisfactory manner by the continental phenomenologists. They have claimed that the pre-reflective self is developed through the body as an infant grows. Through proprioceptive and kinaesthetic feedback, the body creates the 'zero point' of space from which the perspective on the world of the pre-reflective self can be achieved. However there are results, from recent neuroscience experiments, that show such a claim is unlikely: the proprioceptive/kinaesthetic feedback is treated by the brain just as any other. Moreover there are results from de-afferented people indicating no loss of the sense of self at the moment of their de-afferentation (Taylor, 2003d). Thus the detailed nature of the PRS is still unclear.

To help explore the PRS further, I propose to relate it to states observed in meditation. In particular the Pure Conscious Experience (PCE) (Forman, 1990) has remarkably similar features to the PRS: the PCE is a state with no content, but is solely of stillness:

> Reports of pure consciousness suggest that, despite the absence of mental content, the subjects were somehow aware that they remained aware throughout the period of pure consciousness (Forman, 1999).

Recent experiments have shown that the PCE has physiological correlates distinguishing it from other states of consciousness, in particular from sleep, drug induction, out-of-the-body experiences and hypnosis (Taylor, 2002a). In particular the following features of PCE have been observed by numerous experiments:

- $\alpha$ wave synchronization;
- skin conduction increase;
- respiratory rate decrease;
- brain imaging in PCE have shown PFC/Parietal activity increases, while activity in sensory areas;

These results support both the existence of PCE as a distinct physiological state, and the further identification of it as an extended form
of the PRS, as I have proposed elsewhere (Taylor, 2002a, b).

Thus we arrive at some core principles for consciousness to be
present in an information processing system as follows:

a)   The system possesses the ability to create estimates of
     attended states of the world in which it inhabits, in terms
     of focusing on certain stimuli and ignoring all others (as
     distracters);

b)   It can be seen to have two components to its conscious
     experience (as it might report or as can be externally
     observed):
     • One possessing content of the external world;
     • The other with no content, equivalent to our pre
       re-reflective (PRS), and giving sense to the personal
       pronoun 'I';

c)   The temporal flow of the PRS and content consciousness
     appear to be turn-and-turn about, corresponding to a
     'gappy' character of the content component;

d)   Under suitable (possibly lengthy) experience the system
     can experience a state of PCE, with no content but not be
     unconscious (as observed or by report).

We now turn to look in more detail at the nature of human attention,
in order to understand how we might be able to model it in a
machine, satisfying the above four principles.

## 2. The Nature of Attention

It is now accepted that attention involves a process of selection of
part of a scene for analysis, thereby acting as a filter on the input.
This is especially important for complex scenes with many
distracters. This is now accepted as being achieved in the brain by
attention, through the process of amplification to the attended input
and inhibition of distracting inputs. These processes occur in various
sensory and motor cortical regions in the brain; they can also be
observed in higher regions (such as temporal lobe face and object
maps in the fusiform gyrus, or goal representations in prefrontal cortex). The temporal dynamics of such amplification signals have been
observed in action (Mehta et al, 2000). Furthermore there are regions
of the brain which have now been accepted as generating the control
signals which produce these amplificatory/inhibitory signals to be

sent to the regions I mentioned earlier. These control regions are sited in parietal and prefrontal cortices. A parietal/prefrontal network for shifting attention has been detected by PET study in an attention movement paradigm (Corbetta & Shulman, 2002). Modulation of cells in V4 by attention to their receptive fields has been observed (McAdams & Maunsell, 1999).

Thus overall, attention movement involves brain sites with two different functions:

1) Amplification/Decrease of sensory input/ motor output (in sensory and motor cortical regions);

2) Creation of control signals to achieve the relevant control signal. This generation is now recognized as occurring in parietal and prefrontal cortex.

As concluded by Kastner and Ungerleider:

> Attention-related activity in frontal and parietal areas does not reflect attentional modulation of visually evoked responses, but rather the attentional operations themselves. (Kastner & Ungerleider, 2001, p 1263; see also ibid 2000)

Given this clear control function that attention performs, it is to be expected that sites with more specific functions will be expected to be observed in the brain (goals, monitors/errors, feedback signals, control generators). In order to bring some order to the increasing number of brain sites being observed as relevant in attention control, it was proposed in 2000 to use the engineering control approach for attention (Taylor, 2000). That has been developed more fully since then (Taylor, 2001a, b; 2002a, b, c; 2003a, b, c; 2005; 2006). This approach will be developed in the next section.

### 3. A Control Framework for Attention

Engineering control theory is now well developed (Phillips & Harbor, 2000). It has many applications across industry and commerce. For the purpose of application to the brain, consider the specific modules of standard control systems:

*a) The Plant.*

This is the system being controlled. It may, for example, be a steel mill, or a moving robot. The control signals would then be the amount of heat being supplied or a command to move so far left or right respectively.

### b) *The Goal Module*

This contains the required goals, set up by some external requirements. A certain temperature range of the steel, or a particular temporal change in this temperature, would be expected to be
considered for the first case (the steel mill). The second example may
have as goals a sequence of actions, such as going to a cupboard, taking out a cup, and making a cup of coffee.

### c) *The Inverse Model Controller*

This is the module which, given the present state of the plant and the
required state involved in the goal set up earlier, generates a control
signal to achieve that desired state of the plant. For the above examples, the controller for the first example specifies how much energy
is required to attain the desired state and the second a sequence of
control actions fed to the robot's actuators.

### d) *The Observer/Forward Model*

To achieve rapid control signals, but in the absence of fast feedback,
there is need to constantly update any estimated state of the plant
without such feedback. This is the purpose of the observer. It provides an early estimate of the state of the plant, determined by the
previous state and the control signal. This state estimate in the
observer can then be used to correct any error that might be expected
to arise on the basis of such an expected future state. The examples
above have obvious observer structures, the first concerned with the
estimated steel temperature, the second with the expected position
of the robot.

Such a control framework has been applied with increasing success to motor control by the brain (Sabes, 2000; Desmurget &
Grafton, 2000; Wolpert & Ghahramani, 2000; Kawato, 1999; Miall &
Wolpert, 1996). Thus all the modules above are clearly in evidence in
a range of paradigms:

1)   The plant exists as the musculature;

2)   The goal structures arise in the prefrontal cortex
     (Willingham, 1998);

3)   The inverse model controller is observed in posterior
     parietal lobes (Desmurget & Grafton, 2000) and in the cer-
     ebellum (Kawato et al, 2000).

4) The forward/observer model is observed in a variety of actions: in eye control and in motor actions on the hand, and in numerous other processes under motor control by the brain (Sabes, 2000; Desmurget & Grafton, 2000; Wolpert & Ghahramani, 2000).

There is also the learning of motor control models that is under considerable investigation.

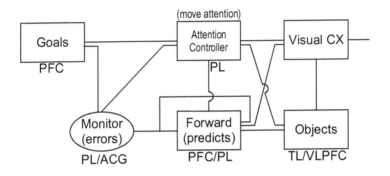

**Figure 1: Basic Attention Control Model**
The modules are described in the text, and their possible siting in the brain placed beneath them. PL = parietal lobe; TL = temporal lobe; PFC = prefrontal cortex; ACG = anterior cingulate; VLPFC = ventro-alteral prefrontal cortex

I now apply the above engineering control framework to the movement of attention. This is shown in figure 1, in which the main modules introduced above from the engineering control framework are included. In detail these modules are plant module, identified with low-level sensory and motor cortices, the goal module for holding goal representations in working memory (in prefrontal cortex), the inverse model controller for generating an attention movement control signal to move the focus of attention (in various portions of the parietal lobes), forward/observer model of state estimation (expected in the sensory buffer sites in parietal cortex), and the error monitor module (in anterior cingulate cortex). The brain identifications given have good support, although need to be refined with further data. In particular the complexity of the parietal lobes indicates there may be more modules than proposed in figure 1, as well as the possibility that each functional module is more likely represented by a distributed network of sites in the brain.

This engineering control framework for attention movement has been applied to simulate the Posner benefit (Taylor & Rogers, 2002). The Posner paradigm uses the movement of focus of attention by a cue to a particular region of space. A target is then presented at either this place (for a valid cue) or an alternate site (for an invalid cue). It was found that cueing attention to a place (as in the valid cueing condition) speeds up response; but response is delayed if attention has to be moved to another site (as in the invalid cueing condition). The simulation uses a very simple architecture, a goal module composed of 3 nodes (L, R, & Central), an IMC module ditto, with lateral inhibition, an object module with similar lateral inhibition. The basic architecture uses the flow of information as:

$$IN \rightarrow OBJ \leftarrow IMC \leftarrow GOAL \leftarrow IN$$

The results of the simulation showed how lateral inhibition in the IMC leads to the delay of the invalidly cued response compared to the validly cued case. Varying the cue-target time difference led to the shapes of the curves of cueing benefit (difference of reaction time to the invalid minus the valid cued cases) reproducing almost exactly the human benefit curves, in the two separate cases of exogenously and endogenously driven attention movement. This and other paradigm simulations give some justification of the presence of the various modules used in the simulation.

There are additional points to consider for an engineering control framework applied to attention:

1)  The control framework can be applied to other sensory modalities;

2)  There is competition/combination between different sensory modalities;

3)  There exists separate control of attention to object features (color, shape, etc) and to space (more basic than object attention movement);

4)  Learning can be guided by a Monitor error signal;

5)  Sub-cortical sites are involved in input representations and goals, as well as Monitor & Forward models (such as Cerebellum);

6)  Sub-cortical and cortical activation crucially uses acetylcholine (from the Nucleus Basalis Meynert);

7) Also Dopamine-based learning will be important (in the Basal Ganglia/Prefrontal Cortex/Amygdala/Hippocampus);

8) Ultimate inclusion is needed of the Thalamus/NRT/Cortex complex (NRT is the nucleus reticularis thalami, and is an inhibitory sheet of cells interposed between thalamus and cortex).

This control framework may be extended from visual attention to visuo-motor control tasks (Taylor & Fragopanagos, 2003), following the numerous results on the sensory/ motor attention control being separated mainly into the right and left hemispheres (Rushworth et al, 1997; ibid, 2001). The structure of this framework is shown in figure 2 below.

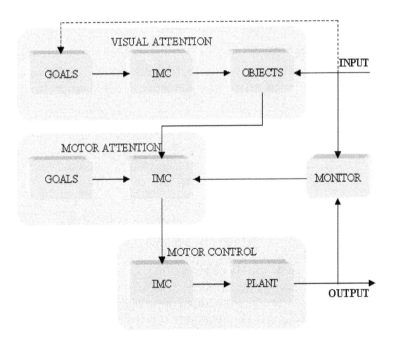

**Figure 2:. Visuo-Motor Attention Control System**
IMC = inverse model controller, to generate the attention movement control signal; plant = muscles/spinal chord

The system is composed of three copies of a control framework: one for visual attention control, one for the control of attention to motor response, and one at an automatic level that is part of the general motor control program mentioned earlier. The justification of introducing two separate attention control system for vision and motor attention (intention)s follows from the experimental observation in a number of experiments on the regions of the brain most involved in separate motor and vision control tasks. These show a clear distinction between the left hemisphere (for motor attention) and right hemisphere (for sensory attention). Thus we use two separate models, one for motor and one for visual attention control.

This general framework has been applied to several visuo-motor tasks. A neural simulation of the choice reaction time task of Schluter et al (2001) appeared in (Taylor & Fragopanagos, 2003). The paradigm was:

- Respond with 1st finger if one particular stimulus object appeared (of two possible such objects), and with the second finger if the second object appeared (of two)

- Learn the correct response by error-based learning

Agreement between the experimental results and the simulation is shown in the table below, with excellent agreement between the two.

**Table 1**
Experimental and Simulation Results for the Choice and Simple Reaction Time Tasks (Schluter et al, 2001; Taylor & Fragopanagos, 2003)

|  |  | Choice RT task | Simple RT Task |
|---|---|---|---|
| Simulation | Result | 544 ms | 265 ms |
| Schluter et al | Right hand | 573 ms | 211 ms |
| ... | Left hand | 572 ms | 210 ms |

The second paradigm simulated was the Posner movement benefit paradigm. This extends the analysis of the benefit of the presence of the focus of attention, in speeding up response to a visual target (as discussed earlier) to the preparation of motor acts. One of the paradigms considered was in (Rushworth et al, 1997), in which two stimuli in the shape of hexagons were presented to a subject; the hexagons appeared, one above, the other below, the fixation point (present throughout). The appearance of a coloured interior to one or other of the hexagons signalled to the subject to press either a left or right button. There was a cue, a little before the colouring of the hexagon, which arose by colouring the periphery of one of the hexagons. As before the cue could be valid if the periphery chosen by prior coloration was that whose interior then was coloured; an invalid cue corresponded to contradiction of the earlier cue by the opposite hexagon interior colouring. The results for the benefit of motor preparation showed a considerably larger increase of reaction time on increase of proportion of invalid trials for subjects with left-hemisphere parietal damage than right-sided damage of controls. The simulation using the general circuit of figure 2 was again successful in fitting the experimental data.

To conclude, we have constructed an engineering control framework for attention, and successfully simulated both sensory (visual) and sensory-motor (visuo-motor) control paradigms. The modules introduced (sensory and motor 'plant' sites, attention movement generators, goal modules, buffer sensory sites and monitors)were supported by these simulations, as well as qualitatively from many neuroscience results analysing attention.

## 4. Creating the Pre-Reflective Self

In the previous section it has been recognised that consciousness has two components, one being the usual part with content, in which we are aware of objects in the world around us. The other was noted as being

- Gappy/discontinuous;
- The gaps being identified with the pre-reflective self (PRS);
- When extended, the PRS leads to the state of pure consciousness reported in Eastern meditation;
- The PRS contributes the essential notion of 'I', that of owning the experiences of awareness of the external world, through immunity to error of misidentification of the first person pronoun (Shoemaker, 1968).

The purpose of this section is to develop a neural network model of both components of consciousness, with the above features. It will bridge the gap between the two components of consciousness by means of the temporal dynamics of the neural activity flowing in the extension of the attention control circuit of figure 1. Such an approach uses the essential feature of attention as the gateway to consciousness. It attempts to determine what extension of the control model of figure 1 is necessary to give ownership and immunity to error to awareness.

The extension I consider here to the attention control framework introduced earlier is the CODAM (Corollary Discharge of Attention Movement) model (Taylor, 2000a, b), and has been developed further since (Taylor, 2002a, b, c; 2003a, b, c). The essential extension of the attention control model of figure 1 that I have made is as follows:

a)   The addition of a working memory buffer, denoted WMSensory, to hold activity for later report; this constitutes the source of content for conscious awareness. It is not a new component, having been considered the site of the creation of content in consciousness for some time by numerous researchers (Taylor, 1999);

b)   The addition of a further buffer, to hold the corollary discharge of attention movement generated by the attention movement controller. This is denoted by WMcd.

The WMcd buffer acts as a predictor of the currently attended input. Attention amplification of a target input (and the related distracter inhibition) takes some hundred to two hundred milliseconds for the amplified input to access the WM Sensory buffer (Mehta et al, 2000). As in motor control models (Desmurget & Grafton, 2000) and standard control theory (Phillips & Harbor, 2000) the presence of a predictor of future input can be used to give fast speed-up of the attention control circuitry, and thereby allow more effective attention movement, leading to an evolutionary advantage to the possessor. The resulting CODAM model is shown in outline in figure 3.

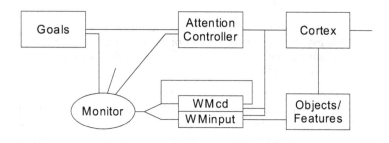

**Figure 3: CODAM Model**
**of Attention Control for the creation of the Pre-Reflective Self**

WMinput = sensory buffer for short term memory storage; WMcd = buffer for storage of the corollary discharge of the attention movement control signal.

To justify the nature of the supposed conscious experience of a system possessing CODAM, it is necessary to construct a set of 'bridging' interpretations to relate neural activity in CODAM to appropriate and essential features of consciousness. This is similar to the process used in scientific analysis of the relation of two theories, such as light and electromagnetism, or heat and thermodynamics, where one theory is expected to explain the other theory. In the former case, Maxwell showed how electromagnetic waves could exist and travel at a velocity which he calculated was identical with that of light. Both this and other similar features (for example refraction or reflection at surfaces of discontinuity of intrinsic electromagnetic properties) led Maxwell to hypothesise that light is a form of EM radiation; this was shown to be so experimentally later.

**Table 2**
Bridging Interpretations to relate mental states to neural brain activity

| PHENOMENAL EXPERIENCE (PE) | NEURAL UNDERPINNING |
|---|---|
| 1) Transparency<br>   a) Look through PE<br>   b) Fully interpreted<br>   c) Infinitely distant<br>   d) Intrinsic<br>   e) Immediately present | a) PE recurrence to lower levels<br>b) PE coded at highest level<br>c) One-way creation of PE<br>d) WMcd unbound to content<br>e) Sharp threshold to reach PE |
| 2) Presence<br>   a) Persistence<br>   b) Latency<br>   c) Seamlessness | a) Temporally-extended activity (WM)<br>b) Takes time to achieve threshold<br>c) Small gap between PE activations |
| 3) Unity<br>   a) Binds parts at a given time/ over time | a) Good couplings between WM sites |
| 4) Intentionality<br>   a) Requires manipulable representations | a) Reps transformable by others (PFC) |
| 5) Perspectivalness<br>   a) Own point of view<br>   b) 'I' infinitely close<br>   c) Privateness | a) WMcd as owner<br>b) One WTA region for IMC/WMcd<br>c) WMcd not bound to content reps |

To proceed on this identification program for consciousness, let me consider the main qualitative features of conscious experience, and see if they can be so related to neural activities in CODAM. Such a set of identifications depend heavily on the choice of the features selected for consciousness. These are still controversial, but they cannot be discussed here in detail; a more detailed discussion is given in (Taylor, 1998; 1999; Taylor, 2001b). The resulting identification is given in Table 2.

The results of this identification are supportive of the overall thrust of the approach taken here and by many others: consciousness arises in various buffer working memory sites, mainly placed in parietal and certain prefrontal sites, with possible contributions from a network of other areas of cortex to provide content.

The ultimate justification of any identification of CODAM with conscious experience must ultimately be brought to a quantitative level. There are a number of detailed paradigms that are relevant here, but to begin with, let me consider a general approach. Across modalities, CODAM predicts that there will be a temporal flow of activity, when an input stimulus is attended to and become conscious, that is of the form

IN → Goal → Attention Movement Controller → Object/Spatial Module

$\qquad$ → WMcd → Monitor $\qquad\qquad\qquad$ ↓

$\qquad\qquad\qquad\qquad\qquad\qquad\qquad\qquad$ WM Sensory

Thus there is early triggering (at about 150 msecs post-stimulus), in the goal module, of target biasing of the attention movement controller. The signal this generates is then sent down to amplify the input stimulus in the object/spatial input module. At the same time there is a copy of the attention movement control signal sent to the WMcd at about 200 msecs post stimulus. Later arrival of the amplified input onto the WM Sensory buffer occurs at around the time of the P3 signal, around 350–500 msecs.

Thus CODAM gives a prediction of expected appearance of a WMcd signal, a little after that from the attention movement control signal in the IMC of figure 3. This may already have been observed as the N2/P2 signal at about 190–250 msecs in attention movement paradigms. From MEG activity in target search (Hopf et al, 2002) the N2 signal is found to consist of two components: one at about 180–200 msecs and one form 220–240 msecs. The former was observed in parietal cortex, the latter in temporal lobe; the former could be identified with the movement control signal, the latter with the WMcd signal.

An important paradigm to help this identification is the Attentional Blink (AB) (Vogel et al, 1998), so-called because it is as if attention had blinked its 'inner eye'. The AB can be observed during a rapid stream of targets, presented every 90–100 msecs. If a particular target, say a white X, denoted T1, is to be detected, and then shortly later, say a further white letter, denoted T2, is to be detected, there is a large reduction of recognition accuracy for the T1 — T2 time separation of about 250–300 msecs. This is when attention 'blinks'.

A detailed CODAM model of the AB has been developed (N Fragopanagos, S Kockelkoren & JG Taylor, 2005). The main source of the AB in the model is the inhibition from the WMSensory activation, brought about by T1, on processing of later targets. T2 is particularly badly hit in the 250 msecs range after T1, especially for the development of the WMcd signal for T2. The presence of the monitor is found essential, in the simulation, to achieve T1 activity protection against degradation by its following mask. In conclusion, the CODAM model of consciousness extends the attention control framework introduced earlier, essentially splitting the WMSensory buffer into two components:

1)   A sensory buffer (WM Sensory)

2)   A Corollary discharge buffer (WMcd)

The interpretation of activity on these two buffer sites is that:

• WM Sens = 'content of consciousness'

• WMcd = 'ownership of that content'
       = pre-reflective self

together with the tentative identification of

• WMcd signal = N2/P2 at 180–240 ms

Support for this flow of information has been recently obtained (Sergent et al, 2005). It was shown in this reference (see in particular figure 6 there) that there was an inhibitory effect of the activity associated with the N2 of the second target T2 on the P3 of the first target T1. It is this interaction which begins to justify the claim that there is a corollary discharge of the attention movement control signal (as used in CODAM), and further that the experimental result also gives support to the detailed architecture of CODAM as used in the simulation of the attentional blink of (Fragopanagos et al, 2005).

It is in this manner that a neural model of consciousness can be developed: CODAM allows an understanding to be obtained of the way the pre-reflective self (in WMcd) helps speed-up creating awareness of the attended input. It can also be seen to allow for development of the meditative state PCE by learning to attend to the activity of WMcd alone (Taylor, 2003 a, b, c).

## 5. Creating Machine Consciousness

We have reached a point in the development of the ideas in which the experimentally supported CODAM model was found, in the previous section, to be complex enough to be able to support a model of the creation of consciousness satisfying the principles adumbrated in section 1. To repeat, these principles and their satisfaction are:

Principle 1 (A complex enough attention control system): This is provided by the CODAM architecture.

Principle 2 (The attention architecture is complex enough to create a PRS): This was shown in terms of the characteristics of the corollary discharge of the attention movement control signal.

Principle 3 (The temporal flow in the attention architecture leads to turn and turn about in PRS and content experience): This was shown to occur naturally in the CODAM architecture, since the attention control signal corollary discharge occurs before the attention-amplified stimulus activity attains its relevant working memory buffer.

Principle 4 (The architecture can support the PCE): This is enabled by suitable long meditation to create a prefrontal endogenous goal causing inhibition of all external sensory input, as discussed in more detail elsewhere (Taylor, 2002).

Having presented an engineering control architecture for attention powerful enough to satisfy the four principles adumbrated in section 1, the next step in building a conscious machine is to implement it on a suitable platform. There are several aspects of the platform that need discussion:

a) Is the software to be run in parallel across the neurons or serially? It could also be programmed in a hybrid form of parallel at semantic level & serial at aware level, as appears to occur in the human brain (where serialisation is brought about by the attention filter).

b) Should it be created in software based on code for CODAM (as running to explain the AB, for example) or on more general principles?

c)   How is detailed coding of objects, external actions and memories of experiences of the machine to be instantiated (especially in terms of the complexity of this coding)?

d)   Are all of the above codes to be learnt from the environment that the machine is in, or is some or all of this to be pre-coded?

e)   What explicit platform is to be used? Is it software or hardware?

f)   If the explicit platform is in software, can there be a powerful enough cluster of computers to create the environmental code?

g)   How will the machine be able to use its software brain (if that is chosen) to develop further in its environment?

f)   There will have to be a disembodied brain if a large cluster is used, so how will the contact (wireless or other) between machine brain and machine body be achieved?

The above relatively long list of questions is mainly about the use of a software system, not hardware. It is clear from the tenor of the questions and the known complexity of the stimuli in the environment that only very large clusters of computers would be needed (upwards of 1,000 nodes). Thus the mobility and adaptability of the machine might not be high. However this need not endanger its ability to encode a modicum of consciousness.

On the other hand, if the hardware route were to be followed there would be such problems for chip implementation as power dissipation, a question already of great importance as increasing numbers of transistors are embedded in a chip. This problem could be handled by using low power with optimisation achieved by activity-driving, although other methods are presently under discussion, such as through the development of nano-chips, with lower power requirements. Reliability, another important feature of chip design, could be achieved by employing: redundancy introduced by population coding, as known to occur in the brain. Reconfigurability: could be achieved by top-down decisions and related attention modulation, such as occurs in CODAM and its extensions to a broader range of executive functions (Fragopanagos et al, 2006). Finally asynchronous computing (needed for very small scale chip processing) could occur at multi-Giga-Hertz: by a variety of methods: local binding/ flexible grouping/ long-range asynchrony/ attention correlation

A further important question to be answered is as to which brain components are to be included in the simulation or in hardware. For the basic building block of the neuron this could be in terms of the basic neuron properties of: neuron/ spikes/ axons/ synapses/ neuro-modulators/ etc. It is the next feature, however, that is the most crucial. It involves the nature of the information being processed: can this be in digital form, as in a digital computer or should it be in analogue form, as in a living neuron.

There is an important analogy to be considered between developing a machine with consciousness and a weather system: the latter is only possible with explicit clouds and rain (and other components of weather). As existing physical entities. It is impossible to obtain the weather by software as only a symbolic representation of it. In the same way, it follows that a machine with consciousness would have to use real-time storage of neuron activation levels. In that way the machine would be able to emulate the processes occurring in the human brain in a physical instantiation, based on an attention control system of CODAM form, with a corollary discharge signal and working memory components able to be activated by this corollary discharge as well as by shortly later content. It was that precise temporal flow of ownership → content in the working memory buffer that brought these two components to life. Without a similar dynamical process in the machine it would be difficult to say if consciousness had occurred or not.

Here we see that the Turing test has been extended to one involving the internal dynamics of the 'brain' of the processing system. External testing just will not be sufficient to settle the matter, but a complete internal analysis of the temporal dynamics of the internal information flow in the machine should allow an external observer, when compounded with the external observational evidence, to decide whether or not the activity in the machine is suitably close to that of the human brain or not.

The criterion for the presence or not of conscious experience developed above is well beyond the original Turing test. But it is completely in accordance with the thrust of information arriving about the nature of the brain and in particular the basis of consciousness in attention and the associated flow of dynamic activity. This allows a far more scientific basis to be given to the test for consciousness than heretofore. That is not to say that the use of the internal dynamics of the machine flow of information is fool-proof or is even yet clarified (as shown by the remarks earlier about the present incompleteness of the CODAM approach). Yet it may be the best we presently possess, as well as being able to be tightened ever further as science advances.

The upshot of the above argument is that it would not be possible to run the machine in software; only hardware emulation would be possible (using the weather analogy). In that manner there would be real-time binding of WM buffer activity to lower level stimulus codes, as well as the achievement of real-time attention control crucial to the timing for consciousness to emerge, as in the CODAM model. The communication of neurons through spike trains would then be natural, since these provide a non-degradable coding of the information to be sent between neurons.

We are thus led to consider active storage techniques with spike production and the methods needed to be employed to transmit spikes suitably between many neurons, to the related learning rules needed to develop suitable stimulus codes, to how to achieve attention modulation, to methods to achieve attention feedback modulation, and to many more. One particularly difficult problem will be that of scaling: as the number of neurons grows to billions then the handling of inter-neuron communication will become a serious hardware problem. The associated timing problems however, present in synchronous chip computing, will not be present provided that completely asynchronous computing methods are used. Finally the manner in which neuro-modulators (a crucial component of brain processing) may be naturally included would have to be considered. It might be that such modulation would not be needed, or easy to include.

It is possible to encapsulate the above discussion and indicate the value of such a system in the following terms:

- Construct 'active neuron' local circuits;

- Embed in overall chip structure (by nano methods);

- Connectivity (by suitable hardware or optic interconnects) by using training of GA/ Hebbian form;

- Can design to help bridge the subsymbolic/ symbolic gap by use of suitable word encodings of various object representations;

- Internal dynamic buffers (WMs) are created as crucial components in the architecture;

- Create input/output space neural SOMs as part of the lower level processing;

- Develop language 'understanding' system ultimately based on these components and the CODAM architecture;

- The resulting chip may be effectively used in mobile robots/guidance systems;

- A range of environments and modalities are possible, in which the modalities would be determined by the sensor capabilities of the machine, the environments by the on-line adaptability of the machine brain in new environments;

- Both 'automatic' and 'attended' (serial) computing architectures would be catered for;

We note the correspondence of the suggested architecture to that of a standard computer:

- Main memory ⇔ LTM (semantic/episodic)

- Memory Buffer ⇔ WM Sensory

- Memory Address ⇔ IMC

- Current Instruction Address ⇔ PFC (index)

- Input coding ⇔ Posterior CX SOMs

- Program counter ⇔ PFC (serial order)

- ALU ⇔ PL/PFC

- Accumulators ⇔ PFC WM systems

- Serial/Parallel ⇔ Attention/Automatic

## 6. Conclusions

Here a set of principles were developed as to the nature of the system needed to construct a machine which would begin to qualify for the epithet of a conscious machine. We developed an attention-based architecture (CODAM) to model human consciousness, where CODAM was based on ideas from engineering control theory. Such a basis is a useful starting point for the creation of machine consciousness. We considered various questions arising in such a quest, and concluded that a hardware approach, based on active neurons was needed to provide real-time activity flow to lead to the give-and-take between the two components of consciousness recognized in section 1: the self of content and the pre-reflective self.

# References

Corbetta M & Shulman GL (2002) Control of goal-directed and stimulus-driven attention in the brain. *Nature Reviews, Neuroscience* 3:201–215

Desmurget M & Grafton S (2000) Forward modeling allows feedback control for fast reaching movements. *Trends in Cognitive Sciences* 4:423–431

Forman RKC (1990) *The Problem of Pure Consciousness.* Oxford: Oxford University Press

Forman RKC (1999) What Does Mysticism Have to Teach Us About Consciousness? pp. 361–378 in *Models of the Self,* eds S Gallagher & J Shear. Exeter, Devon: Imprint Academic

Fragopanagos N, Kockelhoren S. & Taylor J. G. (2005) *A neurodynamic model of the Attentional Blink.* Cognitive Brain Research

Frith CD (1992) *The Cognitive Neuropsychology of Schizophrenia.* Engelwood Cliffs NJ: Erlbaum

Hopf JM, Lucj SJ, Girelli M, Hagnar T, Mangun GR, Scheich H & Heinze H-J (2000) Neural Sources of Focussed Attention in Visual Search. *Cerebral Cortex* 10:1233–1241

Kant I (1933) *Critique of Pure Reason* (transl: N Kemp Smith). London: Macmillan

Kastner S & Ungerleider LG (2000) Mechanisms of visual attention. *Annual Reviews of Neuroscience* 23:315–341

Kastner S & Ungerleider LG (2000) The neural basis of biased competition in human visual cortex. *Neuropsychologia* 39:1263–1276

Kawato M (1999) Internal models for motor control and trajectory processing. *Current Opinion in Neurobiology* 9:718–727

McAdams CJ & Maunsell JHR (1999) Effects of Attention on Orientation-Tuning Functions of Single Neurons in Macaque Cortical Area V4. *Journal of Neuroscience* 19:431–441

Mehta A. D., Ulbert I. & Schroeder CE. (2000) *Intermodal Selective Attention in Monkeys: II: Physiological Mechanisms of Modulation Cerebral Cortex* 10:359–370

Miall, R. C., Wolpert, D. M. (1996). Forward models for physiological motor control. *Neural Networks*, 9 (8), 1265–1279.

Parnas J (2999( Self and Intentionality. pp. 125–147 in *Exploring the Self,* ed D Zahavi. Amsterdam: John Benjamins

Phillips CL & Harbor RD (2000) *Feedback Control Systems* (4th ed). New Jersey: Prentice Hall

Rushworth, M. F. S., Ellison, A., Walsh, V. (2001). Complementary localization and lateralization of orienting and motor attention. *Nature Neuroscience*, 4 (6), 656–661.

Rushworth, M. F. S., Nixon, P. D., Renowden, S., Wade, D. T., Passingham, R. E. (1997). The left parietal cortex and motor attention. *Neuropsychologia*, 35 (9), 1261–1273.

Sabes M (2000) The planning and control of reaching movements. *Current Opinion in Neurobiology* 10:740–746

Sass LA & Parnas J (2002) Phenomenology of Self-Disturbances in Schizophrenia: Some Research Findings and Directions. *Philosophy, Psychiatry and Psychology*, 9:347–356

Schluter ND, Krams M, Rushworth MFS & Passingham RE (2001) Cerebral dominance for action in the human brain: the selection of actions. *Neuropsychologia* 39:105–113

Shoemaker S (1968) Self-reference and self-awareness. *Journal of Philosophy* 65:556–570

Spence SA, Brooks DJ, Hirsch SR, Liddle PF, Meehan J & Grasby PM (1997) A PET study of voluntary movement in schizophrenic patients experiencing passivity phenomena (delusions of alien control) *Brain* 120:1997–2011

Taylor JG (1998) Cortical activity and the explanatory gap. *Consciousness and Cognition* 7:393–409

Taylor J. G. (1999). *The Race for Consciousness*. Cambridge MA: MIT Press.

Taylor J. G. (2000) A Control Model for Attention and Consciousness. Soc. *Neurosci. Abstr.*, 26, 2231#839.3.

Taylor, J. G. (2001a). Attention as a neural control system. *Proceedings of International Joint Conference on Neural Networks* (pp. 272–276), IJCNN'01, IEE Cat#01CH37222C, ISBN#0–07803–7046–5.

Taylor J. G. (2001b) The central role of the parietal lobes for consciousness. *Consc.& Cog.* 10:379–417 & 421–4

Taylor, J. G. (2002a). Paying attention to consciousness. *Trends Cog. Sci.* 6 (5), 206–210.

Taylor, J. G. (2002b). Models of computation in cerebral cortex. In R. Hecht-Nielsen (Ed.), to appear. Springer.

Taylor JG (2002c) From Matter to Mind. *Journal of Consciousness Studies* 6:3–22

Taylor JG (2003a) Consciousness, neural models of. pp. 263–7 in *The Handbook of Brain Theory and Neural Networks*. Ed MA Arbib. Cambridge MA: MIT Press

Taylor JG (2003b) *The CODAM model and Deficits of Consciousness I: CODAM (KES'03)*

Taylor JG (2003c) *The CODAM model and Deficits of Consciousness II: CODAM and Diseases of the Self*

Taylor JG (2005) From Matter to Mind: A Final Answer to Consciousness. *Physics of Life Reviews*

Taylor JG (2006) *The Mind: A User's Manual*. London: John Wiley

Taylor, J. G., Rogers, M. (2002). A control model of the movement of attention. *Neur. Net.*, 15, 309–326.

Taylor JG & Fragopanagos N (2003) Simulations of Motor and Sensory Attention. *Proceedings IJCNN'03*, IEEE Press.

Vogel EK, Luck SJ & Shapiro KJ (1998) Electrophysiological Evidence for a Postperceptual Locus of Suppression During the Attentional Blink. *Journal of Experimental Psychology: Human Perception and Performance.* 24:1656–1674

Willingham, D. B. (1998). A neuropsychological theory of motor skill learning. *Psych. Rev.* 105 (3), 558–584.

Wolpert DM & Ghahramani Z (2000) Computational principles of movement neuroscience. *Nature neuroscience* 3:1212–7

Zahavi D (1999) *Self-Awareness and Alterity.* Evanston, Ill: Northwestern University Press.

Zahavi D & Parnas J (1999) Phenomenal Consciousness and Self-Awareness: A Phenomenological Critique of Representational Theory. pp. 253–272 in *Models of the Self,* eds S Gallagher and J Shear.

Tom Ziemke

# What's Life Got To Do With It?

Hardly surprising in the context of a book on machine conscious-ness[1], the 'it' in the title[2] refers to consciousness. More specifically, here I will address the *self*, and in particular the question what, if anything, the living body contributes to the constitution of the natu-ral self, and subsequently consciousness, that artificial, robotic bod-ies or computer programs might be lacking for an artificial self. Raising this issue is partly motivated by the fact that the majority of machine consciousness researchers today probably would say that the answer to the above question is in fact 'nothing' (or perhaps 'very little'), i.e. life has got (practically) nothing to do with consciousness, and therefore machine consciousness researchers need not be overly concerned with low-level mechanisms underlying homeostasis, sur-vival, etc. in living organisms. At the machine consciousness sympo-sium at AISB 2005 in Hatfield, for example, a simple 'vote' was held regarding the question if (machine) consciousness required life or *'autopoiesis'* (see details below) which only three people, including myself, out of perhaps 30–40 participants thought to be the case. Probably needless to say, I have not changed my mind in the mean-time and will therefore dedicate the rest of my chapter to explaining why one might think that the living body plays a crucial role in the constitution of the self, and subsequently probably many, if not

---

[1]  Although it has been argued quite convincingly that humans, as well as other organisms, are also machines (e.g. Searle, 1980; Harnad, 2003; Ziemke, 2001a), I will here follow most of the machine consciousness literature and use the term 'machine consciousness' for artificial/man-made machines only.

[2]  Unlike the 'it' in the Tina Turner song *'What's love got to do with it?'* that inspired the title.

most, forms/aspects of consciousness, not least phenomenal, subjective experience.

When it comes to theories of the self, there are really too many to even briefly discuss them here properly (cf., e.g., Gallagher, 2000). However, following Gallagher (2002) we can roughly distinguish between *psychological* approaches and *bodily* or *biological* approaches. About the former we can say that they more or less 'dismiss the body as an important element for explaining the self', but instead argue that 'psychological rather than physical continuity is what counts in the constitution of the self', and that 'the only thing about the brain relevant to the … self is the psychological information (or syntactical functions) it instantiates' (Gallagher, 2002). Bodily/biological approaches to the self, on the other hand, assume that 'embodiment contributes in essential ways to the contribution of the self' and that in fact the 'physical nature of the body, and how the body operates, completely conditions conscious activities' (Gallagher, 2002).

However, the above distinction between psychological and biological/bodily approaches cannot straightforwardly be applied to machine consciousness researchers and approaches. Some clearly fall into the psychological category and, following the longstanding functionalist/computationalist tradition in cognitive science (e.g. Simon, 1957; Feigenbaum & Feldman, 1963; Newell & Simon, 1976; cf. Pfeifer, 1995; Pfeifer & Scheier, 1999, Ziemke, 2001a) believe that the psychological processes underlying cognition, self, consciousness, etc. could equally well be implemented in a computational substrate as in a biological brain and body. Others — relatively few if you take the above vote to be roughly representative — believe that consciousness, or at least some of its central aspects, requires a living body, and thus could be said to fall into Gallagher's biological approach category. A third class of machine consciousness researchers do agree that embodiment is essential, would however not agree that a biological/living body is required, but would argue instead that consciousness is a property of *autonomous agents*, living or artificial ones. In fact in the second part of the abovementioned 'vote' at the AISB 2005 machine consciousness symposium the majority of participants agreed to this view, which to some degree overlaps with both of the other two.

In a nutshell, the argument presented is as follows: Even if, from an observer's perspective, we refer to both living organisms and robots as 'autonomous agents', it is important to keep in mind that their 'autonomy' and 'agency' are fundamentally different. More importantly, and less obviously, these differences are highly relevant to the mechanisms underlying the constitution of the self in certain types of living bodies, i.e. the claim is that *the way an organism constructs itself also shapes the way it constructs its self.*

The next section briefly addresses artificial 'autonomous agents' and some of their limitations. The following section then discusses the autonomy and agency of living organisms, and why these might be necessary, though not necessarily sufficient, conditions for at least some forms of self and consciousness. The final section then summarizes the argument and discusses some of the implications for machine consciousness research.

### Robotic Bodies, Computational Minds

So, what exactly is an *autonomous agent* then? As for many concepts in the cognitive sciences today, there are a large number of different definitions which cannot possibly all be discussed here, so let us just take a quick look at a couple of representative examples. Beer (1995), for instance, defined autonomous agents as follows (not in the context of machine consciousness research though):

> By *autonomous agent*, I mean any embodied system designed to satisfy internal or external goals by its own actions while in continuous long-term interaction with the environment in which it is situated. The class of autonomous agents is thus a fairly broad one, encompassing at the very least all animals and autonomous robots. (Beer, 1995)

Similarly, in a paper specifically devoted to identifying the various meanings the concept 'agent' had acquired by the mid-1990s, Franklin and Graesser (1997) provided the following somewhat broader definition that includes software agents and has also been used in the context of machine consciousness (e.g. Franklin, 2003):

> An autonomous agent is a system situated within and a part of an environment that senses that environment and acts on it, over time, in pursuit of its own agenda and so as to effect what it senses in the future. (Franklin & Graesser, 1997)

As these examples indicate, the attribution of agency to artificial systems, such as robots, or software agents, hinges much on certain surface similarities, i.e. properties that are considered characteristic for living organisms, i.e. natural autonomous agents, and can be attributed, by analogy, to their presumed artificial counterparts. These properties include:

- some form of 'autonomy' ('own agenda', 'own actions', cf. above),
- goal-directed behavior,
- some form of 'situatedness' (essentially being located interacting with an environment; cf. Ziemke, 2001b),
- some form of 'embodiment', although not necessarily a physical body[3] (cf. Chrisley & Ziemke 2002; Ziemke, 2001a, 2003),
- and some might add capacities for adaptation, development and/or learning (cf. Sharkey & Ziemke 1998).

It is fairly obvious that few, if any, of these properties are actually exactly the same in living and artificial agents (cf., e.g., Sharkey & Ziemke, 1998; Moreno & Etxeberria, 2005). For example, few would deny that there are a number of differences between living bodies and robot bodies, let alone software agents. Many, however, would argue that these differences do not play any significant role when it comes to some body's/substrate's capacity to support or implement the mechanisms underlying cognition, consciousness, etc. For example, many would consider a human body and a sophisticated humanoid robot body, which have a number of obvious structural similarities, as more similar than, let us say, the bodies of a human being and a snail, or even some unicellular organism, which presumably have little in common apart from their biological, carbon-based nature (e.g. Zlatev, 2001).

However, as discussed in more detail elsewhere (Ziemke, 2004), when it comes to embodied AI and autonomous agents research as an approach to modeling cognition and consciousness, it remains unclear, and is rarely discussed in the field, what conception of embodiment and embodied cognition AI researchers, including machine consciousness researchers, are actually committed to (cf. Sharkey & Ziemke, 2001). On the one hand, much of embodied AI, in particular the widespread emphasis on physically embodied computational models (e.g. Steels, 1994; Pfeifer & Scheier, 1999), is very compatible with the view of *robotic functionalism* (Harnad, 1989), according to which embodiment is about *symbol grounding* (Harnad, 1990) or, more generally speaking, *representation grounding*, whereas cognition/thought can still be conceived of as computation, i.e. syn-

---

[3]  Franklin (1997), for example, argues: 'Software systems with no body in the usual physical sense can be intelligent. But, they must be embodied in the situated sense of being autonomous agents structurally coupled with their environment.'

tactically driven internal manipulation of representations (cf. Anderson, 2003; Chrisley, 2003), in line with psychological approaches to the self in the above sense. On the other hand, much of the rhetoric in the field of embodied AI, in particular its rejection of traditional notions of representation and cognition as computation (e.g. Beer, 1995; Clark, 1997; Sharkey & Ziemke, 1998; Pfeifer & Scheier, 1999; Ziemke, 2001a), suggests sympathy for more radical notions of embodied cognition that view *all* of cognition as embodied and/or rooted in the mechanisms of the living body (e.g. Varela et al., 1991; Stewart, 1996; Clark, 1999; Nunez, 1999; Ziemke, 2001a; Zlatev, 2002; Gallagher, 2005; Ellis, 2005), in line with bodily/biological approaches to the self.

As pointed out elsewhere (Ziemke, 2000, 2001a, 2004), a problem with embodied AI and autonomous agents research is that, despite its strong biological inspiration it has focused on establishing itself as a new paradigm *within* AI and cognitive science, i.e. as an alternative to the traditional functionalist/computationalist paradigm (e.g. Pfeifer, 1995; Pfeifer & Scheier, 1999). Relatively little effort, on the other hand, has been made to make the connection to other theories, outside AI, e.g. in theoretical biology, addressing issues of autonomy, embodiment, etc. For example, artificial autonomous agents are 'autonomous agents' in the sense that, unlike most traditional AI systems, they possess some of the above aspects of autonomy and agency, or at least easily can be attributed with them from an observer's perspective, not in the sense that they actually possess many of the features of biological autonomy and agency. Similarly, much embodied AI and autonomous agents research distinguishes itself from its traditional AI counterpart in its interactive view of *knowledge*. For example, work on adaptive robotics, in particular evolutionary (Nolfi & Floreano, 2000) and epigenetic/developmental robotics (e.g. Zlatev & Balkenius, 2001; Berthouze & Ziemke, 2003; Lungarella et al., 2003), is largely compatible with the constructivist/enactivist/interactivist view (e.g. Piaget, 1954; Varela et al., 1991; Bickhard, 1993; Ziemke, 2001a) of knowledge construction in sensorimotor interaction with the environment with the goal of achieving some 'fit' or 'equilibrium' between internal behavioral/conceptual structures and experiences of the environment. However, the organic roots of these processes, which were emphasized in, for example, the theoretical biology of von Uexküll (1928, 1982) or Maturana and Varela's (1980, 1987) theory of autopoiesis (cf. next section), are often ignored in embodied AI, which still operates with a view of the body that is largely compatible with mechanistic theories and a view of control mechanisms that is still largely compatible with computationalism (cf. Ziemke, 2000, 2001a). That means, the robot body is typically viewed as some kind of input- and output-device that provides physical grounding to the internal computational mechanisms. Thus, in practice, embodied AI has become a theoretical hybrid, or in fact a 'tribrid', combining a mechanical/behaviorist view of the body with the constructivist notion of interactive knowledge, and the functionalist/computationalist hardware-software distinction and its view of the activity of the nervous system as computational (cf. Ziemke 2001a).

The mechanical view of the body is of course also of particular importance when it comes to embodied AI/autonomous agent models of consciousness. As Greenspan and Baars (2004) have recently discussed in detail (cf. also Sharkey & Ziemke, 1998, 2001; Ziemke, 2001a), the mechanistic/reductionistic approach to biology and psychology of leading early 20th-century researchers like Loeb (1918) and Pavlov (1927) paved the way for the strong dominance of behaviorism in psychology, as pursued by Watson (1925) and Skinner (1938), which essentially suppressed the study of consciousness for several decades. At a first glance, it might seem that with the rise of cognitivism and the computer metaphor in cognitive science, mechanistic behaviorism has been 'overcome', but Costall (in press) recently pointed out that:

> ... it is not the case that mainstream cognitive psychology entirely replaced the traditional mechanistic model. It retains the old mechanistic image of the *body*. The new mechanism of mind has been merely assimilated to the old dualism of mind and body, along with the existing conception of the body as a passive machine. This dualism is now, however, reformulated in terms of two radically different kinds of machines — a machine with a machine, a new mechanical mind implanted with the old mechanical body. However, we have all been so fixated upon how to theorize the mind in terms of the new mechanism that this retention of the old mechanistic schema of the body has been systematically overlooked. (Costall, in press, original emphasis)

Although Costall's critique is directed mainly at cognitivist/computationalist AI, rather than embodied AI, it should be noted that the mind/body or hardware/software dualism that he accuses modern psychology of is the exact same dualism that Searle (1980) in his famous *Chinese Room* argument accused AI of. And, as Searle pointed out already back then in his *robot reply*, whether or not the computational mind resides in a slightly less passive robotic body, i.e. a physical/mechanical container that allows the computational mind to interact with its environment through sensors and actuators, really does not make much of a difference when it comes to such computational/robotic systems as models of human intentionality, consciousness, etc. In a similar vein, Parisi (2004) has recently argued for the need for an *internal robotics* in the modelling of cognition (cf. Di Paolo, 2003):

> ... behaviour is the result of the interactions of an organism's nervous system with both the external environment and the internal environment, i.e. with what lies within the organism's body. While robotics has concentrated so far on the first type of interactions (external robotics), to more adequately understand the behaviour of organisms we also need to reproduce in robots the inside of the body of organisms and to study the interactions of the robot's control system with what is inside the body (internal robotics). (Parisi, 2004, p. 325)

The next section addresses the supposed crucial difference(s) between living and robotic bodies, and why biological autonomy is relevant to the perhaps most basic form of self - a non-conscious, pre-reflective 'proto-self' (Damasio, 1999) that keeps track of the living body and its homeostasis, and subsequently presumably is underlying higher levels/other forms of self and consciousness.

## Living Bodies

So, what is so special about biological autonomy and agency then? And why should the differences be relevant to self and consciousness? Let us start with the first question, and then get back to the second question later.

In a nutshell, the answer to the first question is that living organisms have a particular *organization*[4], i.e. depending on which theoretical framework and terminology you prefer, they are *autopoietic* systems (Varela et al., 1973; Maturana & Varela, 1980, 1987; Varela, 1979, 1997; Luisi, 2003; Di Paolo, 2005), or (recursively) *self-maintenant* systems (Bickhard, 1993, 2000, 2004), or simply *autonomous* systems (Christensen & Hooker, 2000). The first and the third of these terms will below be elaborated in some more detail below.

---

[4]    Following Maturana and Varela (1987), the term *organization* here refers to 'those relations that must exist among the components of a system for it to be a member of a specific class' whereas the term *structure* refers to 'the components and relations that actually constitute a particular unity, and make its organisation real'.

There are two things to note here: Firstly, for the present purpose, the above theories can be considered to be more or less equivalent. The term 'autopoietic' will be used primarily in the following, but this should not be taken to reflect a commitment to a particular theoretical framework, but rather reflects the fact that that concept of autopoiesis is more commonly used than 'recursive self-maintenance' and less ambiguous than 'autonomy'. Secondly, these more or less modern theories have a number of historic precursors, such as the concept of autonomy in von Uexküll's (1928, 1982) theoretical biology and theory of meaning (cf. Ziemke, 2000, 2001a; Ziemke & Sharkey, 2001), or even much earlier than that, Spinoza's concept of the *conatus*. Damasio (2003) recently described the latter as follows:

> It is apparent that the continuous attempt at achieving a state of positively regulated life is a deep and defining part of our existence — the first reality of our existence as Spinoza intuited when he described the relentless endeavor (*conatus*) of each being to preserve itself ... Interpreted with the advantages of current hindsight, Spinoza's notion implies that the living organism is constructed so as to maintain the coherence of its structures and functions against numerous life-threatening odds.
>
> The conatus subsumes both the impetus for self-preservation in the face of danger and opportunities and the myriad actions of self-preservation that hold the parts of the body together. In spite of the transformations the body must undergo as it develops, renews its constituent, and ages, the conatus continues to form the *same* individual and respect the *same* structural design. (Damasio, 2003, p. 36)

Some more modern theories of exactly how the above works will be elaborated below. But probably already at this point some of the (supposed) differences between biological and artificial 'autonomous agents' are fairly clear: Living organisms are autonomous in the sense of self-construction and -preservation (from which, arguably, all other goals derive), and they have and maintain an inherent identity/unity, i.e. the organism striving for homeostasis/survival.

The theory of *autopoiesis* (Varela et al., 1973; Maturana & Varela, 1980, 1987; Varela, 1979, 1997) explains these phenomena as follows:

> An autopoietic system — the minimal living organization — is one that continuously produces the components that specify it, while at the same time realizing it (the system) as a concrete unit in space and time, which makes the network of production of components possible. More precisely defined: An autopoietic system is organized (defined as a unity) as a network of processes of pro-

duction (synthesis and destruction) of components such that these components:

(i) continuously regenerate and realize the network that produces them, and

(ii) constitute the system as a distinguishable unity in the domain in which they exist. (Varela, 1997, p. 75)

Accordingly, biological '[a]utonomy is the distinctive phenomenology resulting from an autopoietic organization: the realization of the autopoietic organization is the product of its operation' (Varela, Maturana & Uribe, 1974, p. 188; cf. Varela, 1979). The prime examples of autopoiesis are living cells and organisms, which have also been referred to as 'first-order' and 'second-order autopoietic unities' respectively (e.g. Maturana & Varela, 1987). The concept of autopoiesis has also been extended to social systems (e.g. Luhmann, 1990), such as states and societies, which could possibly be conceived of as third-order autopoietic unities, but this is not fully in line with the original theory of autopoiesis as put forward by Maturana and Varela. Another controversial issue is that Maturana and Varela (1980, 1987) actually consider *all* living systems to be cognitive systems. For obvious reasons, this has been criticized by a number of authors who wish to reserve the term 'cognitive' for higher-level psychological processes (cf., e.g., Barandiaran & Moreno, 2006). Varela (1997) defended/motivated the use of the term as follows:

> The reader may balk at my use of the term cognitive for cellular systems. But from what I have said it should be clear that the constitution of a cognitive domain links organisms and their worlds in a way that is *the very essence of intentionality* as used in modern cognitive science, and as it was originally introduced in phenomenology. My proposal makes explicit the process through which intentionality arises: it amounts to an explicit hypothesis about how to transform the philosophical notion of intentionality into a principle of natural science. The use of the term cognitive here is thus justified because it is *at the very base of how intentionality arises in nature.* (Varela, 1997, pp. 80–81, emphases added)

It should be noted that the controversial question of whether or not cells and simple organisms, by definition, should be considered cognitive, is not relevant here since cognition as such is not actually the topic here and the term is not particularly well defined anyway (cf., e.g., Prinz, 2004). Arguably, in line with the formulations highlighted in the above quote, Varela and Maturana might have been well advised to suggest autopoiesis as a *necessary* condition (for intentionality and self) rather than a *sufficient* condition for cognition (cf., e.g., Barandiaran & Moreno, 2006).

For a competing, though closely related theory, let us also have a quick look at Christensen and Hooker's (2000) theory of autonomy, which aimed to propose a naturalistic theory of intelligent agency as an embodied feature of organized, typically living, dynamical systems. According to this theory, agents are entities which engage in normatively constrained, goal-directed, interaction with their environment. More specifically, '[l]iving systems are a particular kind of cohesive system ... in which there are dynamical bonds amongst the elements of the system which individuate the system from its environment'. Since *cohesion* is a central concept in Christensen and Hooker's (2000) theory, let us have a look at some examples: A gas has no internal cohesion, its shape and condition are imposed by the environment. A rock, on the other hand, has internal bonds and behaves as an integral whole. However, these *cohesive bonds* are *passive* and *rigid* (i.e. stable deep-energy-well interactions are constraining the constituents spatially), and they are *local*, (i.e. there are no essential constraints on the boundary of the system). A cell, finally, has cohesive bonds and acts as an integrated whole, but those bonds are *active* (i.e. chemical bonds formed by shallow-energy-well interactions and continually actively remade), *flexible* (i.e. interactions can vary, are sensitive to system and environmental changes), and *holistic* (i.e. binding forces depend on globally organized interactions; i.e. local processes must interact globally to ensure the cell's survival).

*Autonomous systems* then, according to Christensen and Hooker (2000), are cohesive systems of the same general type as the cell. Their examples of autonomous systems include, as for autopoiesis, cells and organisms, but also molecular catalytic bi-cycles, species, and colonies (for details see Christensen & Hooker, 2000). Regarding the differences between their theory of autonomy and the theory of autopoiesis, Christensen and Hooker (2000) state that the paradigm case of autopoiesis is the operationally closed system that produces all its components within itself, whereas their theory of autonomy emphasizes agent-environment interaction and a 'directive organisation [that] induces pattern-formation of energy flows from the environmental milieu into system-constitutive processes'. However, as Varela (1997: 82) pointed out, in the theory of autopoiesis the term *operational closure* 'is used in its mathematical sense of recursivity, and not in the sense of closedness or isolation from inter-action, which would be, of course, nonsense'.

The question of operational closure and interaction, in fact, also brings us back to the issue of the *self*. Much has been said by now about the autonomy of organisms, i.e. autopoietic systems, and the lack thereof in man-made artefacts, such as robots and software agents, i.e. *allopoietic* systems whose components are produced by other processes that are independent of the organisation of the system (cf. Ziemke, 2001a; Ziemke & Sharkey, 2001). But this, so far, only covers the first question raised in the beginning of this section, whereas the second question, i.e. issue of the self, and why we should consider biological autonomy as necessary for a self, has so far been left relatively open. Varela (1997) had the following to say about this:

> The operational closure of the nervous system then brings forth a specific mode of coherence, which is embedded in the organism. This coherence is a cognitive identity: a unit of percep-tion/motion in space, sensory-motor invariances, mediated through the interneuron network. The passage to cognition hap-pens at the level of a behavioral entity and not, as in the basic cel-lular self, as a spatially bounded entity. The key in this cognitive process is the nervous system through its neuro-logic. In other words the cognitive self is the manner in which the organism, through its own self-produced activity, becomes a distinct entity in space, but always coupled to its corresponding environment from which it remains nevertheless distinct. A distinct coherent self which, by the very same process of constituting itself, configures, an external world of perception and action. (Varela, 1997, p. 83)[5]

The above provides us with an idea of how the coherence, unity and identity of an organism comes about and makes it interact with its environment as a behavioural entity (and thus constitutes the 'cogni-tive self', where, as discussed above, the label 'cognitive' might be controversial). This also seems closely related to what Spinoza referred to as the conatus (cf. above) as well as what Nossal (2001) called the 'immunological self', i.e. the mechanisms of self-recogni-tion that allow the immune system to identify what belongs to the own body and what does not. However, all of these mechanisms are usually considered unconscious, and the question remains in what sense biological autonomy and an unconscious 'organismic self' in the above sense(s) can be considered to be underlying or contribut-

---

[5]    Cf. also Bourgine and Varela (1992).

ing to the subjective experience of consciousness and self-awareness.

The answer comes from *somatic theories* of emotion and consciousness, such as the work of Damasio (1998, 1999, 2003a, 2003b),
Panksepp (1998, 2005), Prinz (2004), or their historical predecessors,
James (1884) and Lange (1885). What these theories agree on is, in a
nutshell and somewhat oversimplified, that emotions arise from the
homeostatic regulation of bodily activity, and emotional feelings are
feelings of such bodily changes (cf. Prinz, 2004).

Damasio (1999), for example, has developed the concept of the
*proto-self*, as a link between the unconscious homeostatic activity of
the living body and the subjective experience of the core self and core
consciousness. The proto-self, according to Damasio (1999), is distributed over several brain regions, including brainstem (cf. Parvizi
& Damasio, 2001) and hypothalamus, but also parts of cerebral cortex, and functioning as a '*coherent collection of neural patterns which
map, moment by moment the state of the physical structure of the organism
in its many dimensions*' (Parvizi & Damasio, 2001, p. 138, original
emphasis). The proto-self itself, however, at least according to
Damasio's theory, is not conscious.

> It should be noted at the outset that the proto-self is not the sense
> of self in the traditional sense, the sort of self on which our cur-
> rent knowing is centered, that is, the core self (the protagonist of
> core consciousness), and the autobiographical self (the extended
> form of self which includes one's identity and is anchored in our
> past and anticipated future). The proto-self is the preconscious
> biological precedent of both core and autobiographical self.
> (Parvizi & Damasio, 2001, p. 138)

Regarding core consciousness then, Parvizi and Damasio (2001),
summarize their theoretical framework as follows:

> The basic form of consciousness, core consciousness is placed in
> the context of life regulation; it is seen as yet another level of bio-
> logical processing aimed at ensuring the homeostatic balance of a
> living organism; and the representation of the current organism
> state within somato-sensing structures is seen as critical to its
> development. Core consciousness is conceived as the imaged
> relationship of the interaction between an object and the changed
> organism state it causes. (Parvizi & Damasio, 2001, p. 135)

Damasio's idea that 'self-awareness emerges from an image of the
homeostatic state of the body' is also supported by Craig (2003), who
recently argued that primates have an *interoceptive* system, associated with autonomic motor control, i.e. 'a distinct cortical image of

homeostatic afferent activity that reflects all aspects of the physiological condition of all tissues of the body'. He further suggested that
this system provides 'the basis for the subjective image of the material self as a feeling (sentient) entity, that is, emotional awareness'
(Craig, 2003, p. 500; cf. also Craig, 2004).

Exactly how the phenomenal quality of such experiences comes
about is of course still an open question. However, it might be worth
noting here that the above theories do not actually fully agree on
where and how the phenomenal conscious experience actually 'occurs'. Panksepp (2005) contrasted the view of Damasio who situates
the 'capacity for emotional feelings quite high in somatosensory
body representation areas of the cerebral cortex' with his own view
that 'core *emotional* feelings ... reflect activities of massive
subcortical networks that establish rather global states within primitive body representations that exist below the neocortex' (Panksepp,
2005, p. 64).

## Conclusion

The argument presented can roughly be summarized, backwards, as
follows: Somatic theories of emotion and consciousness present
what Panksepp, with reference to Damasio's and his own work,
called 'a *multi-tiered affectively embodied view of mind*' (Panksepp,
2005, p. 63, emphasis added). Within this type of theoretical framework the 'mental self' (Damasio, 2003b) emerges from the
homeostatic regulation of bodily activity in complex living organisms (not necessarily in all organisms), through what Craig (2003)
referred to as interoceptive sense of the homeostatic state of the
body. Homeostatic regulation of both body-internal activity and the
interaction of autopoietic unities with their environment as coordinated entities, in its turn, according to the theory of autopoiesis (e.g.
Varela, 1997), is a natural consequence of the realization, and the
continuous regeneration, of the autopoietic organization of living
organisms. Artefacts, such as robots and software agents, on the
other hand, are allopoietic systems whose components are produced
by other processes that are independent of the organisation of the
system, and thus lack the autonomy of living systems.

For the sake of clarification you might want to ask if perhaps the
emphasis on the autonomy of the living organism implies any form
of *vitalism*. This, however, is not at all the case. Varela explicitly
referred to autonomous/autopoietic systems as 'mechanistic
(dynamic) systems defined as a unity by their organization' (Varela,

1979, p. 55) and elsewhere explicitly rejected 'the need to resort to a central agent that turns the handle from the outside, like an *élan vital*' (Varela, 1997, p. 80). For the same reasons, the above also does not imply any dualism—you might say, there simply is no ghost in the machine—quite the opposite, the above argument avoids the mind/body or hardware/software dualism that, for example, Searle and Costall have accused the computational/robotic functionalist framework of (cf. above). You might also want to ask if autopoietic systems necessarily need to be biological/organic in the usual sense. There does not seem to be any principle reason to assume this though, in particular since, in Maturana & Varela's terms, autopoiesis is about the organization, not the structure realizing it: 'the phenomena they generate in functioning as autopoietic unities depend on their organisation and the way this organisation comes about, and not on the physical nature of their components (which only determine their space of existence)' (Maturana & Varela, 1987, p. 51).

What then are the implications of the argument presented here for machine consciousness research? Well, if you are committed to what Gallagher (2002) referred to as the psychological approach to the self (cf. introductory section), i.e. you believe in (some sort of) independence of the self from the physical/biological body, then of course none of the discussions of biological autonomy are likely to impress you much, and you can happily go on building computational models of consciousness (with a growing body of neurobiological evidence against you though). If, on the other hand, you are at least to some degree committed to what Gallagher (2002) called a bodily approach (i.e. you believe that embodiment is relevant) and you were planning to build a truly conscious robot, in the sense of a 'strong AI' (Searle, 1980), i.e. with actual human-like intentionality, etc., some time soon, then the argument here presented might cause you some serious headaches. However, if you are committed to a bodily/biological approach, but are mainly interested in building robotic and/or computational models as cognitive-scientific models of self, consciousness, etc. in the sense of a 'weak AI' (Searle, 1980), i.e. without the ambition to actually (re-) produce the phenomena modelled[6], then you are more likely to interpret the argument as saying something about the appropriate unit of analysis in modeling

---

[6]   Just like very few, if any, meteorological modelers are interested in producing actual artificial weather in their computers.

self, consciousness, etc. (cf. Morse & Ziemke, subm.)[7] Just like since
the late 1980s some AI researchers have taken theories of embod-
ied/situated/distributed cognition as reason to build 'complete'
'autonomous' agents (cf., e.g., Dennett, 1978; Meyer et al. 2005) to
take into account the 'external' context of sensorimotor interaction
with the environment, some researchers argue now that the 'internal' context of the embedding of embodied cognition in homeostatic
regulation of bodily activity should be taken into account as well
(e.g. Di Paolo, 2003; Parisi, 2004; Barandiaran & Moreno, 2006;
Herrera et al., 2006). The arguments presented here suggest that this
interaction between the 'external' context of the world and the 'internal' context of the body — or, more specifically, the interaction
between the sensorimotor, emotional, and homeostatic dimensions
of embodied cognition — is crucial to our understanding of self and
consciousness in living organisms, and should naturally also be
taken into account in the way we build scientific models of these
phenomena.

## Acknowledgements

This work has been supported by a European Commission grant to
the project 'Integrating Cognition, Emotion and Autonomy' (ICEA,
IST-027819, www.his.se/icea) as part of the European *Cognitive Systems* initiative. The author would also like to thank the organizers
(Ron Chrisley, Ricardo Sanz & Aaron Sloman) and participants of
the 2003 'Models of Consciousness' workshop in Birmingham where
an early version of this chapter was presented. The chapter has also
benefited from collaborations and discussions with Mark Bickhard,
Stan Franklin, Carlos Herrera, Tony Morse, and Mikkel Sørensen.

## References

Anderson, M. (2003). Embodied Cognition: A Field Guide. *Artificial
Intelligence*, 149(1), 91–130.
Barandiaran, X. & Moreno, A. (2006). On what makes certain dynamical
systems cognitive: A minimally cognitive organization program.
*Adaptive Behavior*, 14(2), 171–185
Beer, R.D. (1995). A dynamical systems perspective on agent-environment
interaction. *Artificial Intelligence*, 72, 173–215.
Berthouze, L. & Ziemke, T. (2003). Epigenetic robotics: Modelling Cognitive
Development in Robotic Systems. *Connection Science*, 15(4), 147–150.

---

[7]  For example, see Bosse et al. (2005, 2006) for formal models of several of
Damasio's concepts.

Bickhard, M.H. (1993). Representational Content in Humans and Machines. *Journal of Experimental and Theoretical Artificial Intelligence*, 5, 285-333.

Bickhard, M.H. (2000). Autonomy, Function, and Representation. *Communication and Cognition – Artificial Intelligence*. 17(3–4), 111–131.

Bickhard, M.H. (2004). Process and Emergence: Normative Function and Representation. *Axiomathes – An International Journal in Ontology and Cognitive Systems*, 14, 135–169.

Bourgine, P. & Varela, F.J. (1992). Toward a practice of autonomous systems. In: Varela, F.J. & Bourgine, P. (eds.) *Toward a practice of autonomous systems – Proceedings of the First European Conference on Artificial Life* (pp. xi–xvii). Cambridge, MA: MIT Press.

Bosse, T., Jonker, C.M. & Treur, J. (2005). Simulation and Representation of Body, Emotion, and Core Consciousness. In: *Proceedings of the AISB 2005 Symposium on Next Generation approaches to Machine Consciousness: Imagination, Development, Intersubjectivity, and Embodiment*, (pp. 95–103). AISB, UK.

Bosse, T., Jonker, C.M. & Treur, J. (2006). Formal Analysis of Damasio's Theory on Core Consciousness. In: Fum, D., Del Missier, F. & Stocco, A. (eds.) *Proceedings of the Seventh International Conference on Cognitive Modelling, ICCM'06* (pp. 68–73). Edizioni Goliardiche.

Chrisley, R. (2003). Embodied Artificial Intelligence. *Artificial Intelligence*, 149(1), 131–150.

Chrisley, R. & Ziemke, T. (2002). Embodiment. In: *Encyclopedia of Cognitive Science* (pp. 1102-1108). London: Macmillan Publishers.

Christensen, W.D. & Hooker, C.A. (2000). Autonomy and the emergence of intelligence: Organised interactive Construction. *Communication and Cognition – Artificial Intelligence*, 17(3–4), 133–157.

Clark, A. (1997). *Being There*. Cambridge, MA: MIT Press.

Clark, A. (1999). An embodied cognitive science? *Trends in Cognitive Science*, 9, 345–351.

Costall, A. (in press). Bringing the body back to life: James Gibson's ecology of agency. In. Ziemke, T., Zlatev, J. & Frank, R. (eds.) *Body, Language and Mind. Volume 1: Embodiment*. Berlin: Mouton de Gruyter.

Craig, A.D. (2003). Interoception: The sense of the physiological condition of the body. *Current Opinion in Neurobiology*, 13, 500–505.

Craig, A.D. (2004). Human feelings: Why are some more aware than others? *Trends in Cognitive Sciences*, 8(6), 239–241.

Damasio, A.R. (1998). Emotion in the perspective of an integrated nervous system. *Brain Research Reviews*, 26, 83–86.

Damasio, A.R. (1999). *The Feeling of What Happens: Body, Emotion and the Making of Consciousness*. London: Vintage.

Damasio, A.R. (2003a). *Looking for Spinoza: Joy, Sorrow and the Feeling Brain*. Orlando, FL: Harcourt.

Damasio, A.R. (2003b). The person within. *Nature*, 423, 227.

Dennett, D.C. (1978) Why not the Whole Iguana? *Brain and Behavioral Sciences*, (1): pp. 103–104.

Di Paolo, E.A. (2003). Organismically-inspired robotics: Homeostatic adaptation and natural teleology beyond the closed sensorimotor loop. In: Murase, K. & Asakura, T. (eds.) *Dynamical Systems Approach to*

*Embodiment and Sociality* (pp. 19-42). Advanced Knowledge International: Adelaide, Australia.

Di Paolo, E.A. (2005). Autopoiesis, adaptivity, teleology, agency. *Phenomenology and the Cognitive Sciences*, 4(4), 429-452.

Ellis, R. (2005). *Curious Emotions: Roots of Consciousness and Personality in Motivated Action*. Amsterdam: John Benjamins.

Feigenbaum, E. & J. Feldman (eds.) (1963). *Computers and Thought*. New York: McGrall Hill.

Franklin, S.A. & Graesser, A. (1997). Is it an Agent, or just a Program? A Taxonomy for Autonomous Agent. In: Müller, J., Wooldridge, M. & Jennings, N. (eds.) *Intelligent Agents III: Agent Theories, Architectures and Languages* (pp. 21-35). Berlin: Springer.

Franklin, S.A. (1997). Autonomous agents as embodied AI. *Cybernetics and Systems*, 28(6), 499-520.

Franklin, S.A. (2003). IDA – A conscious artifact? *Journal of Consciousness Studies*, 10(4-5), 47-66-

Gallagher, S. (2000). Philosophical conceptions of the self: Implications for cognitive science. *Trends in Cognitive Sciences*, 4(1), 14-21.

Gallagher, S. (2002). The Self: Philosophical Problems. In: *Encyclopedia of Cognitive Science*. London: Macmillan.

Gallagher, S. (2005). *How the Body Shapes the Mind*. Oxford: Oxford University Press.

Greenspan, R.J. & Baars, B.J. (2005). Consciousness eclipsed: Jacques Loeb, Ivan P. Pavlov, and the rise of reductionistic biology after 1900. *Consciousness and Cognition*, 24, 219-230.

Harnad, S. (1989). Minds, Machines and Searle. *Journal of Theoretical and Experimental Artificial Intelligence*, 1(1), 5-25.

Harnad, S (1990). The Symbol Grounding Problem. *Physica D*, 42, 335-346.

Harnad, S. (2003). Can a machine be conscious? How? *Journal of Consciousness Studies*, 10(4-5), 67-75.

Herrera, C., Moffat, D. & Ziemke, T. (2006). Emotions as a bridge to the environment: On the role of the body in organisms and robots. In: Nolfi et al. (eds) *From Animals to Animats 9: Proceedings of the Ninth International Conference on Simulation of Adaptive Behaviour* (pp.3-14). Berlin: Springer.

James, W. (1884). What is an emotion? *Mind*, 9, 188-205.

Lakoff, G. & Johnson, M. (1999). *Philosophy in the Flesh*. New York: Basic Books.

Lange, C.G. (1885). *Om sindsbevægelser – Et psyko-fysiologisk studie*. Copenhagen: Jacob Lunds.

Lindblom, J. & Ziemke, T. (2003). Social situatedness of natural and artificial intelligence: Vygotsky and beyond. *Adaptive Behavior*, 11(2), 79-96.

Lindblom, J. & Ziemke, T. (2006). The Social Body in Motion: Cognitive Development in Infants and Androids. *Connection Science*, 18(4), 333-346.

Loeb, Jacques (1918). *Forced movements, tropisms, and animal conduct*. Philadelphia: Lippincott Company.

Luhmann, N. (1990). *Essays on Self-Reference*. Columbia University Press.

Lungarella M., Metta G., Pfeifer R. & Sandini G. (2003). Developmental robotics: a survey. *Connection Science*, 15(4), 151-190.

Luisi, P.L. (2003). Autopoiesis: A review and a reappraisal. *Naturwissenschaften*, 90, 49-59.

Maturana, H. R. & Varela, F. J. (1980). *Autopoiesis and Cognition*. Dordrecht: Reidel.

Maturana, H. R. & Varela, F. J. (1987). *The Tree of Knowledge - The Biological Roots of Human Understanding*. Boston, MA: Shambhala.

Meyer, J.-A., Guillot, A., Girard, B., Khamassi, M., Pirim, P., & Berthoz, A. (2005). The Psikharpax project: Towards building an artificial rat. *Robotics and Autonomous Systems*, 50(4): 211–223.

Moreno, A. & Etxeberria, A. (2005). Agency in Natural and Artificial Systems. *Artificial Life*, 11, (1–2), 161–175.

Morse, A.F. & Ziemke, T. (subm.). On the Role(s) of Synthetic Modelling in Cognitive Science. Submitted for journal publication.

Newell, A. & Simon, H. (1976). Computer Science as Empirical Inquiry: Symbols and Search. *Communications of the ACM*, 19, 113–126.

Nolfi, S. & Floreano, D. (2000). Evolutionary Robotics. Cambride, MA: MIT Press.

Nossal, G.J.V. (2001). A purgative mastery. *Nature*, 412, 685–686.

Nunez, R. (1999). Could the Future Taste Purple? Reclaiming Mind, Body and Cognition. *Journal of Consciousness Studies*, 6(11-12), 41-60.

Panksepp, J. (1998). The periconscious substrates of consciousness: Affective states and the evolutionary origins of the self. *Journal of Consciousness Studies*, 5(5-6), 566–582.

Panksepp, J. (2005). Affective consciousness: Core emotional feelings in animals and humans. *Consciousness and Cognition*, 14, 30–80.

Parisi, D. (2004). Internal robotics. *Connection Science*, 16(4), 325–338.

Parvizi, J. & Damasio, A.R. (2001). Consciousness and the brainstem. *Cognition*, 79, 135–159.

Pavlov, Ivan P. (1927). *Conditioned Reflexes*. London: Oxford University Press.

Pfeifer, R. (1995). Cognition—Perspectives from autonomous agents. *Robotics and Autonomous Systems*, 15, 47–70.

Pfeifer, R. & Scheier, C. (1999). *Understanding Intelligence*. Cambridge, MA: MIT Press.

Piaget, Jean (1954). *The Construction of Reality in the Child*. New York: Basic Books. Originally appeared as Piaget (1937) *La construction du réel chez l'enfant*. Neuchâtel, Switzerland: Delachaux et Niestlé.

Prinz, J.J. (2003). Level-headed mysterianism and artificial experience. *Journal of Consciousness Studies*, 10(4-5), 111–132.

Prinz, J.J. (2004). *Gut Reactions—A Perceptual Theory of Emotion*. Oxford: Oxford University Press.

Sharkey, N.E. & Ziemke, T. (1998). A consideration of the biological and psychological foundations of autonomous robotics. *Connection Science*, 10(3-4), 361–391.

Sharkey, N.E. & Ziemke, T. (2001). Mechanistic vs. Phenomenal Embodiment: Can Robot Embodiment Lead to Strong AI? *Cognitive Systems Research*, 2(4), 251–262.

Simon, H.A. (1957). *Models of Man*. New York, NY: Wiley.

Skinner, B.F. (1938). *The behavior of organisms*. New York: Appleton-Century-Crofts.

Steels, L. (1994). The artificial life roots of artificial intelligence. *Artificial Life*, 1, 75–110.

Stewart, J. (1996). Cognition = Life: Implications for higher-level cognition. *Behavioral Processes*, 35, 311–326.

Tani, J. (1998). An interpretation of the `self' from the dynamical systems perspective. *Journal of Consciousness Studies*, 5(5-6), 516–542.

Turing, A. (1950). Computing machinery and intelligence. *Mind*, 49, 433–460.

Varela, F.J. (1979). *Principles of Biological Autonomy*. New York: Elsevier.

Varela, F.J. (1997). Patterns of Life: Intertwining Identity and Cognition. *Brain and Cognition*, 34, 72–87

Varela, F.J., Maturana, H.R. & Uribe, R. (1974). Autopoiesis: the organization of living systems, its characterization and a model. *Biosystems*, 5, 187–196.

Varela, F.J., Thompson, E. & Rosch, E. (1991). *The embodied mind: Cognitive science and human experience*. Cambridge, MA: MIT Press.

von Uexküll, J. (1928). *Theoretische Biologie*. Berlin: Springer Verlag.

von Uexküll, J. (1982). The Theory of Meaning. *Semiotica*, 42(1), 25–82. Originally appeared as von Uexküll, J. (1940). *Bedeutungslehre*. Leipzig: Verlag J.A. Barth.

Watson, J.B. (1925). *Behaviorism*. New York: Norton.

Ziemke, T. (2000). *Situated neuro-robotics and interactive cognition*. Doctoral dissertation, University of Sheffield, UK.

Ziemke, T. (2001a). The Construction of 'Reality' in the Robot. *Foundations of Science*, 6(1), 163–233.

Ziemke, T. (2001b). Are Robots Embodied? In: Balkenius, C.; Zlatev, J.; Brezeal, C.; Dautenhahn, K. & Kozima, H. (eds.) *Proceedings of the First International Workshop on Epigenetic Robotics: Modelling Cognitive Development in Robotic Systems* (pp. 75–83). Lund University Cognitive Studies, vol. 85, Lund, Sweden.

Ziemke, T. (2003). What's that thing called embodiment? In: Alterman, R. & Kirsh, D. (eds.) *Proceedings of the 25th Annual Conference of the Cognitive Science Society* (pp. 1305–1310). Mahwah, NJ: Lawrence Erlbaum.

Ziemke, T. (2004). Embodied AI as Science: Models of Embodied Cognition, Embodied Models of Cognition, or Both? In: Iida, F., Pfeifer, R., Steels, L. & Kuniyoshi, Y. (eds.) *Embodied Artificial Intelligence* (pp. 27–36). Heidelberg: Springer.

Ziemke, T. (2005). Cybernetics and Embodied Cognition: On the Construction of Realities in Organisms and Robots. *Kybernetes*, 34(1/2), 118-128.

Ziemke, T. & Sharkey, N. E. (2001). A stroll through the worlds of robots and animals. *Semiotica*, 134(1–4), 701–746.

Ziemke, T., Zlatev, J. & Frank, R. (eds.) (in press). *Body, Language and Mind. Volume 1: Embodiment*. Berlin: Mouton de Gruyter.

Zlatev, J. (2001). The epigenesis of meaning in human beings, and possibly in robots. *Minds and Machines*, 11(2), 155–195.

Zlatev, J. (2002). Meaning = Life (+ Culture) — An outline of a unified biocultural theory of meaning. *Evolution of Communication*, 4 (2), 175–199.

Zlatev, J. & Balkenius, C. (2001). Introduction: Why 'epigenetic robotics? In: Balkenius, C.; Zlatev, J.; Brezeal, C.; Dautenhahn, K. & Kozima, H. (eds.) (2001). *Proceedings of the First International Workshop on Epigenetic Robotics: Modelling Cognitive Development in Robotic Systems* (pp. 1–4). Lund University Cognitive Studies, vol. 85, Lund, Sweden.

# Igor Aleksander & Helen Morton

# *Depictive Architectures for Synthetic Phenomenology*

## 1. Introduction

In searching for computational models of being conscious, the detailed nature of internal representation is an important facet of the way that modelling is to be approached. We suggest that synthetic phenomenology is involved when two conditions are fulfilled: first there is some sense in which a first person may be ascribed to the model and second when the architecture caters for an explicable and action-usable representation of 'the way things seem' within the machine. We avoid that this should be too distant from reality by insisting that this representation be as close an approximation to 'the way things are' as permitted by the sensory apparatus of that organism. This is assumed to be sufficiently close to reality to enable the organism to take appropriate action in its world. This is likely to be true of successfully evolved organisms, as too many errors of action do not augur well for successful evolution.

The chapter first reviews the reason that in philosophy, phenomenology proves to be a useful concept despite the fact that the appellative became used in a variety of ways. We recognise its meaning first as a way of discussing first person phenomena (in contrast with 'ontology'), second as a basis for 20th century discussions, and finally in the sense of Block's use of the word in the descriptor of 'Phenomenal consciousness' as being distinct from 'Access consciousness'. We particularly single out the way that such concepts could feature in computational systems.

The concept of a 'depictive' representation is developed beyond that which has been discussed to date (Aleksander, 2005) to show that this is a central requirement for an architecture to be synthetically phenomenological. A set of architectural tests is then developed that determines whether an architecture could be said to be phenomenological or not. Two known architectures are submitted to these tests: Shanahan's embodied concept of Baars' Global Workspace architecture (Shanahan, 2005) and the *kernel* architecture of Aleksander (2005). This concludes that the issue of phenomenology can be considered at different levels of mechanistic description, of which the two architectures are distinct examples. Also in the conclusion we argue that phenomenology in computational architectures leads to both explanatory discussions about consciousness and some practical advantages of the way in which synthetic phenomenology might lead to new functional artefacts. We shall first review issues that go under the heading of Phenomenology *and italicise strands that are taken up in discussing the implication for synthetic systems and their architectures discussed later.*

## 2. Phenomenology

### 2.1  Definition

In the broadest terms, we interpret 'phenomenology' as the word given to studies of consciousness which specifically start with the first person. Importantly from a modelling standpoint this implies that introspection is an important facet of the discussion. This distinguishes phenomenology from other forms of approach, where one is concerned with what it is for an object to be conscious. One should also distinguish 'a phenomenon' from other constructs such as 'qualia' which relate to sensational primitives such as 'redness' or 'the sweet smell of a rose'. In general, phenomenologists like to extend the definition beyond the directly sensory to more compositional structures of experience such as enjoying a game of tennis or the experience of having dated a new person.

*The 'kernel' architecture we raise here was synthesised through a process of using introspection to discover design principles. This led us to look at ways that this work contributes to the formation of a synthetic phenomenology paradigm.*

## 2.2 Past Usage

In attempts to operationalise phenomenology it sometimes seems to be the same problem as the operationalisation of consciousness in general. For Franz Brentano (1874) phenomena *are* acts of consciousness, they are the contents of mind. They stand in relation to physical phenomena that are perceived in the world *by intentionally* creating meaning of the physical in the mind. This first-person character of a phenomenon has remained the hallmark of the work of later phenomenologists. Of these, Edmund Husserl (1913), stressed the meanings the mind creates when contemplating the real world. This intentionalist position focuses on the mental object irrespectively of its real-world character. So if the meaning of a stick is its ability to dislodge a banana off the branch of a tree, the phenomenology of the stick appears to become enshrined in a mental vignette of the action of dislodging the banana.

Martin Heidegger (1927) maintained that if ontology (as the search for what there is in being conscious) is set apart from phenomenology, this could be an error. He suggests that it is actually linked to the phenomenology of the first person sensation of being a self in an external world. Putting aside Sartre's observations on phenomenology as a literary examination of one's own experience, Maurice Merleau-Ponty's linking of phenomenology to personal experiences of one's own body (1945) becomes important particularly for those who discuss consciousness in the context of embodied robots.

*The body's muscular activity is a key element in the 'kernel' architecture to create 'depictions', that is sensations of being an entity in an out-there world. As will be seen, Shanahan argues that embodiment is essential to have an experiencer.*

## 2.3 Materialist Concerns

Gilbert Ryle in *Concept of Mind* (1949) argued that linguistic descriptions of mental states are a direct way of expressing phenomenology. But taken to an extreme this creates a doubt about phenomenology through total materialism where mental states are posited to be identical with neural states. The suspicion that this re-kindles dualism has only recently had a helpful solution through a structure put forward by Crick and Koch (2003). Only some parts of the entire neural state are responsible for personal sensation, the parts that are not, have been called by the authors the 'Zombie' regions of the brain. This appears to beg the question of how one distinguishes a neuron that contributes to conscious sensation from one that does not. *A possible answer was developed by Aleksander and Dunmall (2003) and Aleksander (2005). This draws attention to the fact that in the visual system only some neurons, those indexed by the motor areas of the brain, can fire in a way that correlates with elements of the visual sensation of being an entity in an 'out-there' world.*

## 2.4 Access and Phenomenal Aspects

Ned Block (1995) has identified at least two salient functions of consciousness. For the first he used the term 'Phenomenal' consciousness (P-consciousness) to indicate the personal function of experiencing a mental state. He contrasts this with 'Access' consciousness (A-consciousness) which is characterised as that function of consciousness which is available for use in reasoning, being poised for action and the generation of language. Although he argues that both are present most of the time, conflating the two when studying consciousness is a severe error. Some evidence of Block's distinct formalisation is drawn from the phenomenon of 'blindsight' where individuals with a damaged primary visual cortex can respond to input without reporting an experience of the input. This is A without P. P without A is the effect that some unattended experience had happened previously (a clock striking) but the individual had only realised this later. That is, P without A covers the case that unattended input can be retrieved. This creates a mechanistic difficulty for the definition of phenomenal consciousness as, were it never to be brought into access format, it could not in any way be described as 'the way things seem'. In hard-nosed synthetic phenomenology it might be politic to concentrate only on things that have seemed to be or seem to be like something.

*This implies that in studying the function of cognitive architectures it is important to be clear about the way in which immediate perceptual consciousness interacts with awareness of past experience, which bears on the A/P discussion.*

Blindsight has also entered the theories of 'enacted' vision proposed by Kevin O'Regan and Alva Noë (2001) who have largely argued that thinking of 'representing' the visual world in any architecture, living or synthetic, is an error, as the world itself is representation enough for the system to act on it in a physical way. Consciousness is then a 'breaking into' this somewhat reactive, autonomic process through mechanisms of attention.

*It is known that in the brain there are unconscious sensorimotor pro-*
*cesses of the O'Regan and Noë description that work in conjunction with*
*conscious phenomenal processes. For example the oculo-motor loop that*
*involves the superior colliculus is such a mechanism. We are not conscious*
*of the retinal maps that are projected onto the superior colliculus. They lead,*
*also unconsciously, to the saliency maps that partly determine eye move-*
*ment which eventually leads to reconstructions of world-fixed representa-*
*tions much deeper in the visual cortex (the extrastriate regions according to*
*Crick and Koch, 2003). The enacted-unconscious/depicted-conscious inter-*
*action is a useful concept that may be used in synthetic systems. We find it*
*difficult to accept the 'hard' sensorimotor view that complete access to a*
*visual world can be achieved without any phenomenal representation at all.*

## 3.  Phenomenology in Computational Models

There are two important computational issues we wish to stress
here. The first is the relationship of a third-person design of an object
that is capable of first person representation, and the second is the
relationship of depiction to synthetic phenomenology.

### 3.1   *Third Person Design with a First Person Within It.*

Where, in philosophy, phenomenology starts with the first person
sensation, we suggest that in computational modelling, a
phenomenological model must, in the broadest terms, sustain representations that have first person properties for *the model itself.* There
is no dualist slight of hand here as the designer of the system can
happily retain a third-person view of what is being designed, given a
theory of what in the design is necessary to achieve a first person for
the mechanism. That is, in the way that we are able to develop a phenomenal argument that, despite starting with our own first-person
sense, allows us to speak of the first person of others, we can speak of
the first person of a machine. This implies that, in vision, for example, there is a need to differentiate mechanisms that mediate the
sense of presence of the organism in the world from those that are
due to previous experience: memory of various kinds and imagination (for example, states induced by literature). That is, there needs
to be computational clarity about how a first-person phenomenal
state relates to the current world event, how meaning is assigned to
this, how meaningful states arise even in the absence of meaningful
sensory input and how a personal sensation of decisions about 'what
to do next' can arise. In Aleksander and Dunmall, 2003 and

Aleksander 2005 we have referred to a necessary property for the machine having a first person at all as being a 'depiction'. Here we set out this concept in a systematic way.

### 3.2   *Depiction and Phenomenology.*

Our central hypothesis is framed as two definitions which define what we mean by a *synthetically phenomenological system.*

**Def 1**: To be **synthetically phenomenological**, a system S must contain machinery that represents what the world and the system S within it *seem* like, from the point of view of S.

The word *seem* has been transferred from the phraseology used above to stress that perfect knowledge of the world cannot be achieved if only because of the weaknesses of sensory transducers. But, it is stressed that living creatures, if we believe that they have phenomenal representations, will come to our notice only through successful evolution. Again we stress that this is due to some sufficiency in the similarity between what things seem like and how, in some reality that does not depend on observation, *they are*. To achieve this it is necessary that such a representation should fully compensate for bodily movement. In earlier work we have called this a 'depiction' rather than a representation. To extend this prior work we develop a series of definitions and assertions about depictions that positions this work within the framework of phenomenology addressed earlier.

**Def 2**: A **depiction** is a state in system S that represents, as accurately as required by the purposes of S the world, from a virtual point of view within S.

**Assertion 1**: A depiction of Def. 2 is the mechanism that is necessary to satisfy that a system be synthetically phenomenological according to Def. 1.

**Assertion 2**: If S is mobile and has mobile sensors, a depiction as in Def. 2 can only be achieved if the mobile nature of S is encoded into the information carried by the sensors. That is the 'where' of the elements of the world needs to be indexed by the 'body' parameters of S. (In vision, eye-movement needs clearly to be compensated to achieve a depiction).

**Assertion 3**: 'As accurately as required ...' in Def. 2, indicates that, given effectors with which to act on the world, the depiction should carry all the information needed to be deployed on arbitrarily selected elements of the world.

**Assertion 4:** 'As accurately as required ...' also sets an upper limit on the granularity with which the depiction may be achieved.

**Assertion 5:** While Def. 2 makes no call on a topological representation, it does require that differently positioned elements within the representation carry the indexing addressed in assertion 2. In animal vision it is known that different attributes of a visual element (e.g. the colour and motion of a dot) are represented in different parts of the brain.

What 'binds' them in our analysis is the indexing as clarified in the example below.

**Example of indexing:** Participant X is fixating a cross in the centre of a screen. She is asked to identify the shape $s$ and colour $c$ of an object that will appear briefly on some other part of the screen. Shape is represented in area P of her brain and colour in area Q. The eye driven by the superior colliculus will saccade to the position of the object. The signal issued by the eye movement is, say, a 2-dimensional vector $v$. Then the depiction in P will be $s$ indexed by $v$, say $sv$. Similarly, in Q we have $cv$. Assertion 5 states that the binding of $s$ and $c$ is due to the common indexing by $v$: that is, $(s,c)v$.

It is the deeper contention of the depictive approach that $(s,c)v$ uniquely encodes X's phenomenal experience of the appeared object. Of course, away from this experimental example, the indexing, as indicated by a great deal of physiological evidence (e.g. Galletti & Battaglini, 1989) occurs over many areas of the cortex, giving the phenomenal experience of one sensory modality several bound dimensions. Touch together with vision is a common experience.

## 4. Architectures

By 'architecture' we refer to a structure that first, is made of several internal parts each of which performs a specified distinct function, and second, includes a full specification of the interconnections among these parts the inputs and a variety of outputs (e.g. language generators, physical actuators etc.). It is the contention of these pages that there exists a set of architectures that can support phenomenology for the organism that embodies the architecture. We shall first look at two specific architectures to assess some of the definitional material presented in section 3.

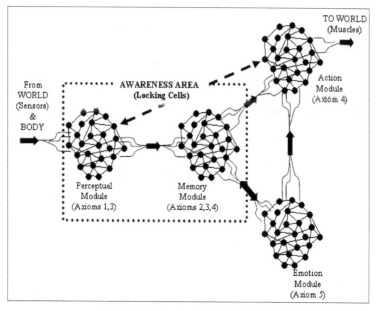

**Figure 1: The 'Kernel' Architecture**

## 4.1 The 'Kernel' Architecture

It is hardly a coincidence that a prototypical architecture we have recently suggested (Aleksander, 2005) should be based on the notion of a depiction and can, therefore, be said to have phenomenal consciousness according to our criteria. We take a closer look at this scheme that is shown in Figure 1.

This architecture is based on the axioms of consciousness published in Aleksander and Dunmall (2003). For completeness, they are briefly listed in the Appendix. These axioms start from a phenomenological standpoint as they are derived through an introspective decomposition of the most significantly felt aspects of being conscious. Then, it has been argued, the decomposition eases the transfer of these features into the synthetic domain. Fig.1 is the result of this process. It consists of five modules each of which is considered to be a neural state machine (NSM) that operates in binary mode. That is, each connection carries a binary signal. We have often argued that any loss of generality due to the binary synthesis will be minor with respect to the behaviours that are being researched.

The binary NSM is specified as a six-tuple:

$$<C_i, C_o, C_f, C_t, I, O, F, T>n$$

where, n is the module index, Ci is a connection pattern of inputs (which may come from other modules or sensory inputs); Co is a connection pattern of outputs (to other modules or system outputs); Cf is the pattern of internal feedback connections. Ct is the set of 'teaching connections' that determine the state of Co and Cf that become associated with Ci. I, O, F, and T are the state sets of Ci,Co,Cf and Ct respectively.

Then, in the usual way with neural state machines, the states of F(t) and O(t) become functions of F(t-1) and I(t). These functions are determined by a training strategy which is expressed through T during a 'training phase'. For example, an 'Iconic' mode of training is conventional with neural state machines of this kind (Aleksander and Morton, 1995). This ensures that, given that Ct and Cf have the same dimensions and Co=Cf, the network learns F(t)=T(t) as a function of I(t) and F(t-1). Returning to Fig.1, the four axioms are implemented as follows.

P is a 'Perceptual' NSM which is made to be phenomenological in the sense of the earlier definitions through the following design. The state F(t) is a reconstruction of the sequences of attended world inputs from sensory transducers over defined time windows (sometimes sliding time windows). The muscular effort required to attend to the elements of the world is shown as the link from the 'action' NSM, A. In the animal visual system it is surmised that attentional shifts are driven by saliency maps in the superior colliculus. In specific studies of the visual system, this has been modelled as an additional part of the kernel architecture (See Igor Aleksander et al., 2001).

M is the memory and 'imagination' module. It is connected to P in such a way that for every reconstruction in P, a state in M is created. Sequences of reconstructed states in P can therefore be stored as state trajectories in M—they will have inherited the depictive, hence phenomenal properties of P. P and M together form what we have dubbed 'the awareness areas' of the architecture. In the sense that one can perceive and recall at the same time, the two areas both contribute to the same phenomenal state.

The remaining modules of the kernel architecture are not depictive, hence not phenomenal, but add to the phenomenal existence of the system in the following way. As mentioned, A is the action area in which links between the state trajectories of the phenomenal areas are translated into action. But this is not automatic, it is surmised that volition and emotion as implemented in module E mediate this link. (See Aleksander, Lahnstein and Lee, 2005.)

In summary, the kernel architecture is based *ab initio* on the intention of synthesising an architecture with phenomenological properties. This has also been guided by those who, like Crick and Koch (2003) have been researching the neural correlates of consciousness in living organisms. We now consider a model that is more closely related to computational approaches of the functional kind.

## 4.2 Embodied Global Workspace

Bernard Baars' (1988, 1997) Global Workspace models have held sway in computational modelling of consciousness for some years. Baars considered how a large number of unconscious processes might collaborate to produce a continuum of conscious experience. In very broad terms, he answers the question through the architecture of Figure 2.

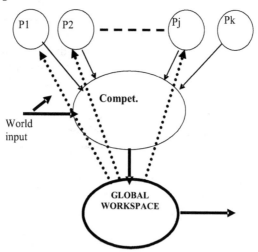

**Figure 2: A Sketch of Baars' Global workspace**

The separate processes, P1 to Pk, said to be unconscious, compete to enter 'The Global Workspace'. Such processes are often thought of as memory activities, say, episodic memory, working memory and so on. The competition is won by the process that has the greatest saliency at a given moment. This saliency is predicated by world input which sets the context for the competition. World input is also assumed to have direct influence on the unconscious processes P1 -

Pk. Having entered the global workspace, the winner of the competition becomes the conscious state of the system. This is continuously 'broadcast' back to the originating processes that can change their state depending on the conscious state. This results in a new conscious state and so on, linking sensory input to memory and the conscious state. It is both general and useful for these separate processes to be modelled as NSMs as was done for the kernel architectures

Murray Shanahan (2005) points out that modelling of a conscious organism cannot proceed without that organism being embodied in some palpable world. Using the above Global Workspace (GW) model he argues that there can be no 'experiencer' in GW unless the model takes account of the 'spatial unity of the body'. It is this localization in space that for Shanahan gives the model its 'viewpoint on the world' which according to def. 1 makes it a candidate for phenomenal consciousness.

Shanahan argues that denying this possibility, as is done by Block (1995), revives the dualist stance, putting phenomenal consciousness in the Chalmers-like 'hard problem' class, that is, a problem that cannot be reduced to physical structure and hence cannot be synthesized. And yet, the claimed 'point of view' of the embodied organism is undoubtedly a claim that this accords with definition 1 above of a phenomenal system.

In terms Block's division into access and phenomenal consciousness, Shanahan implies that the embodied GW model addresses access consciousness, treating the phenomenal element as being an unnecessary appeal to a dualistic concept.

## 4.3   GW and Synthetic Phenomenology

While it seems entirely correct that without embodiment, GW does not include an experiencer, the question remains of how the experience stream in GW relates to the real world. We recall that in section 3.2 we have argued that a synthetic phenomenological system is achieved through a compositional representation of the world that is sufficiently accurate for the system be able to use its embodiment to act on this world as accurately as possible. That is, it is the contention of our chapter that depiction is the missing ingredient in making GW phenomenal. That is, phenomenal consciousness can occur in functional, physical systems, and the implication for the embodied GW system is that *all* the P1-Pk states need to be *depictive* for the GW state to be truly a model of a conscious state. Were this not the case, some translation into depiction would have to go along with the winning of the competition. Otherwise the specter of purely arbitrary representations in GW remains. Shanahan is aware of this by requiring that the conscious broadcast back to the competing processes be in some way intelligible to these processes. But this still makes it hard to see how the states of the processes remain non-depictive when the state of GW might be depictive.

The reason for including these observations is to lead into a discussion of the validity of the concept of synthetic phenomenology by setting conditions under which it can occur.

## 5. Discussion

Here we have developed and explored the concept of synthetic phenomenology mainly by attempting to define the necessary features of an architecture that supports phenomenal consciousness within the broadest definition of the term. We brought the definitions to ground by considering two models that might be candidates for possessing these features.

To conclude we raise and, using the presented material, attempt to answer five general questions that may be central to the existence of a synthetic phenomenology. The first of these addresses the architectures presented above.

*Can non-depictive representations be phenomenal?*
It is the firm implication of this chapter that this cannot be the case. It is depiction in a functional area which determines that the area contributes to the phenomenal sensation of the organism. Were this not the case, a human description of a state would require translation into phenomenal terms as such descriptions are of phenomena and not encoded states. Such translators would have to have depictive states negating the argument for lack of depiction.

*What is the difference between 'depictive kernel' and GW architectures in terms of synthetic phenomenology?*
Clearly the depictive kernel architecture was designed with the purpose of creating a phenomenal representation within the system according to the definitions set out. This has the computational advantage of being able to be display on a screen the current phenomenal state of the machine. This allows a designer to assess the interactions between both postulated conscious and postulated unconscious mechanisms in the generation of the phenomenology.

The rules used in the synthesis involve depiction. Originally no phe-nomenal claims were made for GW, particularly in its practical form as synthesized by Stan Franklin (2003). However with the embodied GW work of Murray Shanahan, the question of the presence syn-thetic phenomenal consciousness acquires a new urgency. Here we have maintained that were an architecture based on GW to have a phenomenal character, there needs to be a depictive activity in the processes that compete for entering the global workspace if the sys-tem is to be phenomenological. This creates problems as, in our scheme of things, depiction in an area of the architecture implies phenomenal consciousness and GW sees the competing processes as being non-conscious.

Therefore a phenomenal GW implies some sort of coming into consciousness in the GW area for reasons other than depiction. These have not yet been explained. Of course, the depiction idea can be rejected, but if not depiction, then what?

*What is the use of synthetic phenomenology?*

Given the difficulties mentioned with embodied GW above, it is proper to ask why bother with phenomenology and why not settle for just access consciousness as implied by Shanahan (2005)? In the arguments, phenomenology actually includes the purposes that are attributed to access consciousness. But such purposes are explicit and searchable through attentional mechanisms for reasons of accu-rate interaction with the environment (see assertions 3 and 4).

This is not a Blockian confusion, but rather a suggestion that there may not be as clear-cut a functional/neurological distinction between access and phenomenal consciousness as Block seems to suggest. The A without P and P without A cases may be extreme con-ditions of a central phenomenon. In summary we argue that accurate interaction with, and thought about the real world is the purpose of phenomenology in a synthetic system as it might be in a natural one.

*Is synthetic phenomenology an oxymoron as it is the non-physical experiential side of consciousness and therefore eschews material synthesis?*

Everything we have submitted in this article is a denial of the above proposition. Treating phenomenology as the 'hard' part of con-sciousness simply kicks it out of touch of science into some mystical outfield. We maintain that addressing it as a constructible concept removes the mysticism with which it might otherwise be associated.

*Is synthetic phenomenology an arbitrary design option for models of consciousness?*

This chapter regards models of consciousness without synthetic phenomenology as being valid only in a behavioural sense. That is, it is possible for a model to be given attributes of being conscious from its behaviour. Stan Franklin's Intelligent Distribution Agent (2003) is a good example of this class of system. Users think that they are dealing with an entity conscious of their needs. But if one were to argue that an architecture throws light on the mechanisms of consciousness in the brain it becomes mandatory to include phenomenal, that is depictive functions.

*What research needs to be done in developing architectures with synthetic phenomenology?*

Referring to the kernel architecture there is much work to be done on modes of interaction between the modules. Current work includes a clarification of the way the emotion module E controls the link between the phenomenological P and M modules and the non-phenomenological action module, A. (fig. 1).

Illusions, ambiguous and 'flipping' figures are situations where phenomenology and reality part company. We are pursuing the mechanisms that, in the kernel architecture, would lead to the kind of perceptual instabilities associated with perceiving the Necker cube. This underlines the usefulness of synthetic phenomenology, as perceptual reversals may be measured in the depictive machinery and the conditions for such reversals studied. This is revealing of the interaction between phenomenal and non-phenomenal processes in the brain.

In GW, architectures it would be interesting to clarify the causes of phenomenology in the GW area which are not present in the supporting competitive processes.

## Appendix: Axioms of Being Conscious.

This is an introspective partitioning of five important aspects of being conscious

1.  I feel as if I am at the focus of an out there world.

2.  I can recall and imagine experiences of feeling in an out there world.

3.  My experiences in 2 are dictated by attention, and attention is involved in recall.

4.  I can imagine several ways of acting in the future.

5.  I can evaluate emotionally ways of acting into the future in order to act in some purposive way.

## References

Aleksander, Igor (2005), *The World In My Mind, My Mind In The World*. Exeter: Imprint Academic.

Aleksander, Igor and Dunmall, Barry (2000), 'An extension to the Hypothesis of the Asynchrony of Visual Consciousness', *Proceedings of the Royal Society of London B* 267: 197–200.

Aleksander, Igor and Dunmall, Barry (2003), 'Axioms and Tests for the Presence of Minimal Consciousness in Agents', *Journal of Consciousness Studies*,10 (4–5), pp. 7–18.

Aleksander, Igor , Lahnstein, Mercedes and Lee, Rabinder (2005), 'Will and Emotions: A Machine Model that Shuns Illusions', *Proc AISB 2005 Symposium on New Generation Approaches to Machine Consciousness.*

Aleksander, Igor and Morton, Helen (1995), *Introduction to Neural Computing (2nd Edition)*, London: Thomson Computer Press.

Aleksander, Igor, Morton, Helen and Dunmall, Barry (2001), 'Seeing is Believing', *Proc. IWANN01*, Springer.

Baars, Bernard (1988), *A Cognitive Theory of Consciousness*, Cambridge: Cambridge University Press.

Baars, Bernard (1997), *In the Theater of Consciousness: The Workspace of the Mind* , New York: Oxford University Press.

Block, Ned (1995), 'On a Confusion about a function of Consciousness', *Behavioural and Brain Sciences*, 18, pp. 227–287.

Brentano, Franz (1995), *Psychology from an Empirical Standpoint*, Trans: Rancurello et al. Routledge. Orig in German 1874.

Crick, Francis and Koch, Christof (2003), 'A Framework For Consciousness' *Nature Neuroscience* ,6, pp. 119–126.

Franklin, Stan (2003), 'IDA a Conscious Artifact?', *Journal of Consciousness Studies*,10 (4–5), pp. 47–66.

Galletti, Claudio and Battaglini, Paolo (1989), 'Gaze-Dependent Visual Neurons in Area V3A of Monkey Prestriate Cortex',. *Journal of Neuroscience*, 6, pp. 1112–1125.

Heidegger, Martin (1975), *The Basic Problems of Phenomenology*, Trans Hofstadter, Indiana University Press. Orig in German, 1975.

Husseil, Edmund (1963), *Ideas:A General Introduction to Pure Phenomenology*, Trans. Boyce Gibson, Collier. Orig in German, 1913.

Merleau-Ponty, Maurice (1996), *Phenomenology of Perception*,Trans Smith, Routledge. Orig in French, 1945.

O'Regan, Kevin and Noë, Alva (2001), 'A Sensorimotor account of vision and visual consciousness', *Brain and Behavioural Sciences*, 24(5).

Ryle, Gilbert (1949), *A Concept of Mind*, London: Hutchinson's.

Shanahan, Murray (2005), 'Global Access, Embodiment and the Conscious Subject', *Journal of Consciousness Studies*, 12, No 12, pp. 46–66.

# Andrea Lavazza

# Sense as a 'Translation' of Mental Contents

## 1. Introduction

The majority of philosophers, psychologists and scientists would agree that 'it makes sense to try to explain consciousness', or 'it makes sense to reject the mind-body dualism on the basis of contemporary science'. The meaning of the statements is clear, and the latter also holds true. The expression 'it makes sense' to say or do something frequently appears in English and in most other languages. The concept of having or finding 'sense' in a certain state of things, either by choice or by their very existence, is often used. Even for a scientist, this would not entail begging the question, with the exception perhaps of logical-positivists who, in the words of Schlick (1936), should simply disregard them as lacking in meaning.

The word and concept of *sense* are exceptionally broad, although its meaning is often vague and ambiguous in colloquial speech. The first examples provided below introduce the definition we will use here. First of all, *sense* is an internal (non-sensory) experience of coherence (or rightness), a feeling of affective resonance linked to assessing something, an experience of fitting something, and a strong experience of unity between object and subject (Potworowski and Ferrari, 2002). *Sense* is linked to understanding but, it must be added, not strictly amounting to *meaning*, insofar as meaning is linked to semantics, i.e. to the relation between words (and thoughts) and their reference regardless of the theory of meaning adopted (the primary positions debated today have their roots in the works of Frege, 1918; Quine, 1953; Wittgenstein, 1953; Putnam, 1975; Grice, 1989; and Dummett, 1991). These attempts in defining the expression are still unsatisfactory, and we still might paraphrase it with the word *purpose* (when we say 'the sense of life') or the words *motive* and *reason* (when we say 'in what sense?') or the words *plausibility* and *coherency/consistency* (when we say 'a theory makes sense'). Nevertheless the inclusion of the word *sense*, albeit in rather hazy instances, in the autobiographies of all human beings forces us to take it seriously.

Obviously one must accept that people use blurry concepts, which science has corrected or re-formulated or revealed to be inaccurate. However it is legitimate to assume that, if we take consciousness seriously enough to want to reproduce it artificially, we must also take into account that the word *sense*, in the manner detailed below, is included in the mind's catalogue.

Accordingly sense might be an important element of phenomenal consciousness, i.e. a first-hand experience of 'how it feels', 'what it is' to be ... a bat (Nagel, 1974).

This might appear to be an ambitious, useless or untimely effort; but it must be said that there are very few points of contact with the theoretical positions that, in the past, gave sense/meaning a precise collocation in the philosophy of the mind. In particular, notwithstanding fecund ideas by Husserl (1912–29) and Merleau-Ponty (1945), which even now exert some influence, to date, we are moving from a different view from the one they explored. Here *sense* is seen, hypothetically, as an 'emerging' aspect of the phenomenal mind, embedded in the brain, and probably the upshot of biological evolution. As such, in principle, it can be studied and reproduced inside of artifacts that include pre-established constraints.

I would like to outline a theory that attempts to explain sense in more rigorous philosophical and scientific terms in order to ensure that it is fully accepted in the mental catalogue.

This entails devising an approach that might be useful in the ongoing debate about the construction of artificial consciousness as well as shedding light on the social perspective of natural consciousness.

I will start by defining sense in terms of the philosophy of the mind and then neurobiologically. Finally I will hint at its artificial reproducibility.

First of all, we must remember that, by axiom, the very character of a definition excludes essentialist or foundational descriptions of individual terms. And that a certain amount of circularity is presupposed from the beginning within the definition.

(1) Sense is the assembly of the mutual inter-translatability of a group of mental contents (sensory and non-sensory — or phenome-

nal; representational, and non-representational). Sense emerges locally from given content configurations when it interrelates to a series of cross-references, with the associated bodily feelings. There are two underlying premises:

    a)    The human mind is able to have sensory and non-sensory content, and

    b)    Sense is one of the distinctive features of human consciousness.

Excluding essentialist descriptions means that individual elements do not constitute components of reality that are final or no longer decomposable but that need other parts for their existence. Excluding foundational descriptions means that individual elements do not make up the minimum building blocks necessary for the understanding of their level of reality but that they need additional elements in order to be intelligible. Thus the definition has elements characterized by a holistic-inferential circularity in the same way that the philosopher Robert Brandom explained in the construction of concepts and meaning (Brandom, 1994; 2000).

It is enough to mention the additional complication that the entire inferential system linked to the definition of sense that will be proposed only *exists* — with a strong ontological value here — within the individual human consciousness that faces it, independent from the way it faces it. The way of posing this issue is one of the central conundrums in explaining consciousness, which will be explored below.

It must be stated that sense is not the same as information and that translatability is not the same as integration. Therefore, the underlying idea is not that sense (or consciousness) is some form of information integration: in this case, we accept the definitions that are commonly accepted at a cognitive science level of information and integration, regardless of what happens in our brain or inside a machine.

## 2. Two Examples of Sense

Before proceeding, let us take two cases in order to test the concept of sense in the field of philosophy of the mind and in the field of artificial intelligence, respectively.

In the first case, we are dealing with the so-called eliminative theories of consciousness. Ultimately, such theories affirm that 'mental states characterized by common sense are mere theoretical structures postulated by an incorrect theory, the so-called folk psychology, on the same level as now abandoned concepts like phlogiston and caloric fluid' (Paternoster, 2002:14). Talking about *beliefs* in actual fact means using empty language labels, which are utterly devoid of reference. So to talk about *sense*, playing on words, does make sense (however, it must be noted that for us the above play on words makes perfect sense).

If we listen to a coherent explanation of the eliminativism, we feel that it has a meaning (i.e. that the terms used have a reference) and makes overall *sense.*

(I am aware that we are still moving at an insufficient level of formalization, but it is a fact that all those who speak with average linguistic and cognitive knowledge do not have a problem 'understanding' everything that is being said. And we will ignore for a moment that fact that even the concept of understanding may seem problematic.)

It is rather trivial to say that the meaning and sense we perceive in the explanation of the eliminative theory are only and always refer to a knowing and animated being, say to the listeners who, by way of a physical medium, were reached by the presentation of the very eliminative theory. If the theory is right, if it describes objective reality (and also in this case, let us set aside, at least temporarily, the multitude of suppositions and issues which arise from it), then it highlights a fallacy in our self-description. Phenomenal consciousness is merely a word that we should abandon together with the idea of sense, which, in this case, should be described as the feeling of intuited coherency, of a perceived rightness. As such, it has nothing to do with the motivated endorsement we would express, for instance, in a review of a book dealing with the eliminative theory.

In such a hypothetical instance of epistemic 'freedom' (since, if eliminativism is correct, there is nothing at all, there has never been anything to discard in ontology), the theory itself should acquire an even stronger overall *sense.*

If we were deprived of the concept of consciousness as we know it in favor, for instance, of the idea of modules competing to obtain the provisional command of brain processes (Dennett, 1991), it is reasonable to suppose that one must be well aware of the *meaning* and the *sense* of it all. And the application of the eliminative theory in a properly formed sentence appears equally certain, not as a first-hand presumed certainty — we are assuming that eliminativism is right — but as an experiential feeling that 'occurs' — which we might be able to translate, albeit hazily and not in a rigorously formalized way.

For instance, the expression might state that we are making an important step forward in the field of scientific knowledge or that we are losing a piece of our ancient, incorrect vision of human beings equipped with a soul. It must be made clear that this thought experiment is difficult to explain since, to date, eliminativism itself lacks a new non-mental vocabulary able to express its approach. We are not being prosaic when we say that it is difficult, if not impossible, to imagine how such translations of meaning and ascription of sense might be abandoned, even hypothetically, without eliminativism itself becoming utterly unfathomable, absolutely de facto 'nonsensical,' thereby reverting to the earlier epistemic condition (Baker, 1997).

In other words, we are dealing with a mental experiment endorsing the view that it is not possible to dispose of *sense* as an operative concept, even if we remove it from our vocabulary. Indeed the apparent resulting contradiction does not mean that we have proved that eliminativism is implausible. Indeed, we are assuming that it is legitimate to continue talking about mental states. I must make it clear that this issue has many points in common with Nagel's (1974) views when he says that 'physicalism is a position we cannot understand because we do not at present have any conception of how it might be true.'

Moving on to artificial intelligence, let us start with the famous Chinese Room thought experiment devised by Searle (1980). Does the person inside the room, who translates using formal syntactic rules, understand Chinese or not? The view that privileges semantics and intentionality says that, *prima facie*, she does not understand the meanings since she only produces syntactic computations on symbols. However we are interested in *sense*. We are assuming that the person inside the room does nothing but decoding/recoding the texts she cannot understand; given such assumptions, it is reasonable that she might see the sense of her activity in the context defined above. Not sense arising from the manipulation of portions of text. In addition, I am not saying there is an external and banal sense. In that case, our human translator is reduced to a level of an employee-robot who mechanically moves from one symbol to the next using the rules supplied while he/she thinks 'I don't know what I am doing, but after one year here I will have earned enough to enjoy life'. We are not talking about this. Rather, our translator, reduced to an ideal microchip, must be equipped with other conceptual content in order to perform the operations and receive the necessary sensory inputs to execute and conclude them; in line with the non-technological example provided by Searle, she sees the papers being pushed under the door, grabs a pencil, uses the translation rules and controls her body to write incomprehensible signs, and then slides the messages back under the door ...

In other words, she has mental contents that may locally give rise to *sense* if they occur in previously specified conditions, even while performing activities whose meaning she does not understand. If the contents available can be mutually inter-translated and if they cause a number of references and the relating sensations of embodiment and situatedness (Clark, 1997), then Chinese is meaningless, but the manipulation of symbols may have a locally associated sense.

This does not mean that a computer feels a private or phenomenological sense, but it does allow us to claim that, theoretically, an embodied and situated machine might implement the conditions required for the emergence of sense, which can be compared to the one typical to humans.

### 3. Sense as a Social Concept

Let us now return to the definitions proposed at the onset. Sense is the assembly of inter-translatability of interconnected mental contents. Sense emerges from a given configuration of content when it is interlinked by a series of references. So, at a given moment, for certain people a thing, an object might 'make' on not 'make sense.' And then 'making sense' recalls the inter-translatability of contents. From this point of view, there is also a social aspect, which by definition is not limited to one individual and her mind but to the culture of a given group. Indeed, if the conditions of inter-translatability disappear at a given moment in time, either the external reference changes, or the corpus of theoretical knowledge is altered, or the focus of cognitive capacities are modified, or the environmental pressure on embodiment and situatedness vary — accordingly altering the individual's phenomenal content — some things or concepts cease 'making sense' since the contents are no longer inter-translatable.

This also holds true for meaning if one accepts the analogy with Robert Brandom's (1994; 2000) holistic-pragmatic-inferential semantics. This theory operates on an inter-subjective level, while the scope of sense is by definition strictly personal. The assumed similarity between man's mental configurations and their partial empirical and experimental communicability enable one to view sense (specific sense connected to a group of mental content) as private with regards to its origin and inter-subjective with regard to its dissemination (Cf. Rapaport, 1995).

For instance, prehistory might fall into this category; we are no longer able to understand the sense of actions or expressions of primitive man since his universe of mental contents (or even of meanings) was very different from ours. Equally, we do not understand why certain Ideas or gestures make sense, or have such a strong sense for some people, unless we access their mutually inter-translatable universe of contents. Once again, there is a similarity between Nagel's (1974) views concerning the difficulties of understanding the claim that all matter is really energy; despite the fact that we know what 'is' means, most people never form a conception of what makes this claim true because they lack the theoretical background. Here, the issue rests not on the conditions of truth but on the very possibility of understanding linked to sense as defined above.

### 4. Operationalizing Sense

The apparent woolliness of this idea can be diminished by referring to attempts made to operationalize facts into psychological experiments like the one that showed that high school students in the Southern United States, mostly from strongly Christian Fundamental families, who understood Darwin's theory of evolution perfectly well but who simply did not value or believe the theory to be true (Jackson *et al.*, 1995).

An example of operationalizing the concept of common sense in AI can be seen in the Cyc project. Douglas Lenat's (1998) aim was to give a system shared knowledge and an experience so that it could understand our speech and text. Common sense models provide a context, a way of restricting reasoning to potentially relevant information and excluding irrelevant data. 'Cyc version 10 is now a knowledge-based system designed to efficiently manipulate and reason with a large ontology (over 2.4 million assertions, 200,000 terms and 9,000 relationships). Its symbolic representation language CycL is based on first order predicate calculus with higher-order and modal extensions. CycL contains both atomic and functionally-defined terms. As part of its higher-order extensions, CycL allow assertions in the Cyc knowledge base to occur as terms (Argument) for meta-assertions. CycL assertions are grouped into reasoning contexts called micro-theories, which in turn form hierarchies of assumptions inheritance' (Belasco *et al.*, 2005). Cyc has several applications, including natural language understanding, checking and integrating information in spreadsheets and databases, and finding relevant information in image libraries and on the World Wide Web. We are talking about inference problems, and common sense is not at all *sense* as we defined it. It is not implausible, however, to say that Cyc, in some way, works on 'content translation", although no mind-content translation is involved.

Regarding sense, the issues to be cleared up obviously involve the idea of inter-translation and the idea of reference and the so-called emotional resonance. This includes bodily feelings, as, for example, proposed by Damasio (1994; 1999), who gives an account of emotions in corporeal terms; his 'background feelings' tend to remain at the margins of the mind and reflect the momentary states of the body.

My suggestion is that we are not dealing with computations concerning the syntax of symbols, as Fodor (1975; 1983) suggested, but the possibility that highly different things like representational and phenomenal contents, sensory contents, and abstract content are 'transparent' and can remand one to the other. *Prima facie*, this experience appears even trivial; indeed the experience of sense is both distinctive and typical of the human mind and consciousness. How this happens is what I would call the 'problem of sense'.

### 5. W. James' *Fringe* as a Component of Sense

The concept of fringe—as opposed to nucleus—expressed by William James and later developed by several contemporary cognitive psychologists (Lavazza, 2006) might prove to be a useful way of understanding. The distinction between the two phenomenological aspects of consciousness is not entirely new. In particular, the dual structure between *clear and distinct contents/vague and peripheral experiences or feeling* has been relevant for many philosophers.

James (1890) claims that consciousness is dynamic; it constantly shifts from idea to idea, from thought to thought. He also states that its structure is complex; every explicit thought is related to a fringe or shade of content, which is intuited. The fringe performs an important role in controlling the orderly progress of consciousness from one substantive thought to another. This process is expressed by the well-known metaphor of stream of thought, which, like a bird's life, seems to consist of an alternation between flying and perching, without continuity, or a resemblance of the constant diversity of flowing water (James, 1890, p. 243).

We are aware of both substantive and transitive thoughts, the latter providing a feeling of context and cementing the temporal fractures between substantive thoughts. This feeling has three component parts: a faded memory of previous thoughts, a 'feeling of relation' between the current thought and other potentially relevant ones, and a 'feeling of tendency' of the train of thought. Epstein (2000) lists several fringe experiences taken from James in the attempt to pinpoint our shades of thought. They include the feeling of expectation we have when our attention has been drawn to something, and we have some sense of what it might be but we have not yet determined exactly what it is; the feeling of having a word "on the tip of one's tongue;" the feeling we have when we know that something is familiar; the feeling of intending to say something when we have a perspective scheme of thought that has not yet been articulated; the vague comprehension we have for the overall scheme or form of a book, a work of art, a scientific system; the feeling of being "on the right track" to a conclusion.

The 'classical' fringe, the shade described by James, has a sensory content, albeit vague, blurred and indistinct. The non-sensory fringe, as proposed by Mangan (1991; 1993a; 1993b; 2000; 2001), is, literally, experience without sensory content. A similar position may also be found in Galin (1993; 1994; 2000). The two aspects are closely related; both channel context information to our consciousness and, because of this, contribute to the voluntary recovery of new information within our consciousness. The 'non-sensory fringe' is not peripheral; on the contrary, it pervades the entire realm of our consciousness. Peripheral sensory experience concerns the surrounding environment, while non-sensory experience has to do with just about everything that is cognitively significant for our consciousness. Non-sensory experiences constitute, among other things, those aspects of consciousness that turn a naked focal-sensory content into an interpreted, meaningful perception. On the ground, non-sensory experiences constitute, among many other things, the feeling of imminence, i.e. the feeling that much more detailed information is available for retrieval on the periphery if needed. A typical non-sensory experience relates to the feeling of familiarity.

One of the most important non-sensory experiences is rightness. It shows how the content of consciousness adapts to its context. The detailed information that makes up the complete representation and assessment of a context is almost entirely non-conscious. Accordingly, the purpose of rightness is to show to what extent conscious and non-conscious cognitive domains are invariably integrated. Setting habit aside, a change in the feeling of rightness indicates the reciprocal adjustment of the contents flowing in our consciousness.

What underpins this functional mechanism that we are also able to intuit phenomenologically? Mangan believes that consciousness must come to terms with a kind of conservation principle because of a physical limitation with regards to processing information (using an analogy based on computers, one might say that the working memory has been reduced). This means, also on account of the aforementioned attributes of thought, that when some aspects of experience become more detailed, the other will become less so; or that the focus of attention will shift form one figure to the other, relegating the other to the background. The relatively reduced dimensions of conscious space with the resulting shifting of attention and the consequential effects are also highlighted by Mandler (1975), Baars (1988) and Fromm (2003).

The fringe is the equivalent of condensed information; it implies (by way of 'imminence' phenomenology or potential access) the presence of a large quantity of information that does not burden the focal working space. Its intrinsic 'fleetingness' is explained by the role it plays; when recalled, the information goes to the nucleus and is altered, thus becoming clear-cut and distinct. Rightness 'works as a feedback device, guiding the local and specific activity of focal attention towards increasing conformity with antecedent and unconsciously encoded contextual demands. This process leads to a reciprocal interaction between conscious and unconscious processing: the process of detailed conscious analysis will usually change the context, and this, in turn, will change the evaluative signal that rightness manifests, and so on' (Mangan, 2001:26). Generally speaking, emotions occur in an evaluative context so the emotional tone of the fringe is phenomenologically blended with the feeling of rightness or wrongness.

It has been proposed (Potworowski, Ferrari, 2002) that there are at least two phenomenologically distinct feelings of rightness (or wrongness) — conceptual and value feeling of rightness/wrongness. And the former is possibly divisible into subtypes (e.g., moral and aesthetic). Moreover, one might think that not only such a feeling is split into positive and negative polarities but also that is has a 'neutral' tone. And so on.

Epstein (2000) explored the possible cerebral correlates of the phenomenological aspects described above. He singles out two mechanisms which are mediated by distinct brain structures. The first is the network of associative memory that enables a person to recall information about people, objects, places, and facts linked to the nucleus content. This key role would be carried out by the medial-temporal lobes (including the hippocampus and the para-hippocampal gyrus).

The research performed by O'Keefe and Dostrovsky (1971) and O'Keefe and Nadel (1978) showed that the medial-temporal lobes first sustained external spatial navigation and then evolved to implement internal navigation within the memory. In particular, the hippocampus would sustain the representation of relation between individual elements.

The second mechanism controls the special associations, which are instanced through the assessment of their relevance with regards to the behaviorial context. Its neural correlates are in the frontal lobe. Their activation does not correspond to the recalling of memories as such, but to the guiding mechanism, i.e. the selection of one portion of memory rather than another or storing the piece of information ready for use.

### 6. Itineraries for Research

*Sense* does not coincide with the fringe; the fringe might be part of sense but, perhaps, it is the part that best suits the attempt to reach a greater knowledge that is closer to scientific understanding.

It is not easy to confute the objection according to which sense is only an appearance, a private epiphenomenon. The fringe and feeling of rightness, albeit phenomenological concepts, can instead have an important evolutionary role insofar as they respond, as was mentioned above, to the economy of the mind (thus saving space for the nucleus of consciousness) and to the survival of the subject by providing an indicator of 'adequacy' in its environment.

In this prospective, sense would also be useful for a machine that would be able to produce the human consciousness. At this point, one asks oneself what prevents machines from reproducing sense. Is the problem linked to their computational ability, to their functional architecture, to the impossibility of simulating embodiment and being situated? I do not intend to go into these issues, which are connected to the implementation of various artificial intelligence paradigms.

If this implementation were possible on the basis of a material different from cerebral wetware, we could even maintain that this machine would be able to quantitatively measure the *sense* of a certain constellation of contents, as Tononi (2003) proposed as being theoretically possible for the consciousness. Obviously this will depend on the way this implementation is realized, and the measure for such a comparison would still only be human because the very idea of *sense* is exclusively tied to living material. Therefore how does one generate *sense*? The objection by the theoretician of AI and artificial consciousness to the idea of the inter-translatability of the contents as a distinctive feature of sense should immediately be clear. What is more inter-translatable than the bits of a digital computer or of a simple machine of Turing? All algorithms are expressed using the same language. Have we not precisely returned to the Chinese Room, where it is possible to perfectly translate from one language to another using a language machine?

A possible answer might be come form the concept of transparency as proposed by Metzinger — transparency

> essentially consists only of the content properties of a conscious mental representation being available for introspection, but not its non-intentional or 'vehicle-properties'.

Accordingly this kind of transparency is a property of all phenomenal states. In other words,

> transparency holds if earlier processing stages are unavailable for attentional processing. Transparency results from a structural/functional property of the neural information-processing going on in our brains, which makes earlier processing stages attentionally unavailable ... For every phenomenal state, the degree of phenomenal transparency is inversely proportional to the introspective degree of attentional availability of earlier processing stages ... Transparency of phenomenal content leads to a further characteristic of conscious experience, namely the subjective impression of immediacy (Metzinger, 2005).

This is one of the foundations on which we can affirm that we are no one (Metzinger, 2004). The limited opacity we are provided with (i.e. 'seeing' the material means — neurons and cerebral biochemistry — of phenomenal experience) enables us to understand the illusion of phenomenology. One might apply the approach to machines. Their opacity is maximized, i.e. they cannot see through the physical symbols they use but are constrained by them. Therefore, be the domain of consciousness an illusion or not, machines are not able to access sense and, in general, *prima facie* phenomenal experiences, since they do not have the defect, or what Metzinger refers to as a constraint, characteristic of the human mind, which enjoys transparency. Perhaps by linking fuzzy logic to an enhanced Cyc system with systematically probabilistic inferences (and the required corollaries linked to embodiment), in addition to differently weighted micro-theories following a system historical biography, might start endowing machines with an 'impression' of *senso*. However, the 'hard problem of sense', which I have only touched upon here, deserves to be researched in greater detail by better qualified experts.

Let us finally return to the level of the philosophy of the mind. Maybe somebody would be willing to admit that this entire discussion makes *sense*. But he would say that it is not scientifically rigorous, and it does not add any information nor does it offer a perspective on the matter discussed above. We can answer that the inter-translatability of contents is not the only function of sense. This may certainly have an evolutionary origin and an important adaptive role as a sensation of 'rightness,' but it had been freed afterwards.

The person who sees *sense* in a collection of contents has overcome the threshold of their mutual inter-translatability. At this point, sense is not per se objective in a scientific way, but it has a widespread characteristic of being shared, which allows it to communicate and evaluate the contents and the meaning associated, which are more valid from the point of view of knowledge of external reality and more adaptive for the survival of the individual and the species, and finally more gratifying for wellbeing and personal happiness. I would also add they will be more aesthetically pleasing or morally noble.

### References

Baars, B.J. (1988), *A Cognitive Theory of Consciousness* (Cambridge: Cambridge University Press).

Baker, L. R. (1997) *Saving Belief: A Critique of Physicalism*, Princeton, Princeton University Press.

Belasco, A. J., Curtis, J., Kahlert, R.C., Klein, C., Mayans, C., Reagan, P. (2005), 'Representing Knowledge Gaps Effectively' in *Practical Aspects of Knowledge Management, Proceedings of PAKM 2004*, eds. D. Karagiannis, U. Reimer, Berlin Heidelberg, Springer-Verlag.

Brandom, R.B. (1994), *Making It Explicit*, Cambridge (MA), Harvard University Press.

Brandom, R.B. (2000), *Articulating Reasons. An Introduction to Inferentialism*, Cambridge (MA), Harvard University Press.

Clark, A. (1997), *Being There: Putting Brain, Body, and World Together Again*, Cambridge (MA), The Mit Press.

Damasio, A.R. (1994), *Descartes' Error: Emotion, Reason, and the Human Brain*, New York, Grosset/Putnam.

Damasio, A.R. (1999), *The Feeling of What Happens: Body and Emotion in the Making of Consciousness*, San Diego-New York, Harcourt.

Dennett, D. C. (1991), *Consciousness Explained*, Boston, Little Brown and Company.

Dummett, M. (1991), *The Logical Basis of Metaphysics*, Cambridge (Ma), Harvard University Press.

Epstein, R. (2000), 'The Neural-cognitive Basis of the Jamesian Stream of Thought', *Consciousness and Cognition*, 9 (4): 550–75.

Fodor, J.A. (1975), *The Language of Thought*, New York, Cromwell.

Fodor, J.A. (1983), *The Modularity of Mind*, Cambridge (MA), Mit Press.

Frege, G. (1918) 'Der Gedanke. Eine logische Untersuchung,' Beiträge zur Philosophie des deutschen Idealismus, I:58–77.

Fromm, H. (2003), 'The New Darwinism in the Humanities, Part I: From Plato to Pinker,' *The Hudson Review*, LVI (1): 89–99.

Galin, D. (1993), 'Beyond the Fringe,' *Consciousness and Cognition*, 2 (2): 113–18.

Galin, D. (1994), 'The Structure of Awareness: Contemporary Applications of William James' Forgotten Concept of the Fringe', *Journal of Mind and Behavior*, 15 (4): 375–401.

Galin, D., (2000), 'Comments on Epstein's Neurocognitive Interpretation of William James's Model of Consciousness,' *Consciousness and Cognition*, 9 (4): 576–83.

Grice, P. (1989), *Studies in the Way of Words*, Cambridge (Ma), Harvard University Press.

Husserl, E. (1912–29), *Ideen zu einer reinen Phänomenologie und phänomenologischen Philosophie*, in *Husserliana*, voll. III, IV, V, Den Haag, Martinus Nijoff, 1952.

Jackson, D.F., Doster, E.C., Meadows, L., Wood, T. (1995), 'Hearts and Minds in the Science Classroom: The Education of a Confirmed Evolutionist,' *Journal of Research in Science Teaching* 32 (6): 585–611.

James, W. (1890), *The Principles of Psychology* (reprinted, New York, Dover, 1955).

Lavazza, A (2006), 'L'arte è la mente vista dall'interno. Verso un'estetica neo-jamesiana tra fenomenologia e neuroscienze' *Rivista di estetica*, XLVI, (nuova serie, 31): 191–214.

Lenat, D.B. (1998), 'From 2001 to 2001: Common Sense and the Mind of HAL,' in *HAL's Legacy: 2001's Computer as Dream and Reality*, ed. D.G. Stork, Cambridge (MA), MIT Press.

Mandler, G. (1975), 'Consciousness: Respectable, Useful and Probably Necessary,' in *Information Processing and Cognition*, ed. S. Solso, Hillsdale (NJ), Erlbaum.

Mangan, B. (1991), *Meaning and the Structure of Consciousness: An Essay in Psycho-Aesthetics*, unpublished Ph.D thesis, Berkeley, University of California.

Mangan, B. (1993a), 'Taking Phenomenology Seriously: The Fringe and its Implications for Cognitive Research,' *Consciousness and Cognition*, **2** (2): 89–108.

Mangan, B. (1993b), 'Some Philosophical and Empirical Implications of The Fringe,' *Consciousness and Cognition*, **2** (2): 142–54.

Mangan, B. (2000), 'What Feeling Is the 'Feeling-of-knowing?', *Consciousness and Cognition*, 9 (4): 538–44.

Mangan, B. (2001), 'Sensation ghost. The Non-Sensory 'Fringe' of Consciousness,' *Psyche*, **7** (18), http://psyche.cs.monash.edu.au/ v7/psyche-7-18-mangan.html.

Merleau-Ponty, M. (1945), *Phénoménologie de la perception*, Paris, Gallimard.

Metzinger, T. (2004), *Being No One*, Cambridge (MA), MIT Press.

Metzinger, T. (2005), 'Précis: Being No One', *Psyche*, 11 (5), http://psyche.cs.monash.edu.au/

Nagel, T. (1974) 'What Is it Like to Be a Bat?' *Philosophical Review*, 83:435–450.

O'Keefe, J.M., Dostrovsky, J. (1973), 'The Hippocampus as a Spatial Map: Preliminary Evidence From Unit Activity In the Freely-Moving Rat', *Experimental Brain Research*, 31: 573–90.

O'Keefe, J.M., Nadel, L. (1978), *The Hippocampus as a Cognitive Map*, Oxford, Clarendon Press.

Paternoster, A. (2002), *Introduzione alla filosofia della mente*, Roma-Bari, Laterza.

Potworowski, G., Ferrari, M. (2002), 'Varieties of Rightness Experiences,' *Pyche*, 8 (13), http://psyche.cs. Monash.edu.au/v8/psyche-8-13-potworowski.html

Putnam, H. (1975), 'The Meaning of 'Meaning'', in *Mind, Language, and Reality. Philosophical Papers*, vol. II, Cambridge (Ma), Harvard University Press.

Quine, W. V. (1953), *From a Logical Point of View*, New York, Harper & Row.

Rapaport, W. J. (1995), 'Understanding Understanding: Syntactic Semantics and Computational Cognition', *Philosophical Perspectives*, 9: 49–88.

Schlick, M. (1936), 'Meaning and Verification,' *The Philosophical Review*, 45: 339–69.

Searle, J. (1980), 'Minds, Brains, and Programs,' *Behavioral and Brain Sciences*, 3: 417–57.

Tononi, G. (2003), *Galileo e il fotodiodo. Cervello, complessità e coscienza*, Roma-Bari, Laterza.

Wittgenstein, L. (1953), *Philosophische Untersuchungen/Philosophical Investigations* (eds. G.E.M. Anscombe, G.H. von Wright), Oxford, Basil Blackwell.

Salvatore Gaglio

# Intelligent Artificial Systems

Intelligent systems, both biological and artificial, require sophisticate functionalities, like perception, reasoning, decision making, learning, and communicating, in order to act in complex environments. By constructing artificial intelligent systems a question arises spontaneously: Can human-level intelligence be captured by a computable model? Or rather, is it possible to realize a process of information processing whose behaviour could be defined as intelligent?

As regards the behaviour itself, a topic, considered a landmark in the field of artificial intelligence, is the one known as the Turing Test (Turing, 1950) (Castelfranchi and Stock, 2000) (Nilsson, 1998), also called the *imitation game*. In the simplified version, a machine tries to convince a human interviewer that it is a human. In particular, the interviewer communicates, today we would say via the Internet, with a human being and with an intelligent machine, and, by communicating with them, he has to understand which is the machine and which is the human being. The machine tries to deceive the interviewer, the human being tries to help him. We will be able to say that the machine has an intelligent behaviour if it achieves its goal.

Actually, it is possible also for quite insignificant machines to deceive human interviewers for a while. Significant examples are some software programs that talk in a human way with human beings, such as Joseph Weizenbaum's historic ELIZA (Weizenbaum, 1966) and Mauldin's Julia (Mauldin,1944) and the most recent chatbots (robots on the net) such as ALICE (www.alicebot.org). A prize has even been awarded, namely the Loebner Prize consisting in a sum of $100,000 offered to the author of the first computer program to pass a complete Turing test.

But does the imitation game allow us to say that the machines are able to think, or even to be conscious? Many people think that human intelligence may be too complex, or at least too dependent on the precise human physiology, to exist apart from its embodiment in humans living in their environment.

The philosopher John Searle (Searle, 1980) believes that what we are made of is fundamental to our intelligence. Thinking can occur only in living organisms.

His anecdote of the Chinese room aims to show that in principle it is possible to simulate intelligent behaviour in a mechanical way, such as on a computer, without there being however any awareness or thinking activity. The anecdote regards the setting up of a system which can communicate in a foreign language, such as Chinese for example, carried out with a human being who doesn't know the language, but who is inside a room and receives a sequence of cards from outside, on which there are some symbols in Chinese. By following some fixed rules, which he can read in a handbook, he can recover other cards from appropriate card files inside the room and construct an answer, in Chinese of course, consisting of a new sequence of cards. If the handbook contains enough rules, we have obtained a system which can communicate in Chinese. But Searle asks himself the question: where does thinking activity lie in the act of communicating? The handbook and the cards are inert objects. There is a human being, but he doesn't know Chinese; he only follows some rules regarding the symbols to be recovered depending on the ones he received, and he doesn't even know the subject of the conversation.

According to others, intelligent behaviour is an emergent phenomenon that can be achieved by purely mechanical methods. This position is summarized in the *physical symbol system hypothesis* of Newell and Simon (Newell and Simon, 1976). A physical symbol system is a mechanical system, like a digital computer, that manipulates symbols arranged in expressions, according to processes that follow precise rules. According to Newell and Simon, a system like this has the necessary and sufficient means to act in an intelligent way.

The important aspect, according to such a hypothesis, is that it doesn't matter what is the substrate of the system. It can be either a living organism or a computer made of logic gates.

## Intelligent Systems and Computability

It is possible to study the processing capabilities of the physical symbol systems through an abstract reference model, which, incidentally, is also the reference model for information processing in general. Such a model allows us to study the information processing itself in abstract terms, disregarding details of the systems really constructed. This model is the Turing machine (Turing, 1936–37) (figure 1).

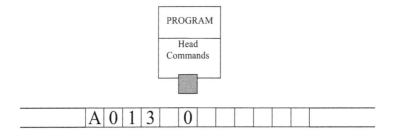

**Figure 1: The Turing Machine**

*A Turing Machine consists of*

1.  a tape of infinite length (in practice for each processing a finite portion is used but not limited beforehand) divided into cells;

2.  a head positioned on one cell of the tape, which is able to move to the left and right of this cell, and to read or write one symbol from a finite alphabet of symbols in the cell on which it is positioned;

3.  a finite set of possible internal states;

4.  a program consisting of a set of possible state transitions, conditioned by the symbol that is read, and of actions that can be taken: the writing of a new symbol in the cell in which the head is positioned or the movement of the head to a cell on the left or on the right.

The machine operates in response to an input of information, encoded in a sequence of symbols contained in adjacent cells starting from the cell to the right of the head. It carries out the transitions defined by the program, and, if necessary, it stops. The sequences of symbols which are in the cells to the right of the head, when it stops, constitute an encoding of the answer. In this way the machine realizes a mathematical function that maps the input configurations in the output configurations.

The interesting aspect of this device is that it can be programmed in such a way as to simulate any another device of the same kind, whose program is given in input on the tape too, thus realizing a universal computer.

But how universal is this machine? The famous thesis of the logician A. *Church* (Church, 1936) asserts that *Every computable function can be calculated by a Turing Machine.* This means that once a problem of information processing has been represented in terms of a function and of an encoding of the input and output information, if a way of resolving it exists, then it is possible to do it with the Turing Machine. This is not a theorem but a fact well corroborated by present mathematical knowledge.

This subject brings us essentially again to the problem of the computability of human-level intelligence. The Turing Machine comes under the class of the physical symbol system, and it is also the universal computer, so the hypothesis enunciated by Newell and Simon requires just the computability Church speaks of in his thesis.

A very interesting recent development connected to the concept of Turing computability and the universal Turing machine is that of *universal artificial intelligence* introduced by Hutter (Hutter, 2005) and which is based also on other basic computational concepts, like algorithmic information theory, Kolmogoroff complexity and Solomonoff universal probability.

The Kolmogoroff complexity (Kolmogoroff, 1968) of an information structure, say for instance a string $x$, is defined

$$C(x) = \min_{p}\{l(p):U(p) = x\}$$

where $p$ is a program that, given as an input to the universal machine $U$, outputs $x$, and $l(p)$ is the length of $p$. In other words, $C(x)$ is the length of the shortest program that generates $x$ as its output on a universal machine. Kolmogoroff complexity is a very general property of an information structure $x$, in the sense that is defined up to an additive constant independent of $x$, which takes into account the particular universal machine.

Solomonoff universal probability (Solomonoff, 1964) of a structure $x$ is defined as

$$\xi(x) \equiv \sum_{p:U(p)=x} 2^{-l(p)}$$

Such a probability expresses the concept that information structures are the result of computational processes originated by casual binary programs, whose single bits are independently and uniformly distributed with an identical probability of 0.5 for 0 or 1. A property of Solomonoff probability (or more correctly a semi-measure) is that it dominates any other computable (recursive) probability ñ in the following sense:

$$\xi(x) \geq 2^{-k(p)} p(x),$$

where $K(r)$ is the so called prefix complexity, a variant of Kolmogoroff complexity, of the probability function r. Accordingly, the semi-measure x can be used as a universal prior probability for every unknown process.

Putting all this together, Hutter has proposed the architecture of figure 2 for a possible universal intelligent agent. This theoretical architecture considers both the environment and the agent as computational entities. They are both modelled as universal machines which share two tapes, which, from the two different perspectives, are input/output tapes: at each cycle, the agent outputs a symbol yi (an elementary action), which is read as an input by the environment, and reads a reward/penalty value ci, and an input xi, both generated by the environment.

The agent estimates from the previous observations, using the Solomonoff universal probability as a prior, the environment function

$$q : Y \to C, X$$

and chooses as its function, i.e. its behaviour, the following function

$$p^* = \arg\max_{p} C(p, q),$$

i.e. the one which maximizes its expected total reward $C(p,q)$.

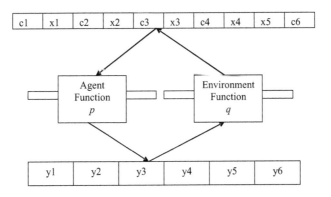

Figure 2: The Universal Agent Model

The Hutter architecture works in principle but is unfeasible in practice: unfortunately Kolmogoroff complexity is a non computable entity and the decision process involved is of a combinatorial nature. What we can do is to resort to approximations and very restricted domains.

### The Symbolic Approach to Artificial Intelligence

Most of the research in the field of artificial intelligence, the so-called *symbolic artificial intelligence,* has been based on an even stronger hypothesis than that of the physical symbol system, namely the fact that intelligence requires knowledge – in order to behave in an intelligent way, a system must have some knowledge about the processes with which it is concerned. This more restrictive hypothesis has been clearly expressed by Brian Smith, and is known as the *Knowledge Representation Hypothesis* (Smith, 1982). It is enunciated in the following way:

> The realization of any intelligent process will base itself on structural ingredients that:
>
> a)    for us external observers represent a propositional description of the knowledge that the process possesses, and
>
> b)    apart from such an external semantic attribution, they have a formal, but also causal and essential role, in producing the behaviour that exhibits such knowledge.

This hypothesis presupposes therefore that what is really needed is an opportune propositional description of the required knowledge, formalized in such a way as to produce the desired intelligent behaviour. Does a formal instrument however exist that can be actually utilized for this purpose? The answer is yes, and this instrument is *mathematical logic.* Even if in the past the subject has been much discussed, mathematical logic constitutes the basic methodology for the various intelligent artificial systems constructed to represent and to use knowledge.

One of the most commonly used logical formalisms is the First-Order Predicate Calculus (Nilsson, 1998). It consists of a language and of a set of rules of inference. We give a brief informal description of it.

The language allows some *facts* to be represented with expressions in which *Terms, Predicates, Logical Operators* and *Quantifiers* appear. Simple facts can be represented through the following association:

Terms        => Entities we talk about

Predicates  => Relationships among entities

Some examples of simple facts are:

read(student, book)
family(father, mother, children)
on(pen, table)

With *Operators* and *Logical Quantifiers* it is possible to construct more complex expressions such as:

(rainy(weather) OR cold(weather))
→ NOT(to go(me, outside))

FOR_ALL(?X, man(?X) → mortal(?X))

which want to represent the propositions 'If it's raining or it is cold then I don't go outside' and 'every man is mortal' respectively. It is clear that if we introduce such expressions into a machine, it doesn't mean that it understands the sense of them at all. In fact we can say without hesitation that for the machine they are nothing more than mere configurations of symbols. But where do intelligence and knowledge lie then?

As we have said, logic also provides us with rules of inference which allow us to perform some operations of automatic deduction. These operations produce some true propositions, called conclusions, starting from other true propositions, called premises.

An example that is reminiscent of the schemes of the Aristotelian syllogism is the following:

*Premise*:

Man(Socrates)
FOR_ALL(?X, man(?X) → mortal(?X))

*Conclusion*:

Mortal(Socrates)

At this point, the mechanism according to which we operate is the following: some true propositions (axioms), which represent basic knowledge, are communicated to the machine; intelligent behaviour is obtained through operations of deduction that the machine is able to carry out in which it produces new true propositions. The whole set of true propositions which the machine contains at a certain moment is called a knowledge base. Let us examine such behaviour in the following example in which the machine is able to answer a question automatically:

*Axioms in the knowledge base:*

> formula_one_driver(Schumacher)
> affiliation(Schumacher, Ferrari)
> FOR_ALL(?X, formula_one_driver (?X) → champion(?X))
> FOR_ALL(?X, affiliation(?X, ?Team)
> 　　　　　　　　AND wins_world_championship(?Team,
> 　　　　　　　　?T) → winner(?X, ?T))
> ..........

> wins_world_championship(Ferrari, 2004)
> ..........

*Question:*

> EXISTS(?T, winner(Schumacher, ?T))
> (Encoding of 'When has Schumacher been a winner?')

*Answer:*

> winner(Schumacher, 2004)

As the example evidently shows, following the hypothesis enunciated by Brian Smith, we have represented some knowledge in propositional form and this representation itself causes the 'intelligent' behaviour, thanks to the power of mathematical logic. Can we say that this machine is able to think? It carries out only some automatic manipulation of symbols, but it is able to reproduce our reasonings, even if the meaning of the propositions remains completely external to the machine.

## Search Problems

Although it seems very natural, the construction of such systems is quite complex. The first problem is the choice of the representation: which entities and relationships do we have to represent and how? This choice is crucial for the behaviour exhibited. A problem that regularly occurs in artificial intelligence is one known as *search problem*. This occurs whenever an automatic procedure in different points requires a choice among possible different evolutions. In this specific case, at every turn several inferences are possible and if the system is left free to choose, its behaviour is like that of a dissociated person who doesn't follow any line of reasoning and churns out a lot of unconnected conclusions.

The evolution of a process like this can be represented by a tree (figure 3). From the initial stage we can proceed towards different subsequent stages and from these towards yet further stages. The problem consists of finding a path which starts from the initial stage and ends in a significant final stage. The final stage represents the attainment of a goal—in the preceding example, finding the answer—the path represents the sequence of steps that lead to the solution, in the example the line of reasoning used to reach the conclusion. It is desirable that this path leads to the solution as directly as possible, without digressions. The criterion followed at every point where a choice must be made is known as *search strategy*. Unfortunately the complexity of these problems is as we say of an *exponential kind* and an inaccurate strategy leads to systems which are unable to give an answer within a reasonable amount of time. In order to understand better the characteristics of problems of an exponential kind, it is sufficient to know that even when the ramifications and depths of the tree in figure 3 are not excessive, the paths requested for the exploration can take even a very fast computer hundreds or thousands of years to complete.

It is therefore necessary to adopt some heuristics in order to deal with the complexity. A heuristics corresponds to the selection of appropriate choice criteria, based upon further in-depth knowledge and analysis of the problem tackled.

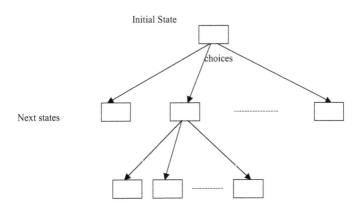

**Figure 3: A search tree**

### The Grounding Problem and the Subsymbolic Level

As we have seen, a drawback of symbolic systems is the fact that the meaning remains external to the representations and to the processes which operate on them. This is quite a general fact, no formal system can really determine its model unequivocally. Everybody knows that a language needs to be interpreted, otherwise it remains incomprehensible. This is shown by the case of the Rosetta stone, that provided the key to the interpretation of Egyptian hieroglyphics.

Human intermediation would therefore seem to be necessary in giving the symbols a meaning. In any case a function of interpretation is needed that maps the representation on entities and relationships of the real world (figure 4). In reality, the representations of a logical kind have the property of being compositional, so the meaning of complex expressions is determined by the component expressions. However, it is necessary to provide from outside the meaning of the simplest expressions from which we have to start, the so called *primitives*.

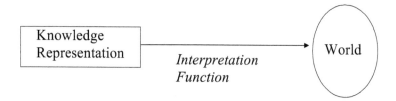

**Figure 4: The symbol grounding problem**

In short:

- An *interpretation function* cannot be defined only in terms of other symbols, because that would cause an infinite regression.

- An *interpretation function* must be calculated, at least for some symbols in the system (the 'primitives'), by a subsymbolic device.

That justifies the need for *subsymbolic cognitive levels* that make it possible to realize functional relationships with the outside world through *perception and action*.

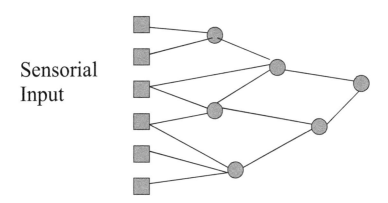

Sensorial
Input

**Figure 5: A subsymbolic device**

Therefore, a possibility for an intelligent system to capture the meaning of the symbols would consist in the so called *anchoring* to perceptive activities and to the actions it is able to perform on the outside world. This anchoring would be done by a subsymbolic device that interacts directly with the outside world (figure 5).

Different systems of subsymbolic processing have been proposed. They have the property of interacting with the outside world through sensors and actuators, by associating some symbols to actions or perceptions. Within them the representations are generally not local, since they are characterized by parameters that do not necessarily and individually represent entities of the outside world, their effect is, so to speak, global: they act in an associative way to mediate correspondences among perceptions or between actions and symbols.

One of the most commonly used models to achieve a subsymbolic processing is based on *neural nets*, which also recalls the way the information is processed in the nervous circuits of biological systems. Like these, the artificial neural nets are realized in terms of circuits interconnecting artificial neurons in various ways and with many *synaptic* connections, the artificial neurons being simplified versions of natural neurons (figure 6).

An artificial neuron is activated if the weighed sum of its inputs is higher than one threshold. The weights model the synapsis among the natural neurons — modulating the inputs — and they can be either positive (exciting synapses) or negative (inhibiting synapses). The activation of a neuron is transmitted through other synapses to

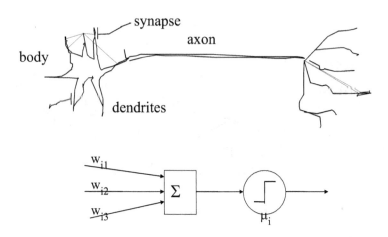

**Figure 6: The artificial neuron**

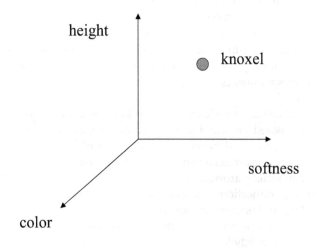

**Figure 7: Conceptual space**

other neurons. Different typologies of neural nets have been studied corresponding to different behaviours, and often evoking functionalities of biological nervous systems.

## Intermediate Cognitive Levels

The construction of perceptions based on signals received from sensors interacting with the outside world requires appropriate reorganization and aggregation of information into significant entities. The same applies to actions and actuators.

Gardenfors proposes as an intermediate cognitive level a *conceptual space* (Gardenfors, 2000) in which the concepts take shape, before symbols are associated with them. A conceptual space is a space similar to our tridimensional space, endowed with some dimensions acting like coordinates. Every dimension corresponds to a quality associated with sensors or actuators. Each point of the space is characterized by the values of the coordinates in the qualitative dimensions and can be considered an elementary concept, we could call it a *knoxel*, like a pixel is an elementary point of an image (figure 7).

In short, in the conceptual spaces

- Information is organized according to qualitative dimensions;
- ... which are divided into *domains* (space, time, temperature, weight, colour, shape ...;
- domains can have a topology or a metrics;
- the similarity is represented by a distance in the conceptual space.

Together with my colleagues Antonio Chella and Marcello Frixione, I proposed a cognitive architecture for visual perception (Chella, Gaglio, Frixione, 1997) organized according to three areas of representation (figure 8). In accordance with such a model, in a conceptual space, halfway between the subsymbolic level and the logic-linguistic one, tridimensional shapes are represented, whose primitives are superquadrics, consisting of volumes characterized by 11 dimensions, corresponding to their position in the space, to the scale, and to the shape respectively. In particular, by varying the shape parameters various types of solids are obtained, such as parallelepipeds, spheres, ellipsoids, cylinders, etc. (figure9).

This way, an elementary concept (knoxel) in our conceptual space related to the shapes is a superquadric. Complex objects are sets of superquadrics which correspond to sets of knoxels in the conceptual space.

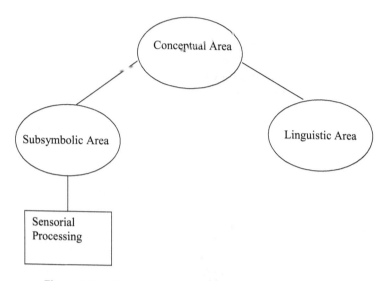

**Figure 8: The three representation areas for visual information
(Chella, Frixione, and Gaglio, 1997–2000)**

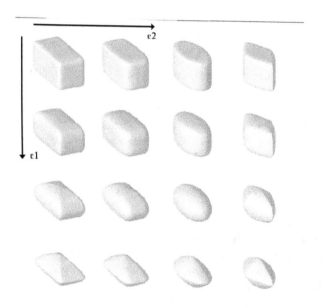

**Figure 9: Superquadrics**

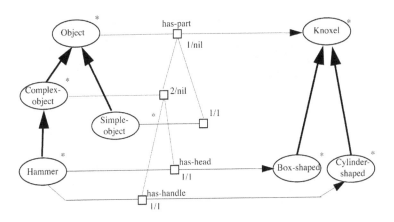

Figure 10: The logic-linguistic representation

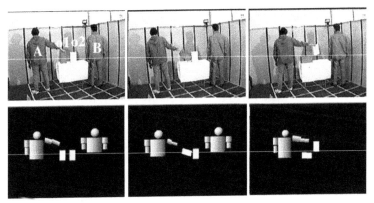

Figure 11: Perception of a scene in motion

The linguistic component assigns some names (symbols) to the shapes, describing their structure with a logical-structural language (figure 10). As a result, all the symbols find their meaning in the conceptual space that is inside the system itself, this way solving the problem of symbol grounding.

A model based upon a conceptual space has also proved to be useful within an artificial system in carrying out attentive and associative tasks peculiar to human perceptive activity, and in particular the comprehension of scenes in motion (Chella, Frixione, and Gaglio, 2000). In figure 11, for instance, a scene in which a person takes an object and passes it to another person is represented with superquadrics in motion, and it is then described automatically in linguistic terms in the following way:

Arm_approach(a1)
Grasp(g1)

Seize(s1)
Part#1_of_Seize(s1, a1)
Part#2_of_Seize(s1, g1)

Rotate(rot1)
Let_go(l1)

... ... ...

## The Self of the Robot

The cognitive architecture that has been described allows us to address one of the major concerns of research in artificial consciousness, i.e. the concept of self (Chella, Frixione, and Gaglio, in preparation). In fact, a robot can also observe himself within the environment that he reconstructs. As a consequence, he can associate an internal representation like the one based on a conceptual space, as discussed above. He can therefore perform reasoning on its internal representation or on those of other robots.

At the same time $t$ two representations coexist: the actual representation of the actual perceived scene, which comprises the robot as an entity, and the representation associated to this perceived entity. In order to avoid well known problematic self-references, we can say that this latter representation is that at a time $t$-$d$ before.

From another perspective, we can say that a given representation of the robot collapses after a time $d$ to an entity (the same robot) within a more external representation (again of the same robot), and, by repeating this process, a sequence of repeated collapses takes shape, as in figure 12. This sequence can be considered as a flow of consciousness. In fact, this flow is the inner personal history of the robot, and is unique to that robot. Even if the robot were cloned at a given instant, we would have a bifurcation and, consequently, two different flows that share only part of their inner personal histories. In this sense we can say that this flow is the *self* of the robot, i.e. a rudimental form of artificial consciousness.

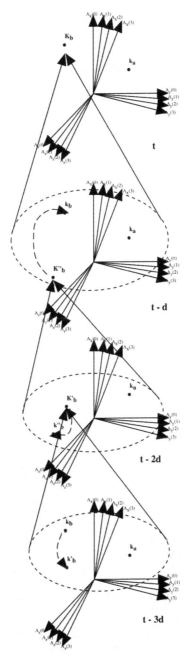

**Figure 12: The self of the robot**

## Conclusions

In this work I have presented the main problems of artificial intelligent systems and the different approaches to their solutions. Apart from the philosophical questions as to whether the machines can actually think like human beings, I have tried to point out how in any case it is necessary to provide solutions to the problem of meaning: intelligent systems cannot be given the meaning from outside by humans. On this point an architecture has also been presented for visual perception realized by the author together with his colleagues Chella and Frixione, in which a solution to the problem is supplied through a conceptual space intermediate between subsymbolic processing and logical-linguistic processing. This architecture can also account for a rudimentary form of artificial self-consciousness.

## References

Castelfranchi, Y. & Stock, O. (2000), *Macchine Come Noi-La Scommessa dell'Intelligenza Artificiale*, Laterza, Bari.

Chella, A., Frixione,M. & Gaglio, S. (1997), A Cognitive Architecture for Artificial Vision, *Artificial Intelligence*, 89, No. 1–2, pp. 73–111.

Chella, A., Frixione, M. & Gaglio, S. (2000), Understanding Dynamic Scenes, *Artificial Intelligence*, 123, pp. 89–132.

Chella, A., Frixione, M. & Gaglio, S. (in preparation), Towards a New Generation of Conscious Autonomous Robots. In preparation.

Church, A. (1936), An Unsolvable Problem of Elementary Number Theory, *American Journal of Mathematics*, 58, pp. 345–363.

Hutter, M. (2005), *Universal Artificial Intelligence*, Springer-Verlag, Berlin.

Kolmogoroff, A.N. (1968), Logical Basis for Information Theory and Probability Theory, *IEEE Trans. Inform. Theory*, IT–14(5), pp. 662–664.

Solomonoff, R.J. (1964), A formal theory of inductive inference, part 1 and part 2, *Inform. Contr.*, 7, pp. 1–22, 224–254.

Frixione, M. & Palladino, D. (2004), *Funzioni, Macchine, Algoritmi*, Carocci, Roma.

Gardenfors, P. (2000), *Conceptual Spaces*, MIT Press, Cambridge, MA.

Mauldin, M. (1994), 'Chatterbots, TinyMUDs, and the Turing Test: Enteringthe Loebner Prize Competition, *Proceedings of Twelfth National Conference on Artificial Intelligence*, Seattle, Washington, August 1994.

Newell, A. & Simon, H.A. (1976), Computer Science as Empirical Inquiry: Symbols and Search, *Communications of the ACM*, 19(3), 113–126.

Nilsson, N.J. (1998), *Artificial Intelligence: A New Synthesis*. Morgan Kaufmann.

Searle, J.R. (1980), Minds, Brains and Programs, *Behavioral and Brain Sciences*, 3, pp. 417–57.

Smith, B.C. (1985), Prologue to 'Reflection and Semantics in a Procedural Language', in *Readings in Knowledge Representation*, edited by R.J. Brachman & H.J. Levesque, Morgan Kaufmann.

Weizenbaum, J. (1966), ELIZA—A Computer Program For the Study of Natural Language Communication Between Man and Machine, *Communications of the ACM* Volume 9, Number 1, pp. 36-35.

Turing, A.M. (1936-37), *On Computable Numbers, with an application to the Entscheidungsproblem*, Proc. Lond. Math. Soc. (2) 42 pp. 230-265.

Turing, A.M. (1950), Computing machinery and intelligence. Mind, 59, pp. 433-460.

Maurizio Cardaci, Antonella D'Amico, & Barbara Caci

# The Social Cognitive Theory

## A New Framework for Implementing Artificial Consciousness

'I'll use the word consciousness to mean the organization of different ways we have for knowing what is happening inside your mind, your body and the world outside.' In this perspective 'some machines are already potentially more conscious than are people' even if 'is one thing to have access to data, but another thing is to know how to make a good use of it.'

Minsky (1991)

### Introduction

Consciousness is one of the most controversial issues in the area of the scientific research. In the past decades, philosophers and psychologists have attempted to define the nature of human consciousness with the aim to design 'conscious' artificial agents. However, there is not still a general consensus about the meaning of the term 'consciousness' and about the best strategies for implementing it in artificial agents (Colombetti & Schiaffonati, 2004; Bechtel, 1995).

For these reasons, we do not think to be exhaustive in defining consciousness: in the present contribution, we focus our attention only on the use of conscious processes in the regulation of motivated behaviour. To this aim, we start from the Minsky's definition (1991) of consciousness, that is somewhat similar to the Bandura's Social Cognitive Theory (Bandura, 1986; 2001).

During the 75th Anniversary Symposium on Science in Society (Canada, 1991) Minsky argued: 'I'll use the word consciousness to mean the organization of different ways we have for knowing what is happening inside your mind, your body and the world outside.' Analogously Bandura (2001) argues that consciousness, the 'very substance of mental life', corresponds to a function that involves purposive accessing to information and deliberative processing of information for selecting, constructing, regulating and evaluating courses of actions. In other words, consciousness is an *experienced cognition* embodied and situated (Gibson, 1966; 1979) in a variety of environments (Carlson, 1997). Literally, a human or an agent is 'conscious' because he/she/it has a *hic et nunc* point of view. In this sense, consciousness is not a special or extraordinary occurrence, but an utterly mundane aspect of human experience. According to Carlson (1997) for understanding consciousness we must refer to the concept of Self as an Agent: 'consciousness is not a thing but a systemic, dynamic property or aspects of persons — typically engaged in purposive activity in an information-rich environment — and their mental states'. Consciousness is a sort of 'primary awareness' that controls the flow of mental events and that is grounded in purposeful, goal-directed action. As claimed by Bandura (1986), agency is the experience of oneself as originator or controller of its activities. Indeed, the human's mind is an *active force* that constructs one's reality, encoding selectively the information, performing behaviours on the basis of values and expectations and imposing structure on its own actions. In particular, the Author points up that people use their sensory, motor and cerebral systems as tools to accomplish tasks and goals that give sense to their life (Bandura, 1997). At the same time, the human brain evolves in its structure and functionality through the action of exploring, manipulating and influencing its 'psychological environment': this position is known as 'triadic reciprocal determinism' that explains the way by which the actions, the cognitive/affective personal factors and the environmental events convey all in a *emergent interactive agency* (Bandura, 1986; 1999).

Consciousness arises from this emergent interactive agency, and its core features are intentionality, forethought, self-reactiveness and self-reflectiveness (Bandura, 2001). *Intentionality* corresponds to a proactive commitment to bring an action. Indeed, one of the key qualities of human agency is the power to originate goal-oriented actions or, in other words, intentions that are centred on plan of actions. Intentionality does not guarantee to individuals to succeed in their projects. People, setting goals for themselves, use also the *forethought* process to anticipate the likely consequences of their future actions; on the basis of the forethought process, individuals select and create behaviours able to produce the desired outcomes and to avoid any possible negative consequence (Bandura, 1991). Forethoughts are formed on the basis of observed conditional relations between environmental events and the outcomes that given actions produce. In this sense, all the previous individuals' experiences are used to create new forethoughts about future behavioural outcomes, which are used to program new actions (Bandura, 1986). With the aim to give shape to these actions and to motivate and regulate their execution, people use a series of *self-reactiveness* skills such as self-monitoring, performance self-guidance via personal standards and corrective self-reactions (Bandura, 1986; 1991). The final core feature of consciousness consists in the *self-reflectiveness* that is the process by which people self-examine their functioning. In other words, it is a meta-cognitive capability to reflect upon oneself and the adequacy of one's thoughts and actions. In this sense, the self-reflectiveness corresponds to a reflective self-consciousness.

Carrying this approach to extremes, the researchers could build up a future generation of conscious artificial agents with the paradoxical property of having access to their own internal data, even more than people. As Minsky writes: 'some machines are already potentially more conscious than are people' (Minsky, 1991).

## Implementing Artificial Consciousness in Goal-Oriented Agents

The above-mentioned theoretical notes allowed us to depict an artificial agent that uses conscious processes in the regulation of its own motivated behaviours. In the human beings motivated behaviours are goal-oriented and the chance that a given behaviour occurs is a function of two combined factors: the first is the expectation that a particular behaviour will obtain a reward or a punishment; the second is the individual perceived value of this reward/punishment. Thus, successes and failures correspond to 'junctures of plans' that may generate in individuals different motivational and emotional states (Oatley & Johnson-Laird, 1987). Individuals with a so-called Internal Locus of Control tend to attribute their success experiences to their own personal efforts and merits and, conversely, their failure experiences to their own incompetence or inadequacy. On the contrary, individuals with a so-called External Locus of Control tend to attribute both success and failure experiences to the external contingencies such as case, fortune, etc. (e.g. Rotter, 1966; 1975; Strickland, 1978; Cardaci, 1988; Marshall, Collins, & Crooks, 1990; Lefcourt, 1991; McLaughlin & Saccuzzo, 1997).

A previous research (Caci, Cardaci, Chella, D'Amico, Infantino & Macaluso, 2005) was aimed at studying the behaviour of a mobile robot equipped with two architectures simulating both the Internal Locus of Control and the External Locus of Control (see Figure 1).

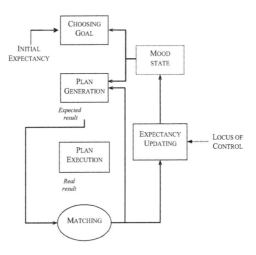

**Figure 1: The robot architecture**

Both the architectures allows the robot to represent the environment by means of a rich and expressive conceptual area, based on the theory of conceptual spaces (Gärdenfors, 2000), and are provided with an *initial expectancy value* and a function by which the robot may *generate plan of actions* in order to produce a desired result. During the *plan execution*, the robot operates a matching between the *expected results* of its actions, and the *real obtained results*. In the architecture that simulates the Internal Locus of Control, the result of this *matching*, expressed as an output number comprised between –1 (Total Mismatching) and 1 (Total Matching), is used to update the *expectancy* variable. On the contrary, in the architecture that simu-

*Artificial Consciousness*

lates the External Locus of Control, the expectancy value is always updated with a random value (in the range of –1; 1). The expectancy-updated value is used by both architectures to increment/decrement the *mood state of the robot*. The mood states, in turn, affects both the execution speed of the following behaviours and the new plan generation and/or the choosing of more difficult or simpler goals.

In Caci, Cardaci, Chella, D'Amico, Infantino & Macaluso (2005), we implemented the described architectures in a mobile robot (RWI-B21) assigned with a navigation task in two different environments. Indeed, to simulate the success/failure experiences, we created: 1) a low-difficulty environment, where the static/predictable position of obstacles produced very high chances to succeed or, in other words, to obtain a reward; 2) a high-difficulty environment, featured by a dynamic/unpredictable position of obstacles, where the chance to succeed, or to obtain a reward, were very low. The results of this study were consistent with the Locus of Control Theory. Indeed, when the robot was assigned with the Internal Locus of Control architecture, it showed a more 'persistent' and 'motivated' behaviour (higher *mood* levels) in high static environments; as above mentioned, indeed, the increasing of the mood level determined both the higher execution speed and the choosing of goals of increasing difficulty. The Internal Locus of Control became, on the contrary, a 'depressing' factor (lower *mood* levels) when the robot explored more dynamic environments. When the robot was assigned with an external Locus of Control, it varied its expectancy value and its mood level independently of the environmental context; this feature leaded it to maintain a more constant mood level, as the robot was less persistent and motivated in predictable environments, but also less emotionally vulnerable in unpredictable ones.

By implementing the above-described architecture, we simulated aspects such as intentionality (i.e. reaching a goal) and forethought (based on the updating of expectancies). However, we still cannot say to have developed something like a 'conscious system', as it lacks of self-reactiveness and self-reflectiveness, the two indispensable aspects of consciousness as defined in the Social Cognition framework. In other words, such architecture lacks of a meta-cognitive level that, using the Minsky's expression, allows the system 'to have access to its own internal data' and that suggests how to 'make good use of it'.

In the Locus of Control framework, which may be the meaning of 'having access to its own internal data and to make a good us of it'? Some other information is necessary to complete the picture: indeed, psychological studies (Bless, Fiedler, 2005) demonstrated that, although people show quite stable 'Locus styles', they often use a sort of *hedonic regulation* of mood with the aim to preserve an optimal self-esteem image. Such hedonic regulation corresponds to a more adaptive Locus style, leading them to attribute the positive outcomes of their action to their own efforts (internal Locus) and the negative outcomes of their action to the contingencies (external Locus).

We tried to represent in operational terms such concept, designing a more complete architecture able to optimise the interaction between the robot internal/external attribution styles and the environmental features. To this aim, the projected architecture will be featured by a more flexible Locus style; in particular, a meta-cognitive function will allow the system to use the environmental feedbacks for 'choosing' which Locus style to adopt in order to develop a more persistent and goal oriented behaviour. Such metacognitive function will help the system in the self-monitoring and self-regulation of its Locus style, via a real-time detection of the matching/mismatching sequences.

In presence of a static/predictable environment (or, in other words, in presence of quite stable matching sequences), the system will self-assign an Internal Locus of Control style, that will make it more persistent in the achievement of goals of increasing difficulty level. In presence of a dynamic/unpredictable environment (when the alternation of matching/mismatching sequences is almost casual), the system will self-assign an External Locus of Control style that will avoid it to experience the 'learned helplessness' mood. In such way the system will be less vulnerable to the 'depressive' effects of unfriendly environments.

Even if this approach is quite simple, it could allow the researchers to equip an artificial agent with the capability to access to the consciousness of its internal states, including affects and motivations. Not always people are able to use conscious process in the self-regulation of their mood, affects and motivation ... as a paradox, a similar architecture may create an artificial agent 'potentially more conscious than are people' (Minsky, 1991).

# References

Bandura A. (1986). *Social Foundations of Thought and Action: A Social Cognitive Theory*. Englewood Cliffs, NJ: Prentice-Hall.

Bandura A. (1991). Self-Regulation of motivation through anticipatory and self-reactive mechanisms. In *Perspective on Motivation: Nebraska Symposium on Motivation*, ed. R.A. Dienstbier, 38·69-161. Lincoln: Univ. Nebraska Press

Bandura A. (1997). Self-Efficacy: The Exercise of Control. New York: Freeman.

Bandura A. (1999). A Social cognitive theory of personality. In Handbook of Personality, ed. L. Pervin, Q. John, pp. 154–196. New York: Guilford, 2nd edn.

Bandura A. (2001). Social Cognitive Theory: An Agentic Perspective. *Annual Review Psychology*, 52:1–26.

Bechtel W. (1995). Consciousness: Perspective from Symbolic and Connectionist AI. Neuropsychologica, vol. 33, n. 9:1075–1086.

Bless H., Fiedler K. (2005), *Mood and the regulation of information processing and behavior*, 8th Sydney Symposium of Social Psychology.

Caci B., Cardaci M., Chella A., D'Amico A., Infantino I., & Macaluso I. (2005). Personality and Learning in Robots. The Role of Individual Motivations/Expectations/ Emotions in Robot Adaptive Behaviours. *Proceedings of the Simposium 'Agents that Want and Like: Motivational and Emotional Roots of Cognition and Action'*, AISB 2005, 12–15 April 2005, University of Hertfordshire, Hatfield, England.

Cardaci M. (1988). *Studi sul Locus of Control*. Contributi del Dipartimento di Psicologia, Università degli Studi di Palermo.

Carlson R. A. (1997). *Experienced Cognition*. Mahwah, NJ: Erlbaum.

Colombetti M., Schiaffonati V., (2004), *Computo, ergo sum*, in D. Galati, C. Tinti (a cura di), *Prospettive sulla coscienza*, Roma: Carocci.

Gärdenfors P. (2000). *Conceptual Spaces*. MIT Press, Bradford Books, MA: Cambridge.

Gibson, J.J. (1966). *The Senses Considered as Perceptual Systems*. Boston: Houghton Mifflin.

Gibson, J.J. (1979). *The ecological approach to visual perception*. Boston, MA: Houghton Mifflin.

Lefcourt H.M. (1991). Locus of Control. In J.P.Robinson, P.R. Shaver & L.S Wrightsman, eds. *Measures of Personality and Social Psychological Attitudes*, Vol. 1:413–499. Academic Press, Inc., CA: San Diego.

Marshall G.N., Collins B.E., & Crooks V.C. (1990). A Comparison of Two Multidimensional Health Locus of Control Instruments. *Journal of Personality Assessment*, Vol. 54:181–90.

McLaughlin S. C, & Saccuzzo D. P. (1997). Ethnic and Gender Differences in Locus of Control. In Children Referred for Gifted Programs: The Effects of Vulnerability Factors. *Journal for the Education of the Gifted*, Vol. 20:268–83.

Minsky M. (1991). Conscious Machines. In Machinery of Consciousness, *Proceedings, National Research Council of Canada, 75th Anniversary Symposium on Science in Society*, June 1991.

Oatley K., & Johnson-Laird P. N. (1987). Towards a cognitive theory of emotions. *Cognition and Emotion*, Vol. 1:29–50.

Rotter J.B. (1960). Some implications of a social learning theory for the prediction of goal directed behavior from testing procedures. *Psychological Review*, Vol. 67: 301–316.

Rotter J.B. (1966). Generalized expectancies for internal versus external control of reinforcement. *Psychological Monographs*, 80.

Rotter J.B. (1975). Some problems and misconceptions related to the construct of internal versus external control of reinforcement. *Journal of Consulting and Clinical Psychology*, Vol. 43:56–67.

Rotter J.B., Chance J.E., & Phares E.J. (1972). *Applications of a social learning theory of personality*, Holt, Rinehart & Winston, New York.

Strickland B.R. (1978). Internal-external expectancies and health-related behaviors. *Journal of Consulting and Clinical Psychology*, Vol. 46:1192–1211.

Antonio Chella

# Towards Robot Conscious Perception

## 1. Introduction

The current generation of systems for man-machine interaction shows impressive performances with respect to the mechanics and the control of movements; see for example the anthropomorphic robots produced by the Japanese companies and universities. However, these robots, currently at the state of the art, present only limited capabilities of perception, reasoning and action in novel and unstructured environments. Moreover, the capabilities of user-robot interaction are standardized and well defined.

A new generation of robotic agents, able to perceive and act in new and unstructured environments should be able to pay attention to the relevant entities in the environment, to choose its own goals and motivations, and to decide how to reach them. In a word, new robotic agents must show some form of artificial consciousness. To reach this result, a robotic agent must be able to simulate different functions of the human brain that allow humans to be aware of the environment that surrounds them.

Epigenetic robotics and synthetic approaches to robotics based on psychological and biological models have elicited many of the differences between the artificial and mental studies of consciousness, while the importance of the interaction between the brain, the body and the surrounding environment has been pointed out (Rockwell, 2005).

The current chapter takes into account the *externalist* (Honderich, 2004; Rowlands, 2003) point of view about artificial consciousness by hypothesizing that the conscious perception process is based on a *generalized loop* between the brain, body and environment. In particular, the perception loop is in part internal and in part external to the robot, and it comprises the interactions among the proprioceptive and perceptive sensor data, the anticipations about the perceived scene, and the scene itself, through a focus of attention mechanism implemented by means of recurrent neural networks.

The perception model has been tested on an effective robot architecture implemented on an operating autonomous robot RWI B21 offering guided tours at the Archaeological Museum of Agrigento (Figure 1). Several public demos, some in the presence of media, validating the capabilities of the robot have been given over the last years. The task of a museum guide is a hard one for the robot because it must tightly interact with its environment which is dynamic and unpredictable; moreover the robot must be able to rearrange its goals and tasks according to the environment itself.

The chapter is organized as follows: Section 2 presents some theoretical remarks about the proposed account of conscious perception; Section 3 describes the implemented robot architecture, and Section 4 presents the robot implementation operating at the Archaeological Museum of Agrigento. Finally, Section 5 outlines some conclusions.

Figure 1: The robot *Cicerobot*
operating at the Archaeological Museum of Agrigento

## 2. Theoretical Remarks

In the recent years, there has been an increasing interest towards consciousness. Following this interest, computational models of *machine consciousness* for autonomous robots have been proposed and discussed, see Trautteur (1995); Buttazzo (2001); Holland (2003) for a review.

More in details, Franklin (2003) proposed the IDA system, a multi agent system employed in the USA navy and based on the Global Workspace Theory (Baars, 1988). Edelman and colleagues built the NOMAD architecture (Edelman et al., 1992; Edelman and Tononi, 2001; Krichmar and Edelman, 2002) based on the Edelman theories about consciousness and neural group selection (Edelman, 1989).

A mobile robot with a notion of *self* has been described by Tani (1998) and based on the theory of dynamic systems. Aleksander (2005) presented over the years several neural networks implementing aspects of consciousness related with visual awareness, imagination and planning from an engineering point of view; Aleksander and Dunmall (2003) summarized these results in a small number of theoretical principles for minimal consciousness in agents.

Based on empirical findings from cognitive neuroscience, Taylor presented neural networks implementing several aspects of consciousness (Taylor, 1999; 2002a); he also discussed about the relationships between consciousness and attention, memory and actions (Taylor and Taylor, 2000; Taylor and Rogers, 2002; Taylor, 2002b). Cotterill (2003) presented the CyberChild project, a complex software architecture aimed at simulating the consciousness of a child. Holland (Holland and Goodman, 2003) presented a robot architecture able to build an internal model of the environment by means of self-organizing maps.

Haikonen (2003) presented a modular system based on nonnumeric neural networks that implement cognitive aspect of consciousness. Steels (2003) presented a robotic framework to investigate the relationships between consciousness and *inner voices*.

Recently, Holland (2006) presented a model of anthropomorphic robot made up of a dorsal spine, tendons, muscles, and so on, in order to conduct experiments on robot consciousness. Shanahan (Shanahan and Baars, 2005; Shanahan, 2006) proposed a computational model for artificial consciousness based on the previously cited Global Workspace Theory.

The first ideas about externalism were mainly due to Gibson (1979), that introduced the *ecological* approach to perception as based on a tight interaction between living entities and the environment. Philosophical introductions to externalism have been proposed by Rowlands (2003) and Honderich (2004). See also Honderich (2006) for a debate about radical externalism.

Several works present suggestions on how to implement an artificial consciousness model based on externalism. The most relevant one is due to O'Regan and Noë (2001) that discusses the process of visual awareness as based on *sensorimotor contingencies* (see also Noë 2004). Following this approach, the robot should be equipped by a pool of sensorimotor contingencies so that entities in the environment activate the related contingencies that define the interaction schemas between the robot and the entity itself.

Some contingencies may be pre-programmed in the robot system by design (*phylogenetic* contingencies), but during the working life, the robot may acquire novel contingencies and therefore novel way of interacting with the environment. Moreover, the robot may acquire new ways of *mastery*, i.e., new ways to use and combine contingencies, in order to generate its own goal tasks and motivations (*ontogenetic* contingencies).

A mathematical analysis of the theory based on a simple robot in a simulated environment is presented in Philipona et al. (2003). The relationships between the sensorimotor contingencies and the minimal axioms for consciousness proposed by Aleksander has been analyzed in Aleksander and Morton (2005).

The *Multiple Drafts* model proposed by Dennett (1991) is a computational model based on agent systems that has several contact points with externalism. In the same line is the *behavioural field* between the brain, the body and the environment proposed by Rockwell (2005) and based on the Dynamic System Theory.

Manzotti and Tagliasco (2001) proposed the *Theory of Enlarged Mind* as an externalist theory covering the phenomenal and the functional aspects of consciousness. Following this line, Manzotti (2006) analyzed in details the human and robotic conscious perception as a process that unify the activity in the brain and the perceived events in the external world.

### 3. Robot Conscious Perception Model

The proposed robot perception model is inspired to the externalist approach to conscious perception. In agreement with Rockwell (2005), the model is based on tight interactions between the robot brain, body and environment.

The model is described in Figure 2. The *Robot Vision System* receives in input the proprioceptive data from internal sensors as the odometric sensor, and the perceptive data from the external sensors, as the scene acquired by the video camera.

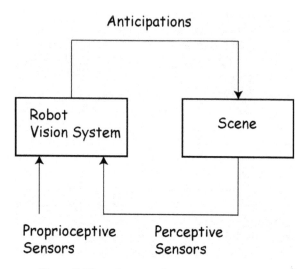

Figure 2: The robot conscious perception model

The perception loop works as follows: the robot vision system receives in input the robot position, speed and so on from the proprioceptive sensors and it generate the scene *anticipations*, i.e., the expectations about the perceived scene. The perception loop is then closed by the perceptive sensors that acquire the effective scene by means of the video camera.

In the current implementation, the process of generation of scene anticipations is performed by a computer graphics simulator that generates the expected 2D image scene on the basis of the robot movements. The mapping between the anticipated and the perceived scene is achieved through a *focus of attention mechanism* implemented by means of suitable recurrent neural networks with internal states. A sequential attentive mechanism is hypothesized that suitably scans the perceived scene and, according to the hypotheses generated on the basis of the anticipation mechanism, it predicts and detects the interesting events occurring in the scene. Hence, starting from the incoming information, such a mechanism generates expectations and it makes contexts in which hypotheses may be verified and, if necessary, adjusted.

In the psychological literature, the focus of attention is sometimes metaphorically described as a spotlight beam (LaBerge and Brown, 1989) which scans the visual field. Objects falling inside the spot are processed; the other objects in the scene are ignored. It is debated (see, e.g., Duncan, 1984) whether the attention selects regions of space independent of the objects it may contain or whether it selects the objects in the scene. According to space-based attention (Posner, 1980, Treisman and Gelade, 1980), the attention may also select empty regions of the scene. According to object-based attention (Kahneman et al., 1992), the attention selects only regions containing some object of interest. Logan (1996) proposes a theory that integrates both these approaches.

Many psychological theories agree that the attention process is serial, in the sense that the focus of attention selects only one or a few items at a time, moving from one to the other. This mechanism is important for visual search tasks (Duncan and Humphreys, 1989). An open problem is the identification of the processes that guide the movements of the focus of attention; models have been proposed by Wolfe et al. (1989), Koch and Ullman (1985) and Taylor and Rogers (2002), among others. Also the relationship between consciousness and attention has been largely addressed in the literature, see (Koch, 2004; Taylor, 2002b) for reviews.

In the proposed perception model, the focus of attention mechanism selects the relevant aspects of the acquired scene by sequentially scanning the image from the perceptive sensors and by comparing them in the generated anticipated scene. The attention mechanism is crucial in determining which portions of the acquired scene match with the generated anticipation scene: not all true (and possibly useless) matches are considered, but only those that are judged to be relevant on the basis of the attentive process.

The match of a certain part of the acquired scene with the anticipated one in a certain situation will elicit the anticipation of other parts of the same scene in the current situation. In this case, the mechanism seeks for the corresponding scene parts in the current anticipated scene. We call this type of anticipation *synchronic* because it refers to the same situation scene.

The recognition of certain scene parts could also elicit the anticipation of evolutions of the arrangements of parts in the scene; i.e., the mechanism generates the expectations for other scene parts in subsequent anticipated situation scenes. We call this anticipation *diachronic*, in the sense that it involves subsequent configurations of image scenes. It should be noted that diachronic anticipations can be related with a situation perceived as the precondition of an action, and the corresponding situation expected as the effect of the action itself. In this way diachronic anticipations can prefigure the situation resulting as the outcome of a robot action.

Two main sources of anticipation are taken into account. On the one side, anticipations are generated on the basis of the structural information stored in the robot by design. In line with Manzotti and Tagliasco (2005), we call *phylogenetic* these kind of anticipations. On the other side, anticipations could also be generated by a purely *Hebbian* association between situations learned during the robot operations. We call *ontogenetic* this kind of anticipations. Both modalities contribute to the robot conscious perception process.

More in details, *ontogenetic* anticipations are acquired by *online learning* and *offline learning*. During the normal robot operations, when something unexpected happens, i.e., when the generated anticipation image scene does not match the scene acquired by the perceptive sensors, the robot vision system learns to associate, by an *Hebbian* mechanism, the current image scene with the new anticipation image through the previously described attentional mechanism. This is the *online* mode of anticipation learning. Figure 3 shows the online learning mode: the generated anticipated image scene *Scene#1* does not match

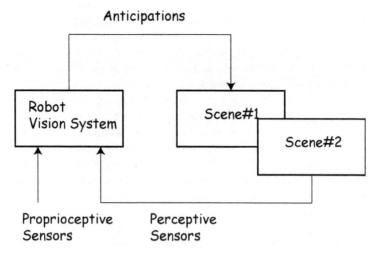

Figure 3: The online mode of learning new anticipations

the scene *Scene#2* acquired by the perceptive sensors. A new anticipation is then learned by the robot vision system.

In the *offline* anticipation learning, the proposed framework for conscious perception is employed to allow the robot to imagine future sequences of actions to generate and learn novel anticipations, as in the system MURPHY proposed by Mel (1990) (see Figure 4). In facts, the signal from perceptive sensors is related to the perception of a situation of the world out there. In this mode, the robot vision system freely generates anticipations of the perceptive sensors, i.e., it freely *imagines* possible evolutions of scenes and therefore possible interactions of the robot with the external world, without referring to a current external scene. In this way, new anticipations or new combinations of anticipations may be found and learned offline by the robot itself through the synchronic and diachronic attentional mechanisms.

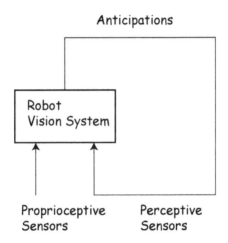

Figure 4: The offline mode of generation and learning new anticipations

The described perception process, which is in part internal and in part external to the robot, constitutes the perception experience of the robot, i.e., what the robot perceives at a given instant. The generalized conscious perceptual loop at the basis of robot experience is the stage in which the two flows of information, i.e., the anticipations data generated by the robot and the perceptive data coming from the scene, coexist and compete for consistency. This kind of perceiving is an active process, since it is based on the generation of the robot anticipations and driven by the external flow of information. The robot acquires evidence for what it perceives, and at the same time it interprets visual information according to its anticipations.

## 4. The Robot Operations

The ideas presented in the current chapter have been implemented in *Cicerobot*, an autonomous robot RWI B21 equipped with sonar, laser rangefinder and a video camera mounted on a pan tilt. The robot has been employed as a museum tour guide operating at the Archaeological Museum of Agrigento, Italy offering guided tours in the *Sala Giove* of the museum (Figure 1).

A first session of experimentations, based on a previous version of the architecture, has been carried out from January to June 2005; the results are described in Chella et al. (2004; 2005). The second experimental session, based on the architecture described here, started in March 2006 and ended in July of the same year.

The robot controller includes a behaviour-based architecture (see, e.g., Arkin, 1998) equipped with standard reactive behaviours as the static and dynamic obstacle avoidance, the search of free space, the path following and so on.

Figure 5 shows the proprioceptive sensors data coming from the robot odometry; Figure 6 shows the perceptive sensors data from the robot camera, and Figure 7 shows the corresponding anticipation image generated by the robot vision system. In both images the focus of attention mechanism is outlined.

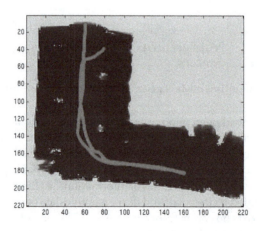

Figure 5: The robot proprioceptive data coming from the odometric sensor

Figure 6: The robot perceptive data coming from the video camera
along with the focus of attention mechanism

Figure 7: The robot anticipations generated by the vision system
along with the focus of attention mechanism

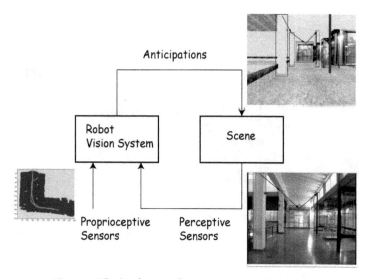

Figure 8: The implemented conscious perception model.

Figure 8 shows the implemented conscious perception loop process. As previously described, the robot vision system receives in input the data coming from the robot odometry and it generates the related anticipation of the scene. The perception loop is then closed by the scene acquired by the robot video camera. To implement the interaction between the robot and the environment, the robot is equipped with a stochastic algorithm, namely a *particle filter* (see, e.g., Thrun et al., 2005). In brief, the robot hypothesizes a set of anticipated positions in the Museum environment. For each anticipated position, the corresponding anticipated image is generated, as in Figure 7. The algorithm thus generates an error measure between the anticipated and the effective image scene, according to the mapping process based on the described focus of attention mechanism. The error thus weights the expected position under consideration; in subsequent steps, only the winning expected positions that received the higher weights are taken, while the other ones are dropped.

When the robot acts in the environment, e.g., it moved forwards, starting from the winning hypotheses, it generates a new set of hypothesized robot positions. The filter iterates until convergence, i.e., until the winning positions converge to a small set of moving points. Figure 9 (left) shows the initial distribution of expected robot position and Figure 9 (right) shows the small cluster of winning positions.

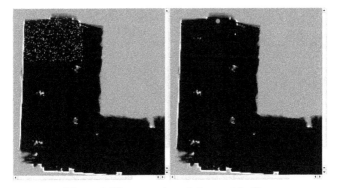

**Figure 9: The operation of the particle filter.**
The initial distribution of expected robot positions (left),
and the cluster of winning expected positions (right)

The *phylogenetic* anticipations are programmed in the robot system by design and stored in the robot memory. They are related to the architectural entities in the Museum scene.

During the working life, the robot may acquire novel anticipations and therefore novel expectations and novel way of interacting with the Museum environment, by means of *ontogenetic* anticipations. During a standard museum visit, the robot activates its own anticipations. In this case, the robot has a low degree of conscious perception. When something unexpected happens, for example the presence of a new object in the Museum, the robot arises its own degree of awareness and it copes the situation by mastering suitable anticipations.

These unexpected situations generate a trace in the robot memory, i.e., they are stored in the neural networks weights related with the focus of attention, in order to allow the robot to generate new anticipations and/or new ways of combining anticipations. In this case, new trajectories of the focus of attention mechanism will be learned by the robot. This is an example of the *online* anticipation learning mode.

Therefore, the robot, by its interaction with the environment, is able to modify its own goals or to generate new ones. A new object in the museum will generate new expectations related with the object and the subsequent modifications of the expectations related with the standard museum tour. Moreover, as previously stated, in the *offline* anticipation learning mode, the robot freely generates and learns sequences of novel Museum situations.

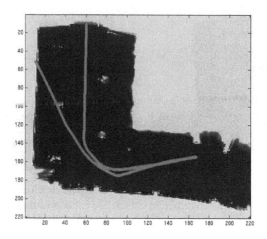

Figure 10: The operation of the robot equipped
with the odometric feedback only

To analyze the perception model, we tested the robot by considering the odometric feedback only; results are shown in Figure 10. It
should be noted that the proposed model based on the conscious
perception loop let the robot to operate more precisely and in a more
satisfactory way. In facts, the described mechanism let the robot to
be aware of its position and of its perceived scene. The robot is therefore able to adjust and correct its own subsequent motion actions.
Moreover, the robot is able to generate anticipations about its future
actions and it is therefore able to choose the best motion actions
according to the current perception.

## 5. Conclusion

The main goal of the current chapter is the proposal of an externalist
generalized loop for conscious perception. The problem of how to
build a robot with perceptual experience on the basis of the framework of externalism has been investigated and an effective robotic
architecture has been proposed. The loop is based on a tight interaction between the robot brain, body and environment. The model has
been implemented on *Cicerobot*, a working robot operating as a
museum guide in the *Sala Giove* of the Archaeological Museum of
Agrigento and results have been reported.

The generalized loop is based on the anticipation generation process performed by the robot vision system by means of the focus of

attention mechanism. The anticipation generation process requires some sort of representation of internal neural networks states in order to sequentially scan and compare the perceived and the anticipated scenes. This is a minimal representation which is necessary for implementing a tight interaction between robot and environment. Clark and Grush (1999) introduce the notion of *Minimal Robust Representationalism*, i.e., the minimal internal representations with the following capabilities: the operative conception is non-trivial; the identification of internal states as representations does explanatory work; the identification is empirically possible; and the identified states figures in biological cognition. It should be noted that the proposed anticipation process owns all the capabilities required by Clark and Grush.

The perception loop of the robot is related to the approach of *sensorimotor* contingencies proposed by O'Regan and Noe. The external environment and also the robot itself activates the anticipations by the attentional mechanism that define the interaction schemas between the robot and the environment. So for example a vase, a window, the visitors, will activate the related robot anticipations by means of suitable scans of the focus of attention. Therefore, in agreement with the approach of O'Regan and Noe, the robot phenomenology grows up from the mastery of contingencies which are at the basis of the task execution of the robot.

A related approach is described by Grush (2004), based on the concept of *emulator* in the fields of motor control and visual perception. The basic cognitive architecture proposed by Grush is made up by a feedback loop connecting a controller, a plant to be controlled and the emulator of the plant. The loop is *pseudo-closed* in the sense that the feedback signal is not generated by the plant, but by the emulator, which parallels the plant and it receives as input an efferent copy of the control signal sent to the plant. A more advanced architecture takes into account the basic schema of the Kalman filter. Comparing the Grush architecture with the described model, the anticipation generation process may be seen as a sort of visual emulator of the robot scene; anyway, the proposed model stresses the role of the focus of attention mechanism as the mapping process between the perceived and the anticipated image scenes.

In conclusion, we maintain that our proposed model is a good starting point to investigate robot conscious perception. An interesting point, in the line of Nagel (1974), is that a robot has a different awareness of the world that we humans may have, because it may be equipped with several perceptive and proprioceptive sensors which have no correspondences in human sensors, like for example the laser rangefinder, the odometer, the GPS, the WiFi or other radio links, and so on.

Therefore, the line of investigation may lead to study new modes of conscious perception which may be alternative to human conscious perception, as for example the conscious perception of an intelligent environment, the conscious perception distributed in a network where the robots are network nodes, the conscious perception of a multirobot team, the robot with multiple parallel consciousness, and similar kinds of robot conscious perception.

*Acknowledgement*

Author would like to thank Salvatore Gaglio and Riccardo Manzotti for discussions about the proposed architecture, and the director and the staff of the Archaeological Museum of Agrigento for their help. Irene Macaluso coordinated the implementation and test phases of the project. The *Cicerobot* project has been partially supported by the *Polo Universitario della Provincia di Agrigento*.

## References

Aleksander, I. (2005), *The World in my Mind, My Mind in the World* (Exeter: Imprint Academic).

Aleksander, I. and Dunmall, B. (2003), Axioms and Tests for the Presence of Minimal Consciousness in Agents, *Journal of Consciousness Studies*, 10, No. 4–5, pp. 7–18.

Aleksander, I. and Morton, H. (2005), Enacted Theories of Visual Awareness, A Neuromodelling Analysis, in *Proc. BVAI 2005*, LNCS 3704, (Heidelberg: Springer-Verlag) pp. 245–257.

Arkin, R.C. (1998), *Behavior-Based Robotics* (Cambridge, MA: MIT Press).

Baars, B.J. (1988), *A Cognitive Theory of Consciousness* (Cambridge: Cambridge University Press).

Buttazzo, G. (2001), Artificial Consciousness: Utopia or Real Possibility?, *IEEE Computer*, July, pp. 24–30.

Chella, A., Frixione, M. and Gaglio, S. (2004), Is Our Robot Self-Conscious?, *Proc. Towards a Science of Consciousness 2004*, Tucson, AZ.

Chella, A., Frixione, M. and Gaglio, S. (2005), Planning by imagination in Cicerobot, a robot for museum tours, *Proc. of AISB Symposium on Machine Consciousness*, 2005.

Clark, A. and Grush, R. (1999), Towards a Cognitive Robotics, *Adaptive Behavior*, 7, pp. 5–16.

Cotterill, R.M.J. (2003), CyberChild — A Simulation Test-Bed for Consciousness Studies, *Journal of Consciousness Studies*, 10, No. 4–5, pp. 31–45.

Dennett, D. (1991), *Consciousness Explained* (New York: Little, Brown).

Duncan, J. (1984), Selective attention and the organization of visual information, *J. Experimental Psychology*, 113, pp. 501–517.

Duncan, J. and Humphreys, G. (1989), Visual search and stimulus similarity, *Psychological Review*, 96, pp. 433–458.

Edelman, G. (1989), *The Remembered Present: A Biological Theory of Consciousness* (New York: Basic Books).

Edelman, G. and Tononi, G. (2001), *A Universe of Consciousness: How Matter Becomes Imagination* (New York: Basic Books).

Edelman, G.M., Reeke, G.N., Gall, E., Tononi, G., Williams, D. and Sporns, O. (1992), Synthetic neural modelling applied to a real-world artifact, *Proc. Natl. Acad. Sci. USA*, 89, pp. 7267–7271.

Franklin, S. (2003), IDA — A Conscious Artifact?, *Journal of Consciousness Studies*, 10, No. 4–5, pp. 47–66.

Gibson, J.J. (1979), *The Ecological Approach to Visual Perception* (Hillsdale, NJ: Lawwrence Erlbaum Associates).

Grush, R. (2004), The emulator theory of representation: motor control, imagery and perception, *Behavioral and Brain Sciences*, 27, pp. 377–442.

Haikonen, P.O. (2003), *The Cognitive Approach to Conscious Machines* (Exeter: Imprint Academic).

Holland, O. (2003), Editorial Introduction — Special issue on Machine Consciousness, *Journal of Consciousness Studies*, 10, No. 4–5, pp. 1–6.

Holland, O. (2006), Artificial Consciousness and the Simulation of Behaviour, *Proc. AISB 06*, University of Bristol.

Holland, O. and Goodman, R. (2003), Robots With Internal Models — A Route to Machine Consciousness?, *Journal of Consciousness Studies*, 10, No. 4–5, pp. 77–109.

Honderich, T. (2004), *On Consciousness* (Edinburgh: Edinburgh University Press).

Honderich, T. (2006), Radical Externalism, *Journal of Consciousness Studies*, 13, No. 7–8, pp. 3–13.

Kahneman, D., Treisman, A. and Gibbs, B. (1992), The reviewing of object files: Object specific integration of information, *Cognitive Psychology*, 24, pp. 175–219.

Koch, C. (2004), *The Quest for Consciousness* (Engewood, CO: Roberts and Co.).

Koch, C. and Ullman, S. (1985), Shifts in selective visual attention: Towards the underlying neural circuitry, *Human Neurobiology*, 4, pp. 219–227.

Krichmar, J.L. and Edelman, G., (2002) Machine psychology: autonomous behavior, perceptual categorization and conditioning in a brain-based device, *Cerebral Cortex*, 12, pp. 818–30.

LaBerge, D., and Brown, V., (1989), Theory of attentional operations in shape identification, *Psychological Review*, 96, pp. 101–124.

Logan, G.D. (1996), The CODE theory of visual attention: An integration of space-based and object-based attention, *Psychological Review*, 103, pp. 603–649.

Manzotti, R. (2006), A process oriented view of conscious perception, *Journal of Consciousness Studies*, 13, No. 6, pp. 7–41.

Manzotti, R. and Tagliasco, V. (2001), *Coscienza e Realtà. Una teoria della coscienza per costruttori e studiosi di menti e cervelli* (Bologna: Il Mulino).

Manzotti, R. and Tagliasco, V. (2005), From behaviour-based robots to motivation-based robots, *Robotics and Autonomous Systems*, 51, pp. 175–190.

Mel, B.W. (1990), *Connectionist robot motion planning: A neurally-inspired approach to visually-guided reaching* (Cambridge, MA: Academic Press).

Nagel, T. (1974), What is it like to be a bat? *Philosophical Revue*, 83, pp. 435–50.

Noë, A. (2004), *Action in Perception* (Cambridge, MA: MIT Press).

O'Regan, J.K. and Noë, A. (2001), A sensorimotor account of vision and visual consciousness, *Behavioral and Brain Sciences*, 24, pp. 939–1031.

Philipona, D., O'Regan, J.K. and Nadal, J.P. (2003), Is There Something Out There? Inferring Space from Sensorimotor Dependencies, *Neural Computation*, 15, pp. 2029–2049.

Posner, M.I., (1980), Orienting of attention, *Quarterly J. Experimental Psychology*, 32, pp. 2–25.

Rockwell, W.T. (2005), *Neither Brain nor Ghost* (Cambridge, MA: MIT Press).

Rowlands, M. (2003), *Externalism – Putting Mind and World Back Together Again* (Montreal & Kingston: McGill-Queen's University Press).

Shanahan, M. and Baars, B. (2005), Applying global workspace theory to the frame problem, *Cognition*, 98, No. 2, pp. 157–176.

Shanahan, M. (2006), A cognitive architecture that combines internal simulation with a global workspace, *Consciousness and Cognition*, 15, pp. 433–449.

Steels, L. (2003), Language Re-Entrance and the Inner Voice, *Journal of Consciousness Studies*, 10, No. 4–5, pp. 173–185.

Tani, J. (1998), An Interpretation of the 'Self' from the Dynamical Systems Perspective: A Constructivist Approach, *Journal of Consciousness Studies*, 5, No. 5–6, pp. 516–542.

Taylor, J.G. (1999), *The Race for Consciousness* (Cambridge MA: MIT Press).

Taylor, J.G. (2002a), From Matter To Mind, *Journal of Consciousness Studies*, 9, No. 4, pp. 3–22.

Taylor, J.G. (2002b), Paying attention to consciousness, *Trends in Cognitive Sciences*, 6, No. 5, pp. 206–210.

Taylor, J.G. and Rogers, M. (2002), A Control Model of the Movement of Attention, *Neural Networks*, 15, pp. 309–326.

Taylor, N.R. and Taylor, J.G. (2000), Hard-wired models of working memory and temporal sequence storage and generation, *Neural Networks*, 13, pp. 201–224.

Trautteur, G. (ed.), (1995), *Consciousness: Distinction and Reflection* (Napoli: Bibliopolis).

Thrun, S., Burgard, W. and Fox, D. (2005), *Probabilistic Robotics* (Cambridge, MA: MIT Press).

Treisman, A. and Gelade, G., (1980), A feature-integration theory of attention, *Cognitive Psychology*, 12, pp. 97–136.

Wolfe, J.M., Cave, K.R. and Franzel, S.L. (1989), Guided search: An alternative to the feature integration for visual search, *J. Experimental Psychology*, 15, pp. 419–433.

Ricardo Sanz, Ignacio López &
Julita Bermejo-Alonso

# A Rationale and Vision for Machine Consciousness in Complex Controllers

Control systems are becoming extremely complex (Aström, 2000). Science and technology of computer-based control is facing an enormous challenge when increased levels of autonomy and resilience are required from the machines that are supporting our ambient environment: electricity networks, cars, telecommunications, etc. All these systems include as a necessary component for the provision of the system functionally an enormous amount of embedded control software. We can say, without doubt, that control systems complexity is boosting and leading to a construction problem. We may even ask the question: Are control systems becoming too complex to be built under the required performance and safety constraints?

In some sense, software intensive controllers are becoming too complex to be built by traditional software engineering methods. Old age engineering processes fall short when dealing with increased levels of required functionality, performance, connectivity, robustness, adaptability, openness, etc. Non-functional requirements are pressing towards a world of control systems that cannot be built by conventional human-based engineering processes.

There are two main effects of this increased complexity that we would like to consider:

- Increase in size, that supposes a necessary increment in effort to build the system and that implies a whole new bunch of development and management practices.

- Decrease in designability (i.e. the capability of effectively calculate and/or predict the characteristics of the system when built). This may suppose a decrease in performance or more worrying a major decrease of dependability.

A decrease in dependability in office software is not a very big problem — as we all know. This is not the case of technical systems where dependability (both as reliability and maintainability) is a critical aspect. A chemical plant control system can be composed of thousands of computers — from intelligent sensors to top level management information systems — and kill thousands of people when not working properly (see Figure 1).

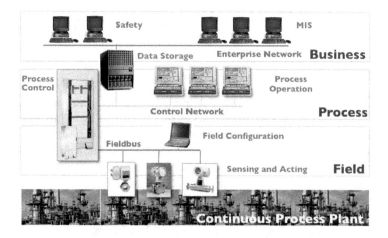

**Figure 1:** A simplified diagram of a distributed control system for an industrial continuous process plant. These systems may include thousands of interconnected computers.

Providing the required dependability is a major problem and the origin of specific information technology practices to build safety-critical systems. The problem is that these methods do not scale well for complex applications and that limitation forces a trade-off between features and robustness (Gunderson, 2003).

Common control system failures may be associated to unexpected events — changes in the plant — or to control design errors — in a sense similar to the former from an epistemological point of view. Many control strategies have tried to cope with this kind of change: robust, self-tuning, adaptive controllers are well known examples.

However, in complex, software intensive controllers, the failure modes due to faults or errors in the software are becoming a very significant part. In these systems the unexpected not only comes from the plant under control and its environment but from the controller implementation itself.

A possible path to the solution of this increasing control software complexity problem is to extend the adaptation mechanism from the core controller to the whole implementation of it.

Adaptation of a technical system like a controller can be seen from two main perspectives: adaptation during construction and runtime adaptation. A paradigmatic example of the first type (construction) is reusable component retargeting to adapt it to a particular execution platform. A paradigmatic example of the second type (run-time) is fault-tolerant control.

We have reached the conclusion that the continuously increasing complexity makes almost impossible the only use of construction-time techniques because they do not scale and prove robust enough. Designers cannot guarantee by design the correct operation of a complex controller (Benveniste, 2003).

The alternative approach is to move the responsibility for correct operation into the system itself. That means moving the adaptation from the implementation phase into the runtime phase. During runtime the control system perceives changes — not only in the plant — and adapts to these changes to keep the mission assigned to it during the design phase.

Analysing the characteristics of this problem — action by reflection — we have identified a common problem structure — isomorphism (Bertalanffy, 1969) — between this situation and the situations analysed in consciousness studies. We hence wonder whether artificial consciousness can be a potential solution to the performance/dependability problem in artificial control systems.

## The Business Case

It may sound strange to claim for the existence of a business case for conscious machines when there is even disagreement on the role that consciousness plays in natural systems and its evolutionary value. This is clearly shown in the fact that there is even a school of thought that claims that consciousness is an epiphenomenon, *i.e.* nothing we cannot live without.

Obviously, we do not think that way, and the best proof of its evolutionary value is our own everyday perception of consciousness:

What do you prefer? a conscious or an unconscious taxi driver? What do you prefer? a conscious or an unconscious neurosurgeon? It is quite clear that consciousness does play an important role in the correct execution of tasks, in the exercising of adequate behaviour in the presence of uncertainty.

But beyond exploring ideas on what consciousness is and how can it be manifested by an artificial agent we may consider the question of real needs for this technology. Is there any real business case for it?

Indeed it is. Not one but many business cases. Let's mention just two in quite different niches and then do some analysis that may serve as a general business drive for this technology.

The first business case is the case of the software systems we use to support human activity processes; our laptops, PDAs and mobile phones are full of software and communications because today's computing environment is changing from the isolated isles of productivity around a productivity toolset to the open sea of web services and dynamic applications. There is no longer a central deity that decides when to release a new complete update of our suite. There is nobody in charge of our whole environment anymore. We must strive for keeping our working environment in line with evolving realities out there. And the task is not easy at all: this new Flash 8 media file that cannot be properly executed on my Linux Firefox browser; this just-released sequencer plug-in that my OS X music software rejects to incorporate. All they are changing in the world out of a coherent configuration management. There is no single authority that can do that.

The second business case is the case of electrical system internetworking between countries. National power production plants, transport and distribution grids are operated by companies or governments that have quite different objectives and strategies. Cross-border interconnection seems necessary from many points of view (e.g. robustness, efficiency, policies, etc.). But, from a purely technical point of view, the task of controlling such a system is hopeless. There is nobody in charge anymore. Subsystems are built using different technologies and operated under different ruling agencies. While the technical issues may be solved relatively easily (standardisation bodies do help in this) the main problem remains: integrated and unified decision-making. The local operation decisions can be contradictory at a system-wide scale. Autonomous distributed decision making processes mine the technically sound operation of the global network. These processes are not only political or commercial decision processes but also include technical, even automatic, decision processes that happen ubiquitously in the network and that can produce electrical ripples that may manifest catastrophically in a remote place. We are engineering systems that suffer butterfly effects. That old wildly free character of some natural realities is becoming a daunting fact of our infrastructures.

What do these two cases have in common? The answer is relatively easy to identify: the behaviour of the global system is driven by interaction of local systems that are not any longer under a common change authority. It may look like the problem is that of proper physical integration, but not only. The main issue, the really daunting thing, is that the bottleneck, or to be more precise, the key of the path to the solution is the capability of cognitive level metareasoning and integration. The question is for a technical system to be able to reason about i) how it is able to think and act ii) how others do the same and iii) how can I communicate with them to achieve my objectives. Some of these topics have been addressed in the agents community, but agent technology still lacks the level of self-awareness that is needed to properly vehiculate these processes.

The business case is clear: software intensive systems -real-time or not- are getting so complex that we're no longer in the position of fully controlling them and their environments to make them robust enough. The classic zero-defect engineering or replicative fault-tolerance approaches do not scale well to systems of such a size and such a rate of uncoordinated change.

The possibility we envision is also clear: make systems responsible for providing their function. Instead of having a single production engineer -producing either software or electricity- in charge of change let the systems take care of themselves. Make the systems self-aware. This is somewhat happening in the field of software (IBM's autonomic computing or Sun's conscientious software). We need it to also happen with physically embedded systems.

It looks like it is better if machines are conscious but, obviously, machines are not humans and hence machine consciousness need not be the same as humans consciousness. For example, we must be aware of the apparent differences between *sensing, perceiving* and *feeling*. Perception and feeling seem tinted with the colours of phenomenology, that seems to be a private, agent specific, issue (at least in biosystems).

We see three major motivations for research on artificial consciousness:

1. *Building artefacts like us*: consciousness, emotion and affect, experience, imagination, etc. This may be the main motivation for consciousness in Robotics.

2. *Studying natural systems with computer laboratory models*: this is one of the main strategies of Cognitive Science.

3. *Making effective machines*: the pursuit of Intelligent Control technologies.

In any case, a deeper, cleaner theory of consciousness is needed to support these objectives.

The focus of our work on machine consciousness is hence on software intensive controllers for autonomous robust behaviour based on self-awareness. Qualia and related issues are left out for future endeavours.

## Approaching Autonomy

As we said before, the selected approach is to simplify the engineering work of building robust systems by moving the responsibility for correct operation into the system itself. This will require complex real-time architectures to support this reflective capability but hopefully they will improve performance and, more importantly, increase resilience of large-scale systems.

Moving the adaptation from the implementation phase into the runtime phase will make necessary for the system to gather self-information to perceive the changes that the systems is suffering: i.e. during runtime the system perceives changes and adapts to these changes to keep the mission assigned to it during the design phase.

Several alternatives have been explored in the past, based on the implementation of architectural mechanisms for self-organisation and/or self-repair. These systems are built and started in a base state and they follow adaptive life-cycles based on the circumstances of the environment that surrounds the computing system (e.g. fault-tolerant systems, automatic learning, genetic programming or autonomic computing)

As an example, let's quote IBM's description of their autonomic computing initiative (IBM, 2003):

> Autonomic computing is the ability of an IT infrastructure to adapt to change in accordance with business policies and objectives. Quite simply, it is about freeing IT professionals to focus on higher-value tasks by making technology work smarter, with

business rules guiding systems to be self-configuring, self-healing, self-optimizing, and self-protecting.

To achieve all these self-x properties, autonomic computing is based on the implementation of reflective control loops to increase operational autonomy of managed computing elements (see Figure 2). The IT elements—computers, printers, switches, etc—are augmented with sensors, actuators and knowledge-based controllers termed autonomic managers. Computing infrastructures are composed by collections of autonomic elements that are able to respond to change autonomously.

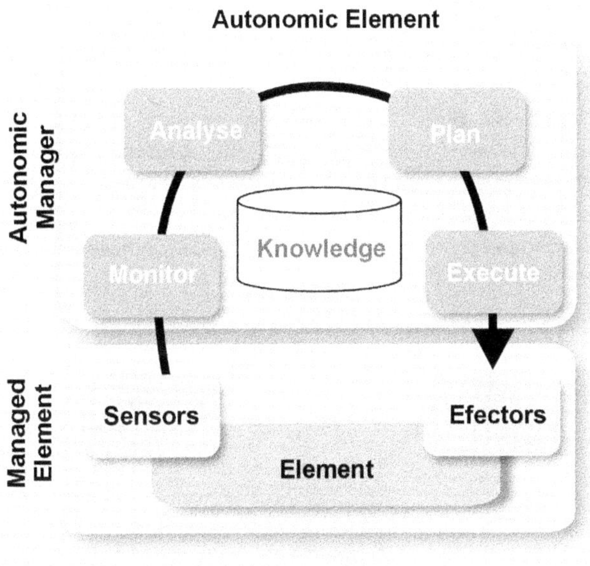

**Autonomic Element**

**Figure 2**: The IBM's vision on autonomic computing is based on the implementation of reflective control loops to increase operational autonomy of managed computing elements.

### The Modelling Approach to System Development

The approach that we try to follow is to implement our equivalents of the autonomic managers using system models as the main knowledge representation of the system itself. Model-driven development (MDD) is a strategy to build systems that is gaining wide acceptance in the construction of complex embedded systems. And we try to use the MDD engineering models as runtime models for the autonomous agent.

*Artificial Consciousness*

In the words of Jonathan Sprinkle:

> [MDD is] A design methodology used to create and evolve integrated, multiple-aspect models of computer- based systems using concepts, relations, and model composition principles to facilitate systems/software engineering analysis of the models and automatic synthesis of applications from the models.

In MDD, deep and multiple system models are built and analysed using tools provided by the modelling environment. These models are later used to (semi)automatically generate the final system (see Figure 3). This means that the models must necessarily capture the semantic aspects of the final system and not just the structural properties. Functional modelling help capture the intention (Leveson, 2000) of the designer and the finality of the artificial system (Bertalanffy, 1969).

If the models capture the semantics of the final system it is possible to use model-based reasoning techniques to make run-time decisions about the system itself. In a similar way to fault-detection systems, discrepancies between system behaviour and expected behaviour may be pointed out identifying differences between reality and model-predicted outputs.

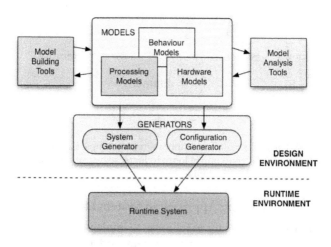

**Figure 3**: In the model-driven approach to system development, multiperspective, semantically-rich models of the system under construction are specified in advance and used to generate automatically the running system, typically by a set of transformation-based generators.

## Model-Based Self-Aware Control Systems

*Analysis of extant control engineering perspectives*

Before introducing our approach to this problem let's consider some basic control patterns that will help set the ground for our work.

Control systems exploit knowledge about the process under control to provide inputs to it that can drive the dynamics of the process to reach certain output state of interest (see Figure 4).

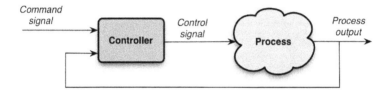

**Figure 4:** A simple feedback control system provides a small amount of operational autonomy [Gancett 2004]

In general, in autonomous agents, we can consider the agent body as the process to be controlled, and the output measurement and control signal generation are mapped into sensing and action processes (see Figure 5). This must be done carefully because the division agent-environment may be not very clear depending on the embodiment and the function of the agent (consider for example the cases of mobile robots or environment control systems).

In the case of model-based controllers, the control box uses a explicit model of the plant under control to improve the performance of the controller going beyond the calculation of the simple control action of a feedback controller. There are many examples of this type of control, e.g. model-reference adaptive controllers and the RCS control model of autonomous agents (see Figures 6 and 7).

A truly adaptive system (e.g. a system with the autonomic properties) must necessarily do a semantic processing of the information it has about itself. This is the type of reasoning that MDD tools help perform over their models if they are semantically precise enough.

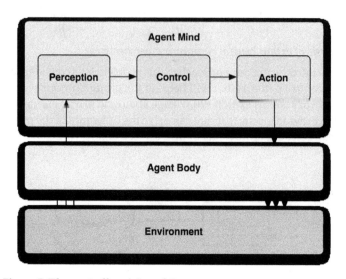

**Figure 5: The controller vision of the autonomous agent**

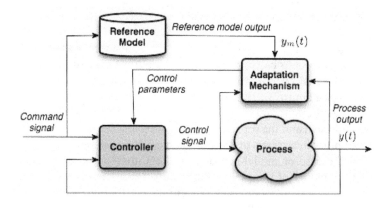

**Figure 6: The controller vision of the autonomous agent**

*The ASys vision: Model-based self-aware control systems*

The vision of the ASys project of our research group can be summarized as follows: *make artificial controllers operate with the same models that humans use to build them.*

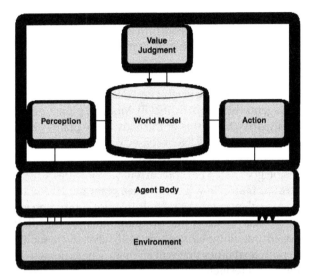

**Figure 7**: The basic structure of the RCS intelligent controller exploits a model of the agent and the world in the determination of control actions [Albus 2001].

In this way, the system would operate with an explicit model of itself and of its environment: an integrated model of its world. A system working in this way would exploit the model for its operation not only in the classical sense of control, but even for interaction with its environment and the other agents of its world.

This vision implies that the tools and models that are being developed to be used by builders at the implementation phase can find their 'autonomic' use by the system itself at the runtime phase. So, the engineering models do constitute the very self-model of the running system and the value system used to make decisions (both *auto*

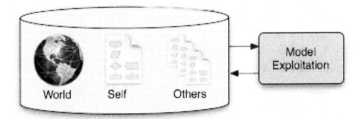

**Figure 8: Model contents and use**

and *allo*) may be included with the model itself because it contains information not only about the world but also about the agent itself and other agents that interact with it (and the system provides value to them).

In this way, the control setpoints of conventional control systems find their place at the same level of any relation of authority between intelligent agents (human or artificial). Model exploitation strategies will not only drive the status of the body — the plant — but also all the interactions with other agents based on semantically sound representation of their own value systems.

This vision goes a step beyond current technologies: Classic adaptive control or fault-tolerant control use plant models to adapt the control to new plant conditions. Fault-tolerant computing uses computation models to keep the computation ongoing. Reflective, model-based autonomous systems will have deep model-based introspection capabilities that will let them achieve a high degree of adaptability and resilience.

Models (of the world, of the self, of others) may be executed by the agent over appropriate virtual machines for different purposes (Self-X operations), for example:

- Decision-making and action calculation
- Diagnosis and reconfiguration
- What-if scenarios (imagination) and risk evaluation
- Abduction, retrodiction and causal analysis
- Coordination, negotiation and agreement
- etc.

We call this technology Self-X. Self-X functionality exploits models of the system itself in the performance of model-based action.

We expect that this vision can break the problematic barrier between the process and the product and bridge the gap between construction and run-time phases to enable life-cycle adaptation. In summary, we can say that Self-X makes the system adaptive using self-models and real-time reflection.

Obviously this vision falls short of explaining the multifarious nature of human consciousness, but one of the main problems we confront is the lack of a systematic characterisation of it with some relevant exceptions [Alexander 2003].

## Conclusions

The rise of control system complexity claims for new technologies that provide the required scalability to address the problems of the technical infrastructure.

We consider that the capability of adaptation is a key issue but without losing the constraining capability of design-based engineering processed. Bounded, semantically-rich self-adaptation is needed for many reasons (in particular for increased dependability). With the required levels of autonomy and complexity, the phases of systems engineering and construction necessarily run short. Complex systems must be able to adapt to their real scenarios of activity as part of their operation.

In this light, the ASys Vision considers that model-driven development technology is a crucial technology for complex controllers. Model-based control is not new at all, but it can be extended to the control system itself and not be restricted to model the plant.

The way to design and to build systems that can operate efficiently and with high degrees of dependability is by making systems exploit their knowledge not only for controlling the plant (as traditionally,) but for controlling themselves. This implies reflexive capabilities, which still have to be highly developed for the artificial world.

Conscious, self-aware controllers will use self models embedded in models of their world for maximising mission-level effectiveness. A question remains, however: *What is it like to be a model-based reflective predictive controller?* There may be something it is like to be such a user of a self-model linked to such a world-model in a machine with a mission.

# References

Albus, James and Alexander Meystel (2001). *Engineering of Mind: An Introduction to the Science of Intelligent Systems*. Wiley Series on Intelligent Systems. Wiley. New York.

Aleksander, Igor and Barry Dunmall (2003). Axioms and tests for the presence of minimal consciousness in agents. *Journal of Consciousness Studies* 10(4-5), 7-18.

Åström, Karl, Isidori, Alberto, Albertos, Pedro, Blanke, Mogens, Schaufelberger, Walter and Sanz, Ricardo, Eds.) (2000). *Control of Complex Systems*. Springer. Berlin.

Benveniste, A., L.P. Carloni, P. Caspi and A.L. Sangiovanni-Vincentelli (2003). *Heterogeneous reactive systems modeling and correct-by-construction deployment*. In: Proc. Int. Conf. Embedded Software (EMSOFT) (R. Alur and I. Lee, Eds.).

Bertalanffy, Ludvig von (1969). *General System Theory*. George Braziller, 1969.

Blum, Alex, Vaclav Cechticky, Alessandro Pasetti and Walter Schaufelberger (2003). A Java-based framework for real-time control systems. In: *Proceedings of 9th IEEE International Conference on Emerging Technologies and Factory Automation*. Lisbon, Portugal. pp. 447-453.

Douglass, Bruce Powell (1999). *Doing Hard Time. Developing Real-Time Systems with UML, Objects, Frameworks and Patterns*. Object Technology Series. Addison-Wesley. Reading, MA.

EUSAI (2004). European symposium on ambient intelligence. http://www.eusai.net/.

Gancet, Jeremi and Simon Lacroix (2004). Embedding heterogeneous levels of decisional autonomy in multi-robot systems. *7th International Symposium on Distributed Autonomous Robotic Systems* (DARS'04), Toulouse (France) 23-25 June 2004.

Gilani, Wasif, Nabeel Hasan Naqvi and Olaf Spinczyk (2004). On adaptable middleware product lines. In: *Proceedings of the 3rd ACM Workshop on Adaptive and Reflective Middleware*. Toronto,Canada.

Gunderson, Lance H. and Jr., Lowell Pritchard, Eds.) (2002). *Resilience and the Behavior of Large-Scale Systems*. Island Press. Covelo, CA.

Haikonen, Pentti O. (2003). *The Cognitive Approach to Conscious Machines*. Imprint Academic. Exeter.

Holland, Owen and Ron Goodman (2003). Robots with internal models — a route to machine consciousness?. *Journal of Consciousness Studies* 10(4–5), 77–109.

Holland, Owen, Ed.) (2003). *Machine Consciousness*. Imprint Academic. Exeter, UK.

Huang, Hui-Min (Ed.) (2004). *Autonomy Levels for Unmanned Systems (ALFUS) Framework*. Volume I: Terminology. Version 1.1. National Institute for Standards and Technology (NIST), 2004.

IBM (2003). *An architectural blueprint for autonomic computing*. Technical report. IBM.

Jacob, Bart, Richard Lanyon-Hogg, Devaprasad K. Nadgir and Amr F. Yassin (2004). *A Practical Guide to the IBM Autonomic Computing Toolkit.* RedBooks. IBM.

Leveson, Nancy (2000), *Intent Specifications: An Approach to Building Human-Centered Specifications.* IEEE Trans. on Software Engineering, January 2000.

Lieberherr, Karl, Doug Orleans and Johan Ovlinger (2001). *Aspect-Oriented Programming with Adaptive Methods.* Communications of the ACM 44(10), 39–41.

Meystel, Alexander (2000). *Measuring Performance of Systems with Autonomy: Metrics for Intelligence of Constructed Systems.* White Paper for the Workshop on Performance Metrics for Intelligent Systems. NIST, Gaithesburg, Maryland, August 14–16, 2000.

Sanz, Ricardo (2004). CO7: Converging trends in complex software-intensive control. In: *Sixth Portuguese Conference on Automatic Control.* Faro, Portugal.

Shrivastava, S.K., L. Mancini and B. Randell (1993). The duality of fault-tolerant system structures. *Software: Practice and Experience* 23(7), 773–798.

Szypersky, Clemens (1998). *Component Software. Beyond Object-Oriented Programming.* ACM Press / Addison-Wesley. Reading, MA.

Taylor, John G. (1999). *The Race for Consciousness.* MIT Press. Cambridge, MA.

Owen Holland, Rob Knight, &
Richard Newcombe

# A Robot-Based
# Approach to Machine
# Consciousness

This chapter describes and explores an approach based on the notion that consciousness may emerge from the structures necessary to support intelligent behaviour in embodied agents. However, rather than dealing with consciousness at the outset, it will be convenient to begin with the problem of producing intelligent behaviour. Consider a physically embodied autonomous agent — a single materially continuous entity, natural or artificial — which exists within a dynamic, hostile, and occasionally novel physical world, and which has to achieve some physically defined mission within that world before its own dissolution. (When the agent's mission is physically defined, it removes from consideration alternative non-physically defined missions such as 'finding inner peace', or 'understanding itself'. From an evolutionary standpoint it is clear that the structures we possess evolved in the context of a physically defined mission — reproduction.)

Most of the possible approaches to achieving a mission can be seen both in biology and in artificial intelligence; they can usefully be analysed in terms of the levels at which they operate. The first level is the baseline strategy of being provided with the means of detecting particular situations through the senses, and of producing a stereotyped reflex or reactive response to each of them. Many invertebrates, especially insects, work mainly at this level, and some of the results can be very good indeed. However, a situation that cannot be sensed cannot be responded to appropriately; successful reactive agents can only exist in environments where there is no real need to deal with counterfactuals.

The next step beyond this level is to provide the agent with some ability to select or modulate its actions by taking into account aspects of the situation not apparent to the senses. For example, female digger wasps seem to be able to set and unset memory flags that serve as functional indications of the previous occurrence and detection of some class of events, such as having fought a particular type of caterpillar. If the flag is set, a digger wasp when presented with a paralysed caterpillar of the correct species will drag it to its nest; if it is not set, it will ignore it. This can be seen as a stereotyped instance of the more general phenomenon of learning: the system changes its response to a given sensory input as a function of previous experience. However, learning in this narrow sense cannot easily accommodate novelty that goes much beyond the constraints of previous experience. The hostility of the environment is also a factor — there are things that cannot easily be learned because the learning process tends to terminate the mission, as for instance in learning not to jump off cliffs.

What is needed for the next level is some way of going beyond experience — of predicting on the basis of experience what would happen in some novel situation. The ability to predict has been identified many times as being of crucial importance to intelligent organisms. For instance, Dennett describes a series of three imaginary creatures, each representing stages in evolution (Dennett, 1995). The first, the Darwinian creature, is the basic model. Its responses to its environment are specified by its genes; those examples with genes producing bad responses die, and those with genes for good responses survive to breed, eventually producing a population with better responses. The second, the Skinnerian creature, is capable of learning, and as a result becomes capable of producing better responses if it is not killed by an early bad response. The one of greatest interest is the Popperian creature, which is able to preselect its responses so that those likely to kill it are inhibited:

> But how is this preselection in Popperian agents to be done? Where is the feedback (about the quality of the proposed action) to come from? It must come from a sort of *inner environment* — an inner something-or-other that is structured in such a way that the surrogate actions it favours are more often than not the very actions the real world would also bless, if they were performed. In short, the inner environment, whatever it is, must contain lots

of *information* about the outer environment and its regularities ...
we must be very careful not to think of this inner environment as
simply a replica of the outer world, with all its physical contingencies reproduced ... The information about the world has to be
there, but it also has to be structured in such a way that there is a
nonmiraculous explanation of how it got there, how it is maintained, and how it actually achieves the preselective effects that
are its *raison d'etre*. (Dennett, 1995, pp. 375–6).

The most capable such methods all depend in one way or another
on the construction of models—representations of situations that
can be manipulated to provide answers to questions beginning:
'What if?' Over 60 years ago, Craik articulated this intuition by stating that:

> If the organism carries a small-scale model of external reality and
> of its own possible actions within its head, it is able to try out vari-
> ous alternatives, conclude which is the best of them, react to
> future situations before they arise, utilize the knowledge of past
> events in dealing with the present and future, and in every way
> to react in a much fuller, safer, and more competent manner to
> the emergencies which face it. (Craik 1943).

Models are exploited by undertaking simulations—running the
models under the hypothetical situations, and observing the
responses, which are predictions of what would happen in the real
world. Of course, prediction by itself is not enough—there must be
some evaluation of the utility of the predicted consequences for the
success of the mission, there may have to be mechanisms for comparing the evaluations of a variety of actions, there may have to be
ways of structuring the search of alternatives, there may have to be
some way of encoding the probabilities of various outcomes to take
account of non-determinism, insufficient knowledge, and so forth,
and there must be mechanisms for the storage, retrieval, and execution of the best evaluated actions, and so on, along with satisfactory
evolutionary accounts of how all these components came into being.
It is outside the scope of this brief chapter to examine all of these features in any detail, but what we can do is to explore certain aspects of
the central method, that of simulation using internal models.

Assuming that prediction is to be achieved through simulation,
what exactly has to be simulated? The answer is both obvious and
interesting: whatever affects the mission, and nothing else. An
embodied agent can only affect the world through the actions of its
body in and on the world, and the world can only affect the mission
by affecting the agent's body. The agent therefore needs to simulate

only those aspects of its body that affect the world in ways that affect the mission, and only those aspects of the world that affect the body in ways that affect the mission.

**Figure 1**

At this point, some simple diagrams may be useful. In Fig. 1, the square represents the embodied agent, and the circle the environment. In order to act intelligently, it will be necessary from time to time for the agent to run an internal simulation of its own possible interactions with the world under various conditions. In some circumstances the starting point of the simulation might be the current state of the agent and the world; in others it might be some possible future state of either or both. The function of the simulation is to predict the outcomes of actions. Once an outcome has been predicted, it must somehow be evaluated for its likely contribution to the mission. After one or more actions have been simulated and evaluated, the information generated must influence the action selected for execution. The processes of choice of action to be simulated, simulation, evaluation, and influencing action selection do not need to be perfect, or even good; for the exercise to be advantageous, the improvement in action selection must merely be sufficient to 'pay the costs' of developing and using the system. As far as the simulation component is concerned, this means that it must at the very least have some predictive value — that the consequences of a simulated action in a simulated situation must be sufficiently representative of the consequences of the real action in that situation so that the information acquired enables better performance than never having simulated at all.

**Figure 2**

Figure 2 represents the simulation component of the system being proposed. The agent contains and exploits an internal model of itself and the environment, and is able to initialise and run the system to predict the consequences of actions, including novel actions in novel situations. The component representing the self-model can be limited to the body and how it can be controlled, because the consequences of interest are the physical consequences. As noted above, the ability to make this simplifying restriction is a direct consequence of having an embodied agent with a physically-defined mission.

The simulation system in Figure 2 is a reflection of reality – a model of the agent in the world – but the encapsulation in a 'thought bubble' implies that it is a single seamless system. Indeed it could be – an example of such a system will be presented later – but the two modelled components, the agent's body and the world, are in many ways very different indeed. The body is well known, and changes slowly, if at all; if it moves, it is usually because it has been commanded to move, and it can be assumed that this information is available to the system as a whole. The world, however, is dynamic, partly unknown, and occasionally novel. The acquisition and processing by the agent of the information from the world necessary to enable control also makes the agent very different from most of the other contents of the world – the exception being of course other agents in the world. A programmer approaching the task of creating this simulation would immediately split his simulation into two interacting components, the agent and the world, along the lines shown in Figure 3. (An additional consideration is that some of the information processing necessary for the model of the agent could be provided by the re-use of the circuitry performing that function for the agent. This is the explicit focus of some approaches to embodied cognition and consciousness, such as Hesslow's 'Simulation Hypothesis' [Hesslow, 2002]).

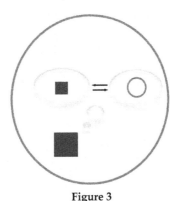

**Figure 3**

## Simulation and Consciousness

It is now possible to explore the possible connections between this architecture and consciousness. For the moment, suppose that the simulations of both agent and world are perfect—that the internal agent model (let us call it IAM) acquires identical information from the model world that the real agent would acquire from the identical situation in the real world. Unless it had information that it was only a model, the IAM would process that information as if it were the agent itself. (The IAM is therefore a transparent model in the sense defined by Metzinger, 2003.) If its internal organisation contained structures representing beliefs, then it would in some sense believe itself to be embodied, just as the real agent would if it too possessed those structures.

The idea that consciousness is a property of certain models in the brain, and in particular of models of self, has been proposed several times in recent years. One of the best articulated points of view is that of Blackmore (1986. 1988):

> What seems real at any time is only a model of oneself in the world. Indeed perhaps consciousness is no more and no less than being a mental model ... If the conscious self is a mental model then it makes sense that there can be selfless states in which no

ordinary model of self is constructed by the system. In this way even quite strange experiences become comprehensible. Since human information processing systems are uniquely capable of constructing complex and flexible models the potential for exploring consciousness is hardly touched upon as yet—not to mention the prospects opened by future developments in artificial intelligence (Blackmore, 1988)

We propose that the IAM in a fully implemented system of the type shown in Figure 3 may be conscious, and that its cognitive contents will reflect those of human consciousness. Its experience will be of the constructed world model, not of the world, yet in the sense described above it will take the world model to be the real thing, and the properties of the model will be attributed to the world. When the real body acts on the real world, the IAM will be configured to execute the same movements, and the changes in the real world will be used to update the world model. To the IAM, it will seem as if its own actions will have affected the only world it knows, whereas in reality both the IAM and the world model are driven by external events. It is possible to identify many other potential correspondences between processes in a system of this general type, and various aspects of consciousness; in fact, much of the analysis of phenomenal self-models in Metzinger's *Being No-one* can be adapted to this context with little or no change. However, our approach at this stage is different; it is synthetic and empirical, and our initial aim is to explore the abilities and disabilities of systems of this type from a functional point of view before examining them more closely for any content related to consciousness.

### A Robot Worth Modelling

What might a self-model have to be like in order to play an effective role in the kinds of system architectures discussed above? An earlier investigation used a very simple simulation of a very simple robot (Holland and Goodman, 2003). Even though we demonstrated that a very low level of information content was adequate to provide for the four functions of internal models we identified, it did not seem likely that a mere quantitative extension of the approach would bring us to a qualitatively different outcome. We therefore went back to first principles.

If an internal self model is involved in human consciousness, then it makes sense to think about what such a model would have to be like. The only component which we can be sure is necessary is the model of the physical component—the human body—and so as a first step we resolved to try to build a robot with a body like that of a human, and then to examine the features of such a body that might need to be represented in an internal self model used for simulated actions as described in the general schema. We are not claiming that it is only the model of the body that is important—indeed, that seems intrinsically improbable—but since the evolutionary proof of the pudding is in the execution of the actions selected with the aid of the internal modelling structure, it would at least be an insurance against providing a substrate inadequate to support the components that perhaps do really matter.

So what are the differences in kinds of bodies that might make a difference to something as apparently abstract as consciousness? In order to answer this, it is necessary to consider the kinds of robot bodies available in practice. Most traditional mobile robots look like dustbins on wheels, and this is for perfectly good engineering reasons. The cylindrical shape is good for manoeuvrability, provides a stable sensor platform, has a low centre of gravity, and so on. More recently, a number of humanoid robots have appeared. These have an external form that mimics the human, but the internal elements are almost always traditional motors and gearboxes controlled using conventional engineering methods. Although humanoid robots look very different from the standard cylindrical models, the way in which they are controlled and actuated makes it clear that the difference is only skin deep. A human body is more than just an external form—its internal structures (bones, joints, muscles, and tendons) seem qualitatively different from those of robots, as do the movements they produce. Our robot, then, should combine a humanoid outer form with human-like internal structures that would have to be controlled in much the same way as the human body is controlled.

The main technical problems we faced in the construction of the robot centred around two key features: the skeleton; and the musculature. Of course, these could not be treated independently, because each imposed constraints on the other. In the event, however, the first strategy we tried worked very well: it was simply to copy the skeleton as best we could—at life size—using purely passive elastic elements to represent the musculature, and then to investigate possible ways of constructing and installing suitable powered muscle analogues.

The adult human skeleton is at first sight extremely complex, containing 206 bones. (Interestingly, we have 275 bones at birth, but many have fused by maturity.) However, since more than half are in the hands and feet, and since our bilateral symmetry means that most bones have a mirror image bone with identical structure and function, the problem of building a working skeleton may just be very difficult rather than completely intractable.

Our first problem followed directly on our decision to model the bones of the skeleton: how could we model bone-like structures? In a conventionally engineered robot, the actuators are built into the joints, and the only constraints on the links between the joints are those of rigidity, clearance, and weight. However, as is clear from any anatomy textbook, bones must also provide the points of attachment for the tendons, and this can be critical in determining how the mechanical advantage of a muscle-tendon-joint system changes as the joint moves. In addition, the joints are not limited to simple hinges or universal joints, but may accommodate rolling or sliding movements. To machine, fabricate, or cast a large number of different such components by conventional methods would be difficult and expensive.

The solution was to use a new type of engineering thermoplastic known in the UK as Polymorph, and in the US as Friendly Plastic. Technically a caprolactone polymer, it is polythene-like in many ways, but when heated to only 60 degrees C (for example, by plunging into hot water) it fuses (or softens, if already fused) and can be freely hand moulded for quite some time, finally resetting at around 30 degrees. It has a distinctly bone-like appearance when cold. Since it is a true thermoplastic, it can be reheated and remoulded as many times as is necessary; it is also possible to soften it locally, which makes it particularly easy to use. It is readily moulded around other components and materials—for example, it can be used to form a ball and socket joint by moulding it around a metal sphere mounted on a rod. Its slight contraction on cooling can be used to ensure tight joints when it is moulded around other components. In practical engineering terms, it is tough and springy. Its tensile strength is good, and it can be further strengthened (and stiffened, if necessary) by adding other materials, such as wire, or metal rods or bars.

Although there are many different types of muscle in biology, the 650 or so human skeletal muscles are fairly stereotyped. A muscle consists of a number of muscle fibres (or cells) arranged in parallel, and connected at each end to a common tendon, the elastic connection to the skeleton. When a muscle fibre is stimulated by its associated motoneuron, it fires and contracts momentarily, exerting force on the tendon. A given motoneuron innervates only a single muscle, but controls a number of muscle fibres within that muscle, typically between ten and a hundred; the combination is known as a motor unit. A given muscle is innervated by a number of motoneurons, in many cases by hundreds of them. A sustained muscular contraction is achieved by repeatedly stimulating individual motor units, and the strength of the contraction is modulated by varying the number of motor units activated. Muscle is elastic tissue, and the force exerted is a function not only of the motor unit activation but also of the length of the muscle, which of course changes if the associated joints change position as a result of the balance between the load and the effort.

The essential nature of many skeletal muscle systems derives from two factors: muscles (and tendons) are elastic, and so can only pull and not push; and most degrees of freedom are controlled by antagonistic arrangements of muscles, where the effect of one muscle is opposed by that of one (or more) others. This has two consequences. First, if a muscle and its antagonist are stimulated together, the affected joint will move, changing the lengths of the muscles, until their effects balance the imposed load. This position is known as the set point. Second, the resistance offered to an externally imposed disturbance at the set point — the impedance — is primarily a function of the tension and elastic properties of the muscles involved. Both of these factors make skeletal muscle systems very different from conventional robotic actuation arrangements; as will be seen, these differences have far-reaching effects.

In designing a muscle-like actuator system, we were constrained by a number of practical factors. The cost and size had to be as small as possible — the torso alone would require at least forty powered degrees of freedom. Maximum performance was critical — ideally, some of the actuators would be required to generate forces of the order of 1000N — enough to lift the average person! In order to avoid problems with the distribution of power, an actuator with a built-in power source was highly desirable. Our solution took advantage of the mass production of a common domestic device — the electric screwdriver. These produce quite large torques (around 3Nm) from specially designed small battery packs. The elastic element is provided by marine grade shock cord — a sleeved natural rubber core available in a number of thicknesses. For light loadings we use a

5mm type, and for heavier duty a 10mm version. The shock cord is terminated at each end by 3mm thick braided Dyneema kiteline with a working breaking strain of 250kg. By winding the kiteline round a 10mm spindle driven by a standard good quality screwdriver motor and gearbox, we can achieve tensions in excess of 520N; by using a rather better but larger motor, we can increase this to around 860N, close enough to the target to be satisfactory.

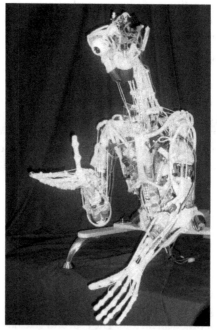

**Figure 4**

### The First Anthropomimetic Robot

The first indication of the nature of an anthropomimetic robot came from the initial prototype, CRONOS, which combined a torso, arm, and head. As can be seen from Figure 4, the sheer profusion of powered and unpowered elastic elements gives a strong qualitative impression of a biological system. This impression soon gives way to the realisation that the robot represents something qualitatively distinct from a conventional robot, even before it is powered up. You take the hand and shake it: it moves easily, and so does the whole skeleton. This multi-degree- of-freedom structure, supported by the tensions between dozens of elastic elements, responds as a whole, transmitting force and movement well beyond the point of contact. You take the arm and push it downward: the elbow flexes, the complex shoulder moves, and the spine bends and twists.

When the robot is powered up, it moves to some equilibrium posture, but the character of the movement is again highly distinctive, because the disturbances due to the robot's own movement are propagated through the structure just like the externally imposed loads. Of course, if all that is wanted is a robot that fits into a human envelope, is able to operate in limited ways on a largely static and predictable world, and is tractable from the point of view of control, this flexibility is nothing but a nuisance. But if the target is a robot that as far as possible also works in the same way as a human – what we call an anthropomimetic robot – then, as engineers, we must face up to the problems that robots like CRONOS present.

At present we are examining the response of the robot's body to programmed movements of a small number of degrees of freedom. Simply moving one degree of freedom, even jerkily, produces what looks like a fluid and coordinated whole-body movement which all observers to date have agreed is very natural and 'biological looking'. This is because the static and dynamic loads produced by the movement are transmitted through the skeleton and the elastic linkages, producing what we call 'passive coordination'. Repeating the same movement command with an applied load produces an equally natural movement, but one in which the weight and inertial forces produce a rather different trajectory and finishing point. This emphasises that the command for such a movement, to be successful, must take account of the anticipated loadings; we believe this is unlikely to be successful if done purely reactively, and that feedforward compensation – anticipating and predictively cancelling the effects of the load – will be necessary for almost any movement, a somewhat daunting prospect when designing the controller. However, from the point of view of an exploration of consciousness that depends on internal models, this new requirement is particularly interesting, because feedforward control depends on the possession and exploitation of forward models; indeed, the use of such models by the nervous system has been advanced by Grush (2002), and earlier by Cruse (1999), as one of the key factors underpinning consciousness.

Of course, in order to respond to the environment, the robot needs sensors as well as actuators. Sensors can be seen as having two related but essentially distinct roles: providing information for building and updating models, and providing information for real-time control. The intention is that, like a human, the robot will be predominantly visual, and so it has been equipped with a visual system that is also anthropomimetic. However, it differs from humans in having a single central eye; this simplifies visual processing enormously, and can be justified by the fact that around 20% of humans do not perform stereo fusion, yet their performance on visual tasks is within the normal range. The imaging unit (currently a 640 x 480 colour webcam with a 25 degree field of view, shortly to be replaced by a specialist high resolution camera with a 90 degree field of view) is mounted in a model eyeball, and is moved by functional analogues of the six extraocular muscles, enabling the control of rotation as well as pan and tilt. The early stages of visual processing are strongly biologically inspired, taking the form of a saliency mapping system similar to that proposed by Itti et al (1998).

## Modelling the Self

In terms of what we need to investigate our theory of consciousness, the robot seems to meet the requirements of the agent, and of course the world meets the requirements of the world. There are two further major components required: an internal model of the robot, and an internal model of the world, and of course the interactions between the two must have predictive value. In addition, in order to be maximally useful, the internal commands that move the IAM should be representable in some form that can be used to generate the commands to move the real robot in a similar enough way. The world is not static, but dynamic; it develops with time—think of a ball bouncing, or a tree falling—and the world model must also develop in similar enough ways. As regards interactions, the model of the robot should affect the model of the world appropriately, and the model of the world should also affect the model of the robot. The world can affect the robot in two ways: by physically enabling or constraining its movements; and by representing the sensory/perceptual information that the real robot would obtain from the real world in that situation and that would be necessary for the robot to use for control or decision.

Although some neuroscientists (e.g. Ramachandran and Blakeslee, 1998) have written about the need for these interacting models to be present in the brain, we have found no information that would assist us in building such models with any degree of biological inspiration. The artificial intelligence literature was similarly unrewarding, in that the standard methods (reasoning over knowledge bases) have serious deficiencies when dealing with unconstrained environments. We decided instead to explore a solution inspired by engineering: physics-based modelling. This a technique for simulating complex deformable or interacting structures and objects by describing them in software in terms of their constituent elements, reducing these descriptions to a large set of equations in physics, and then using numerical techniques to solve these equations. In the past, conventional analytical techniques could only be applied to structures and interactions that were analytically tractable; however, a physics-based approach can be applied to arbitrary objects. Until quite recently, the huge amounts of computation required made such modelling the province of government agencies and large companies, but the inexorable progress dictated by Moore's Law has seen the cost and speed of such techniques change exponentially. In the last year the technique has become applicable to computer games; we decided therefore to implement our internal models using software specifically designed for the games industry, namely the PhysX rigid body simulator from Ageia (http://www.ageia.com/physx/index.html).

We have now completed a full dynamic physics based model of CRONOS, using PhysX. It is somewhat simplified, in that it does not model the shapes of individual bones, but instead abstracts their key physical characteristics: length, mass, and distribution of mass (moment of inertia). Joints are modelled as degrees of freedom with appropriate characteristics. The 'muscles' (motor, gearbox, shock cord, kiteline) are modelled as compound spring/damper assemblies, with parameters set to mimic those of the real implementations as far as possible. The outside of the robot (i.e. the surfaces that will interact with the world model) are for the moment modelled as simple geometric forms—cylinders, spheres, and cuboids. Figure 4 shows the model, which we call SIMNOS, rendered for viewing. (The spiky protuberances and rings are not parts of the body, but indicate the current states of the joints and actuators—this information is very useful for debugging.) The world in this simple model consists of the table on which SIMNOS is mounted. The window at the bottom left shows the view rendered from the viewpoint of the simulated eye—the left and right hands can be seen in a perspective view against the tabletop. Figure 6 shows a more complex world, with more than a hundred simple objects in it. These objects interact with one another and with the robot appropriately; what is more, the whole simulation, robot and objects, runs on an ordinary laptop computer in real time, and this performance can be maintained when many hundreds of interacting objects are present. The model of the robot is convincing not just at the physical level, but in the perceived quality of its movements as well. The fluidity, load sharing, and passive coordination so evident in CRONOS is also seen in SIMNOS.

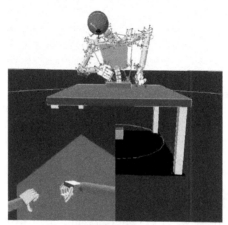

**Figure 5**

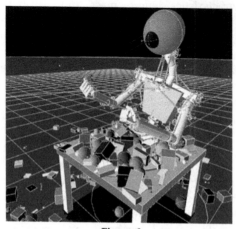

**Figure 6**

We now have the key components of the system in Figure 3: a real (human-like) agent in the real world, an accurate internal model of the agent (the IAM), and a configurable internal world. If the IAM is positioned and actuated in a particular way in a model world which is furnished with a particular configuration of objects, then the ensuing interaction is guaranteed by the integrity of the physics-based modelling system to resemble what would happen if the real robot were actuated in the same way in a corresponding real-world scenario. In addition, because the actuation system of SIMNOS is a reasonably good model of the actuation system of CRONOS, it will be relatively easy to transform a given motor program for SIMNOS in order to produce similar movements in CRONOS.

In order to begin our investigation of the functional (and perhaps phenomenal) aspects of systems of this type, we now need to add a number of supporting features. To enable accurate planning for the current situation—the most frequent requirement—it should be possible to configure the internal models to match the current states of both the robot and the world. Configuring the IAM is in principle relatively simple: CRONOS needs to be provided with ways of measuring the disposition of its skeleton, and the states of its actuators. This can be done by adding a range of joint angle sensors, actuator sensors (position and tension), and an inertial measurement unit (IMU) to track the movements and orientation of the head, which carries the visual sensor. By adding corresponding virtual sensors to SIMNOS, it will be easy to reproduce and track in SIMNOS the current position and orientation (what roboticists call the pose) of CRONOS.

Configuring the world model is more difficult, and at the same time more interesting. Using vision and other sensory information, object and environment models must be 'embedded' in the world model in the appropriate location *and with the appropriate physical characteristics*. In many ways this is close to the problem we face when picking up an object. We obtain cues for its distance from us from many sources—vergence, stereopsis, motion parallax, its known size if it is a familiar object, occlusion of an object at a known distance, and so on. Its size may be known, or may be obtained from its retinal size and its distance. Its mass or weight may be inferred from its size and the known density of objects of its general type. Some or all of this information must be fused to enable us to reach out to the correct position, shape (or preshape) our grasp, and exert sufficient force to grip and lift it. The outcome of all these processes is therefore something very close to the normal meaning of perception, but with the addition of estimates of physical characteristics only indirectly related to the available stimuli. (Of course, once the object has been touched, grasped, and lifted, the additional non-visual information will allow the adjustment of the estimated characteristics — the correction of the internal model.)

## Conclusions

Our pursuit of a simple simulation-driven planning system for a real robot has led us to create an anthropomimetic robot — a radically new and different type of robot. Implementing the main components of the planning system has led us to create a physics-based model of the robot which exhibits the same distinctive behaviour as the real robot, and which is capable in principle of interacting with the modelled world sufficiently accurately to have predictive value. It only remains to add subsystems for configuring the robot model and the world model, and we can begin to investigate the functional characteristics of systems of this general type. We believe that this strongly embodied approach to the study of consciousness, rooted in engineering and computer science, is a necessary complement to more abstract and analytical methods, and we also believe that we have shown that the technical problems, although challenging, are not wholly intractable.

*Acknowledgements*

This work was funded by the Engineering and Physical Sciences Research Council (GR/S47946/01)

## References

Blackmore, S.J. (1988) Do we need a new psychical research? *Journal of the Society for Psychical Research*, 55, 49–59

Blackmore, S.J. 1986 What it's like to be a mental model. Paper presented at the 28th Annual Convention of the Parapsychological Association, 1985, Tufts University, MA. August 1985
   Abstract published in *Research in Parapsychology 1985* Ed. D.Weiner and D.Radin, Metuchen, N.J., Scarecrow, 163–164, 1986

Craik, K.J.W. (1943) *The Nature of Explanation*. Cambridge University Press.

Cruse, H. (1999). Feeling our body — The basis of cognition? *Evolution and Cognition 5*:. 162–73.

Dennett, D.C. (1995) *Darwin's Dangerous idea: Evolution and the Meanings of Life*. Allen Lane, The Penguin Press

Grush, R. (2002) An introduction to the main principles of emulation: motor control, imagery, and perception. Technical Report, Philosophy, UC San Diego: to appear in Behavioral and Brain Sciences.

O. Holland and R. Goodman. Robots with internal models: a route to machine consciousness? *Journal of Consciousness Studies*, Special Issue on Machine Consciousness, vol 10, No 4, 2003

Itti, L., Koch, C., & Niebur, E. (1998). A model of saliency-based visual attention for rapid scene analysis. *IEEE Transactions on Pattern Analysis and Machine Intelligence*, 20(11), 1254–1259

Metzinger, T. (2003) *Being No One: The Self-Model Theory of Subjectivity*. MIT-Bradford.

Ramachandran, V.S. and Blakeslee, S. (1998) *Phantoms in the Brain: Human Nature and the Architecture of the Mind*. Fourth Estate, London.

Riccardo Manzotti

# From Artificial Intelligence to Artificial Consciousness

Thinking and being conscious are two fundamental aspects of the subject. Although both are challenging, often conscious experience has been considered more elusive (Chalmers 1996). However, in recent years, several researchers addressed the hypothesis of designing and implementing models for artificial consciousness — on one hand there is hope of being able to design a model for consciousness, on the other hand the actual implementations of such models could be helpful for understanding consciousness. The traditional field of Artificial Intelligence is now flanked by the seminal field of artificial or machine consciousness.

In this chapter I will analyse the current state of the art of models of consciousness and then I will outline an externalist theory of the conscious mind that is compatible with the design and implementation of an artificial conscious being. As I argue in the following, this task can be profitably approached once we abandon the dualist framework of traditional Cartesian substance metaphysics and adopt a process-metaphysical stance. Thus, I sketch an alternative externalist process-based ontological framework. From within this framework, I venture to suggest a series of constraints for a conscious-oriented architecture.

## 1. Artificial Consciousness and Consciousness

During the last ten years, interest in the scientific understanding of the nature of consciousness has been rekindled (Hameroff, Kaszniak et al., 1996; Jennings, 2000; Miller, 2005). To date, a satisfactory and accepted framework has not been achieved either because experimental data is scarce or because a misleading theoretical standpoint is assumed (Koch, 2004; Kim, 2005; Rockwell, 2005). Further, it is possible that many aspects of consciousness are still framed in a conceptual confused way (Bennett and Hacker, 2003).

The effort for a scientific understanding of consciousness has been flanked by a related field named *artificial consciousness* (sometimes *machine* or *synthetic consciousness*) aimed at reproducing the relevant features of consciousness using non biological components (Haikonen, 2003; Holland, 2003). This new field has strong relationships with artificial intelligence and cognitive robotics.

Most mammals seem to show some kind of consciousness — in particular, human beings. Therefore, it is highly probable that the kind of cognitive architecture responsible for consciousness has some evolutionary advantage. Although it is still difficult to single out a precise functional role for consciousness, many believe that consciousness endorses more robust autonomy, higher resilience, more general capability for problem-solving, reflexivity, and self-awareness (Atkinson, Thomas et al., 2000).

Trying to implement a conscious machine could be a feasible approach to the scientific understanding of consciousness itself. Edelman and Tononi (2000) wrote that:

> to understand the mental we may have to invent further ways of looking at brains. We may even have to synthesize artefacts resembling brains connected to bodily functions in order fully to understand those processes. Although the day when we shall be able to create such conscious artefacts is far off we may have to make them before we deeply understand the processes of thought itself.

According to Owen Holland (2003), it is possible to distinguish between Weak Artificial Consciousness and Strong Artificial Consciousness. Holland defines them as follow:

- *Weak Artificial Consciousness*: design and construction of machine that simulates consciousness or cognitive processes usually correlated with consciousness.

- *Strong Artificial Consciousness*: design and construction of conscious machines.

Most of the people currently working in the field of Artificial Consciousness would embrace the former definition. Anyhow, the boundaries between the two are not always easy to define. For instance, whether a machine could exhibit all behaviours normally associated with a conscious being, could we reasonably deny the status of conscious machine? Conversely, whether a machine could exhibit all such behaviours, would it be really subjectively conscious?

It is quite obvious that the dilemma is similar to the Turing test. Is a behavioural test enough to check the existence of a mind? Of a conscious mind? From the earliest days of digital computers, people have suggested that machines may one day be conscious. Alan Turing was one of the earliest to consider seriously this idea. Although the Turing test has been traditionally considered only a behavioural test unable to check the 'intrinsic intentionality' of conscious states (Searle, 1980), the possibility of suggesting 'operational means to distinguish automatic zombie behaviours from those that require consciousness' has not been completely ruled out (Koch, 2004, p. 227).

Other authors claimed that artificial consciousness will provide a better foundation for complex control whenever autonomy has to be achieved. In this respect, artificial consciousness is not a just branch of cognitive robotics, but it could be, at least in principle, applied to all kind of complex systems ranging from a petrochemical plant to a complex network of computers. The complexity of current artificial systems is such that outperforms traditional control techniques. Artificial consciousness could provide new ways to control. According to Ricardo Sanz, there are three motivations to pursue artificial consciousness (Sanz 2005):

1) implementing and designing machines resembling human beings (cognitive robotics);

2) understanding the nature of consciousness (cognitive science);

3) implementing and designing more efficient control systems.

This careful subdivision of the field has been partially fostered by the most dreaded aspect of consciousness — the so called 'Hard-problem' of consciousness. The term 'hard problem' of consciousness was coined by David Chalmers (1996), when he distinguished between 'easy problems' of understanding consciousness (such as explaining the ability to discriminate, integrate information, report mental states, focus attention, control, etc.) and contrasted them with the 'hard problem' (why does awareness of sensory information exist at all? And why is there a subjective component to experience?).

It is easy to see that the separation between Weak and Strong Artificial Consciousness mirrors the separation between the easy problems and the hard problems of consciousness.

One final issue, which is worth to be mentioned, is the dichotomy between Access Consciousness and Phenomenal Consciousness (often abbreviated in A-Consciousness and P-Consciousness), suggested by Ned Block in a pivotal paper (Block, 1995; 2002). According to him, there is a confusion about the word consciousness regarding its twofold meaning — 'the concept of consciousness is a hybrid or better, a mongrel concept'. This confusion is dispelled distinguishing between access-consciousness and phenomenal consciousness. Access-consciousness or A-consciousness is mostly functional — reportability and control are prominently important. According to Block, A-consciousness is definable as 'poised for control of speech, reasoning and action' (Block, 1995). Other authors suggested defining A-consciousness 'as directly available for global control' (Chalmers, 1997). On the contrary, phenomenal consciousness or P-consciousness is identical to subjective experience — what makes a state phenomenally conscious is that there is something it is like to be in that state (Nagel, 1974). Phenomenal consciousness is subjective and qualitative.

In short there is a strain between the subjective and objective aspect of consciousness as well as between the cognitive and phenomenal aspect of the mind. There has been a lot of overlapping and redundancy between various definitions that contributed to make the whole matter difficult to be understood.

Stuart Sutherland, in a much-quoted remark, wrote that 'Consciousness is a fascinating but elusive phenomenon; it is impossible to specify what it is, what id does, or why it evolved' (Sutherland, 1989). Although many aspects of consciousness are still far from being understood, it is also clear that consciousness represents an exciting and important scientific problem. However, regarding the lack of a common definition for consciousness I will adopt the same attitude recently professed by Cristof Koch (2004), p. 12:

> Historically, significant scientific progress has commonly been achieved in the absence of formal definitions. For instance, the phenomenological laws of electrical current flow were formulated by Ohm, Ampère, and Volta well before the discovery of

the electron in 1892 by Thompson. For the time being, therefore, I adopt the above working definition of consciousness and will see how far I can get with it.

A working standpoint is the following. The conscious mind has an irreducible subjective qualitative and phenomenal aspect whose connection with the functional role has never been completely clarified. The functional role of consciousness partially overlaps with more traditional aspect of the mind — control, learning, representation, reportability.

On the other hand, artificial consciousness is a field of its own, a sort of extension of the traditional artificial intelligence. Whether artificial consciousness aims at understanding, replicating, mimicking the actual human consciousness is not altogether clear. Artificial consciousness could develop into a mere technological endeavour loosely inspired to the features of the human conscious mind.

Of course, the described view does not rule out that artificial consciousness cannot benefit from scientific outcomes of the study of consciousness; as well as it does not rule out that artificial consciousness would not be of inspiration for those trying to develop a true science of consciousness.

In this chapter, I assume that the scientific understanding of the phenomenal aspect of consciousness is mandatory and that phenomenal consciousness is connected with the functional aspects of the mind in ways which, though still to be fully understood, are fruitful to be addressed.

## 2. Internalism *vs* Externalism

Currently, the majority of scientific and philosophical literature on consciousness is biased by a seldom challenged assumption — the separation between the subject and the object. Although it is obvious that the body of the subject is separate from the body of the object, it is by no means so obvious that the mind is confined by the same boundaries of the brain. 'Where does the mind stop and the rest of the world begin? … Someone accepts the demarcations of skin and skull, and say that what is outside the body is outside the mind' (Clark and Chalmers, 1999). Indeed, there are many phenomena which extend beyond the boundaries of the body (behaviours, actions, perceptions, ecological processes). The mind could be one of them.

With regard to the nature of the mind, two very broad standpoints must be considered: internalism and externalism. The former states that our consciousness is identical (or correlated) to the processes, events or states of affairs going on *inside* the boundary of our body (or brain). The latter affirms that our consciousness might depend partially or totally on the events, processes or state of affairs *outside* our head or even *outside* our body.

Most current approaches to the problem of consciousness tend towards the internalist viewpoint (Crick, 1994; Edelman and Tononi, 2000; Metzinger, 2000; Rees, Kreiman et al., 2002; Crick and Koch, 2003; Koch, 2004). However, this approach raises several conundrums. If the mind is entirely located or dependent on events or states of affairs located inside the cranium, how can they represent events taking place in the external world? Consciousness appears to have properties which differ from anything taking place inside the cranium (Place, 1956). Spurred on by common sense, literature has revealed a very strong impulse to 'etherealize' or 'cranialize' consciousness (Honderich, 2000). The internalist perspective has consistently led to dualism and still promotes a physicalist version of dualism by endowing the brain (or a brain subset, the Neural Correlate of Consciousness) with the same role as the dualistic subject. Koch's recent book (Koch, 2004, p. 87), endorses an unabashed internalist view with respect to consciousness and the brain: 'The entire brain is sufficient for consciousness — it determines conscious sensations day in and day out. Identifying all of the brain with the NCC [Neural Correlate of Consciousness], however is not useful because likely a subset of brain matter will do.' This standpoint is a form of Cartesian dualism and it suffers of what has been recently defined the *mereological fallacy* by M.R. Bennett and P.M.S. Hacker (2003), p. 73:

> Mereology is the logic of part/whole relations. The neuroscientists' mistake of ascribing to the constituent *parts* of an animal attributes that logically apply only to the *whole* animal we shall call 'the mereological fallacy' in neuroscience. The principle that psychological predicates which apply only to human beings (or other animals) as wholes cannot intelligibly be applied to their parts, such as the brain, we shall call 'the mereological principle' in neuroscience.

On the other hand, many authors have questioned the separation between subject and object — between representation and represented. They look for a different framework in which subject and object provide two different perspectives on the same process. Often, they embrace some brand of externalism where the relevant part of reality 'responsible for a particular percept' is not confined inside the brain or the body.

Externalism is the view 'that not all mental things are exclusively located inside the head [or mind] of the persona or creature that has these things' (Rowlands 2003, p. 2). According to Mark Rowlands, there are two variants of externalism: content externalism and vehicle externalism. The former corresponds to the 'idea that the semantic content of mental states that have it is often dependent on factors ... that are external to the subject of that content' (Rowlands, 2003, p. 5). The latter is more radical and affirms that 'the structures and mechanisms that allow a creature to possess or undergo various mental states and processes are often structure and mechanisms that extend beyond the skin of that creature' (Rowlands, 2003, p. 6).

The vehicle/content dichotomy was originally drawn by Daniel Dennett (Dennett, 1991; Hurley, 1998) between the content of a state and that content's *vehicle*. As Alva Noe observed (Noe, 2004, p. 221):

> It is a mistake to think you can read off properties of vehicles of content (e.g., neural structures and systems, or sentences for that matter) from the contents of the resulting state. The experience of a cube needn't be carried by a cubical neural structure of vehicle ... In some cases, Clark and Chalmers argue, the vehicles of content cross boundaries, looping out of the head into the world ... I have been arguing hat, for at least some experiences, the physical substrate of the *experience* too may extend out into the world (but not that it must do so).

In the following paragraphs, I will present a radical version of vehicle externalism called 'the enlarged mind'(Manzotti and Tagliasco, 2001; Manzotti, 2006a; 2006b; 2006c).

In the recent past, other authors presented various versions of vehicle externalism (Dretske, 1995; Hurley, 1998; Clark and Chalmers, 1999; Lycan, 2001; O' Regan and Noe, 2001; Noe, 2003; 2004). The main difference between these approaches and the one presented here is the fact that they are not radical enough in abandoning the assumption of the separation between subject and object. For instance, the form of externalism advocated by Kevin O' Regan and Alva Nöe (O' Regan and Noe, 2001) evolves towards a kind of functionalism (Manzotti and Sandini, 2001).

Many authors who advocated externalist standpoints were not recognized as such. The position presented here is related with five different and yet connected viewpoints: ecological perception and the theory of affordances (Gibson, 1977; 1979), externalism

(Rowlands, 2003), process philosophy (Whitehead ,1927/1978; Griffin, 1998), neorealism or direct realism (Holt, Marvin et al., 1910; Holt, 1914; Tonneau, 2004), Brentano's immanent realism (Albertazzi, 2006).

The rationale of the proposal is simple, albeit radical. Traditionally it is assumed that there is a world of things and that there is an experience of such a world of things—the two being different and separate. This view is based on the common belief that the world is made of things which seem to exist autonomously and without any need of being in relation with the rest of their environment. I challenge this belief and show proof of the fact that *in order to exist anything needs to interact with something else*. Then I claim that the existence of things (objects and events) should be re-described as their taking place—thereby adopting a process-based stance. As soon as we drop the belief in a world of things existing autonomously and as soon as we conceive the world as made of processes extended in time and space, experience (and thus consciousness) does not need to be located in a special domain (or to require the emergence of something new)—experience is identical with those processes that make up our behavioural story. Experience is no more constrained to the activity taking place inside the cranium—experience is an extended collection of processes comprehending all those events that are part of our conscious experience. Most concepts—like those of representation or mental causation—get a twist and develop a new perspective.

### 3. Continuity Between Phenomenal Experience and the Environment

The internalist standpoint described above conceives reality as made of relatively autonomous objects or relatively autonomous events. This entails that subject and object, being both instantiated by autonomous set of objects or events, are irremediably separate in time and in space. On the other hand, we—as human beings—perceive the world not as an image of the world but as the world itself.

Consider this. Sabrina sees a flower. As a result, the flower does things that would not do alone. For instance, the flower activates Sabrina's visual cortex. The flower causal powers change because of Sabrina and thus the flower, as it is perceived, comes into existence only when it is in relation with Sabrina. Conversely, Sabrina's phenomenal experience of a flower takes place only when she interacts with the flower. Both do not pre-exist the process endorsing their relations. The process is more fundamental — Sabrina's phenomenal experience and the flower being two ways of describing the process.

Alternatively consider this. Romeo perceives Juliet's face. Her face, as a whole, was not there until it started to produce effects. Similarly Romeo's phenomenal experience did not exist until was the result of her face. Her face, as a whole, cannot be split by Romeo's phenomenal experience. Whether Romeo had had prosopagnosia, Juliet's face would not have existed. Romeo's experience and Juliet's face are two sides of the same coin.

If a subject perceives an external object, the external object produces effects in his/her brain. Because of the brain (and the body and other physical conditions) the object is causally extended. At the same time the experience of the subject is extended to the external object. Why do not consider the whole process spanning time and space and extended across the boundaries of the skin? I suggest to adopt a process view which endorses an externalist view of the conscious mind and its object — the two being alternative perspectives on the same process.

The world is not made of separate events. The world is made of intrinsically related processes. Therefore, subject and object are not separate and there is no longer the problem of (phenomenal) re-presentation, since experience and occurrence of the world are identical.

In all previous cases, the cause does not exist isolated from its effect, and vice versa. They take place as different ways of describing a process which is one. Whenever the examples regard perceptual events (like the perception of an object or a face), the perceived object does not exist in isolation from its perception.

Therefore there is no need to add a phenomenal object to the physical one. Symmetrically, there is no need to suppose a physical rainbow 'noumenically' inaccessible to phenomenal experience.

Subjects and the surrounding environment are made of processes — some of them shared by both. These processes shape both the 'world as we experience it' and 'us as the subject of experience'. The body and the brain are made in such a way that, given the same external phenomena, the same processes take place. Subjects cannot perceive the world without a brain and a body and, as far as we know, a brain and body cannot perceive anything in life-time isolation. There is no evidence at all that a brain in a jar can concoct a phenomenal world all by itself (Bennett and Hacker, 2003).

I elsewhere proposed to call this process — which is constitutive of what there is and what we perceive — an *onphene*, derived from the Greek words *ontos* (what there is) and *phenomenon* (what appears) (Manzotti and Tagliasco, 2001; Manzotti, 2003; 2006a; 2006b). It refers to a process in which the traditional distinction between cause and effect (perceiver and perceived, representation and represented, subject and object) does not hold.

The traditional problems of phenomenal consciousness vanish once an externalist and process-based standpoint is adopted. The world in which each subject lives is no longer a private bubble of phenomenal experiences concocted by the brain. Each subject lives in and experiences the real world — the two being different descriptions of the same process. Each subject lives in that part of the world made by those processes with which s/he is identical with. The subject *is* those processes.

From an empirical point of view, consciousness and existence cannot be split (Albertazzi, 2006). Conscious agents are part of a physical flow of processes possible thanks to their physical structure. These processes have the right properties of our own experiences as well as the right properties of the external world. The need for postulating a noumenic world of primary properties (and their bearer, the object) and a symmetrical world of secondary properties (and their bearer, the subject) arose from the undemonstrated assumption of a separation between subject and object. By using a process-based view such need vanishes.

I introduce here the concept of the enlarged mind. If every phenomenal experience is identical with a process, the sphere of an individual consciousness is identical with a collection of processes. In turn, such collection of processes is identical with that part of the environment which takes place thanks to the physical structure of the subject's brain and body. These processes are identical with those events that are relevant for the subject's behavioural history. If a subject is conscious of a face plus some speech to which s/he is listening to, it means that at least three separate processes take place. In reality, there are countless processes going on in the environment. Only a subset is identical with the subject. The mental life of a subject is no longer constrained inside the cranium, compelled to the creation of a theatrical replica of the external world. Mental life is literally 'enlarged' to those processes constituting everything that mind is conscious of. There is not a mental life and a physical life — there is only a life.

It is possible to discard many classical conundrums. In particular it is possible to discard the television view of the mind (Dretske, 1995). This is not a complete novelty. Other authors criticized the idea that what we have an experience of is an internally generated image of the external world. With respect to direct perception this approach has the advantage of suggesting a solution to all the three classical problems of the mind: the hard problem, epiphenomenalism and the problem of representation. Let's briefly see how.

The hard problem is solved since there is a candidate for the nature of phenomenal experience—the physical processes engaged between the brain and the environment. Dualism is no more needed. The price to pay is to discard the assumption of the separation between subject and object as well as the autonomy of the existence of objects. Such processes are neither objective nor subjective. They are private and public at the same time.

Epiphenomenalism is solved since phenomenal states are no longer separate from the physical world. Every phenomenal event is identical with a physical process that, as all physical processes, has causal powers and exerts its effects on the environment. Mental causation is no longer a problem insofar there is no longer such a thing as 'mental' causation. There is only causation.

The problem of representation is solved since there is no more need to re-produce an internal image of the external world. Phenomenal experiences are identical—they coincide—with the aspects of reality they should represent. More precisely, they do not represent reality—they are the reality. The subject does not perceive *an image* of an object. A process takes place which is constitutive both of subject and object; a process which can be described either as a subjective experience or as an objective event.

This is a view which could be considered a radical externalist one since it exploits a kind of radical externalism of the mind with respect to the boundaries of the body. The mind is literally and physically identical with a collection of processes spanning in time and space beyond the boundaries of the brain and the body. It is also a realist standpoint since it assumes that the experience of the world regards the world itself (*it is the world*) and not a mental representation of it.

## 4. Teleologically Open Systems and Externalism

Is it possible to design and implement an architecture exploiting an externalist-oriented view? Or, more modestly, is it possible to derive some practical constraints from an externalist view? The common ground is a teleological entanglement between the agent and the environment. The continuity outlined by the externalist view could be achieved by a system teleologically open.

Current implementations of artificial systems focus on the implementation of intelligent algorithms to achieve a fixed goal (or a fixed set of goals). Conscious subjects are capable of developing unpredictable and unexpected new goals.

Artificial systems are frequently designed with a fixed set of goals. Designers focus their efforts to find 'how' these goals can be achieved. Learning is usually defined as a modification in agents' behaviour: a modification driven by a goal. Various learning paradigms focus mostly on this modification of behaviour.

For instance, Sutton and Barto claim that 'reinforcement learning is learning what to do — how to map situations to actions — so as to maximize a numerical reward signal' (Sutton and Barto, 1998, p. 3). Here, the goal is embedded in an *a priori* defined reward signal. According to them, 'the basic idea is simply to capture the most important aspects of the real problem facing a learning agent interacting with its environment to achieve a goal ... All reinforcement learning agents have explicit goals' (Sutton and Barto, 1998, p. 4–5). These explicit goals are fixed at design time. Reinforcement learning deals with situation in which the agent seeks to achieve a goal despite uncertainty about its environment.

In a reinforcement learning based agent, developing new goals is equivalent to looking for new reward functions. However, very often this is not the case. In Reinforcement Learning systems 'the reward function must necessarily be unalterable by the agent' (Sutton and Barto, 1998, p. 8). On the contrary many biological systems are capable of developing partially or totally unpredictable goals. There is evidence that such capability is greater in humans and mammals, which are also the species less controversially assumed to have some form of consciousness.

Biological agents are capable of singling out new goals. Developing new goals is important since the environment cannot be completely predicted at design time. Therefore a truly adaptive system must be able to add new goals, not only to modify its behaviour in order to perform optimally on the basis of some fixed criteria.

## 5. A Teleological Taxonomy of Agents

Not all biological systems' goals are fixed at birth. As organisms grow and develop, they generate new goals. A mallard duckling does not have the goal to follow its genetic mother. Yet, via its genetic background, the bird possesses the capability of choosing a bird and selecting it as a goal. That particular bird (hopefully its mother) becomes the goal that will control the learning of the bird. The behaviour of behaviour-based artificial agents depends on experience and goals defined elsewhere at design time (Arkin, 1999). Motivation-based agents begins to show the capability of developing new goals (Manzotti and Tagliasco, 2005). In complex biological systems, behaviour depends on experience and goals; yet, goals are not fixed. Goals are the result of the interaction between the subject and its environment. In many complex biological systems, it is possible to distinguish between phylogenetic aspects and ontogenetic ones, nature versus nurture (Gould, 1977; Elman, Bates et al., 2001; Ridley, 2004).

What is a goal? It is an event whose occurrence is more probable thanks to the agent's structure (cognitive and bodily). In this respect a goal is projected towards the future. On the other hand, it is the result of the past. Goals are embedded in causal structures that link the past with the future, the environment with the agent.

It is possible to classify artificial agents accordingly to their degree of teleological plasticity: fixed control architectures, learning architectures and goal generating architectures. In the first case, the system has no capability of modifying how it does what it does. In the second case, the system is capable of modifying its behaviour in order to fulfil some a priori target. The system is capable of modifying *how* it behaves. In the third case, the system is capable of modifying not only *how* it does what it does, but also *what* it does.

### 5.1. Fixed control architectures (input-output)

In this case, the causal structure of the system is fixed. There is no ontogenesis whatsoever. Notwithstanding the behavioural complexity of the system, everything happens because it has been previously coded within the system structure. A mechanical device and a complex software agent are not different in this respect: both are pre-programmed in what they must achieve and how they must achieve it. Nothing in their structure is caused by their experiences. Suitable examples of this category are Tolam's artificial sow bug,

Braitenberg's thinking vehicles (Braitenberg, 1984), Brooks' artificial insects and recent entertainment robots like Sony AIBO and Honda's humanoid ASIMO (2002).

## 5.2. Architectures for learning ('how')

A different level of dependency with the environment is provided by architectures that can learn *how* to perform a task. Behaviour-based robots can be classified in this category. Systems based on artificial neural networks are well-known examples of this kind of architectures. These systems determine how to get a given result once they have been provided with a specific goal. The goal can be given either as a series of examples of correct behaviour (supervised learning) or as a simple evaluation of the global performance of the system (reinforcement learning) (Sutton and Barto, 1998). In both cases some kind of learning is applied. These systems lack the capability of creating new goals. By controlling its motors a behaviour-based robot can learn how to navigate avoiding static and dynamic obstacles. However the goal behind this task is defined by the *a priori* design of the system. There are several examples of this kind of learning agent: Babybot at LIRA-Lab (Metta, Manzotti et al., 2000), Cog at MIT (Brooks, Breazeal et al., 1999).

## 5.3. Teleologically open architectures ('what')

An agent, which learns both *how* to perform a given task and *what* task, corresponds to a teleologically open architecture. This is the case for most, if not all, mammals; it is true for primates and for human beings. They are systems capable of developing new goals that do not belong to their genetic background. For their development, these systems depend more on the environment than the previous two categories. A system belonging to the first category does not depend on the environment for what it does or for how it does what it does. A system belonging to the second category does depend on the environment for how it does what it does, but not for what it does. A system belonging to the third and last category depends on the environment both for what and for how it does what it does.

The final kind of agents, defined as teleologically open, endorse that kind of causal continuity with the external environment useful for the externalist process-oriented framework described above.

A teleologically open architecture is not separate and autonomous with respect to its environment. On the contrary, it endorses the occurrence and the entanglement of environmental processes in longer and larger. A teleologically open architecture changes accordingly to that part of the environment that acts by means of the interactions with the architecture itself.

Whenever a new goal is added to such an architecture, a part of the environment is singled out as well as a new objective. A teleologically open architecture is causally continuous with its environment — the events taking place inside the architecture and the events corresponding to the external causes being two perspectives on the same process.

For these reasons, suggest adopting a framework neutral with respect to the subject/object dichotomy. Such an externalist and process oriented framework has been labelled 'the enlarged mind' (Manzotti 2006). On the basis of such a framework, a teleologically open architecture could exploit the right king of process continuity with the environment; a continuity that could be the phenomenon called consciousness.

## References

Albertazzi, L. (2006). *Immanent Realism. An introduction to Brentano*. Berlin, Springer.

Arkin, R.C. (1999). *Behavior-Based Robotics*. Cambridge (Mass), MIT Press.

Atkinson, A.P., M.S.C. Thomas, et al. (2000). 'Consciousness: mapping the theoretical landscape.' *Trends in Cognitive Sciences* 4(10): 372–382.

Bennett, M.R. and P.M.S. Hacker (2003). *Philosophical Foundations of Neuroscience*. Malden (MA), Blackwell.

Block, N. (1995). 'On a Confusion about a Function of Consciousness.' *Behavioral and Brain Sciences* 18: 227–287.

Block, N. (2002). Some Concepts of Consciousness. *Philosophy of Mind: Classical and Contemporary Readings*. D. Chalmers. Oxford, Oxford University Press.

Braitenberg, V. (1984). *Vehicles: Experiments in Synthetic Psychology*. Cambridge (Mass), MIT Press.

Brooks, R.A., C. Breazeal, et al. (1999). The Cog Project: Building a Humanoid Robot. *Computation for Metaphors, Analogy, and Agents*. Nehaniv. Berlin, Springer-Verlag. 1562.

Chalmers, D.J. (1996). *The Conscious Mind: In Search of a Fundamental Theory*. New York, Oxford University Press.

Chalmers, D.J. (1997). Availability: The Cognitive Basis of Experience. *The Nature of Consciousness*. N. Block, O. Flanagan and G. Guzeldere. Cambridge (Mass), MIT Press: 421–423.

Clark, A. and D. Chalmers (1999). 'The Extended Mind.' *Analysis* 58(1): 10–23.

Crick, F. (1994). *The Astonishing Hypothesis: the Scientific Search for the Soul.* New York, Touchstone.

Crick, F. and C. Koch (2003). 'A framework for consciousness.' *Nature Neuroscience* 6(2): 119–126.

Dennett, D.C. (1991). *Consciousness explained.* Boston, Little Brown and Co.

Dretske, F. (1995). *Naturalizing the Mind.* Cambridge (Mass), MIT Press.

Edelman, G.M. and G. Tononi (2000). *A Universe of Consciousness. How Matter Becomes Imagination.* London, Allen Lane.

Elman, J.L., E.A. Bates, et al. (2001). *Rethinking Innateness: A Connectionist Perspective on Development.* Cambridge (Mass), MIT Press.

Gibson, J.J. (1977). The theory of affordances. *Perceiving, acting, and knowing: Toward an ecological psychology.* R. E. Shaw and J. Bransford. Hillsdale (NJ), Lawrence Erlbaum Associates.

Gibson, J.J. (1979). *The Ecological Approach to Visual Perception.* Boston, Houghton Mifflin.

Gould, S.J. (1977). *Ontogeny and Phylogeny.* Cambridge (Mass), Harvard University Press.

Griffin, D.R. (1998). *Unsnarling the world-knot: consciousness, freedom, and the mind-body problem.* Berkeley, University of California Press.

Haikonen, P.O. (2003). *The Cognitive Approach to Conscious Machine.* London, Imprint Academic.

Hameroff, S.R., A.W. Kaszniak, et al. (1996). *Toward a science of consciousness: the first Tucson discussions and debates.* Cambridge (Mass), MIT Press.

Holland, O., Ed. (2003). *Machine consciousness.* New York, Imprint Academic.

Holt, E.B. (1914). *The concept of consciousness.* New York, MacMillan.

Holt, E.B., W.T. Marvin, et al. (1910). 'The program and first platform of six realists.' *Journal of Philosophy, Psychology and Scientific Methods* 7: 393–401.

Honderich, T. (2000). 'Consciousness as existence again.' *Theoria* 95: 94–109.

Hurley, S.L. (1998). *Consciousness in Action.* Cambridge (Mass), Harvard University Press.

Jennings, C. (2000). 'In Search of Consciousness.' *Nature Neuroscience* 3(8): 1.

Kim, J. (2005). *Physicalism, or Something Near Enough.* Princeton, Princeton University Press.

Koch, C. (2004). *The Quest for Consciousness: A Neurobiological Approach.* Englewood (Colorado), Roberts & Company Publishers.

Lycan, W.G. (2001). The Case for Phenomenal Externalism. *Philosophical Perspectives, Vol. 15: Metaphysics.* J. E. Tomberlin. Atascadero, Ridgeview Publishing.

Manzotti, R. (2003). A process based architecture for an artificial conscious being. *Process theories.* J. Seibt. Dordrecht, Kluwer Academic Press. Process Theories: Crossdisciplinary studies in dynamic categories: 285–312.

Manzotti, R. (2006a). 'An alternative process view of conscious perception.' *Journal of Consciousness Studies* 13(6): 45–79.

Manzotti, R. (2006b). 'Consciousness and existence as a process.' *Mind and Matter* 4(1): 7–43.

Manzotti, R. (2006c). A radical externalist approach to consciousness: the enlarged mind. *Mind and Its Place in the World. Non-reductionist Approaches to the Ontology of Consciousness*. A. Batthyany and A. Elitzur. Frankfurt, Ontos-Verlag.

Manzotti, R. and G. Sandini (2001). 'Does Functionalism really deal with the phenomenal side of experience?' *Behavioral and Brain Sciences* 24(5): 994–994.

Manzotti, R. and V. Tagliasco (2001). *Coscienza e Realtà. Una teoria della coscienza per costruttori e studiosi di menti e cervelli*. Bologna, Il Mulino.

Manzotti, R. and V. Tagliasco (2005). 'From 'behaviour-based'' robots to 'motivations-based' robots.' *Robotics and Autonomous Systems* 51(2–3): 175–190.

Metta, G.,R. Manzotti, et al. (2000). *Development: is it the right way towards humanoid robotics?* ISA–6, Venezia, IOS Press.

Metzinger, T. (2000). *Neural correlates of consciousness: empirical and conceptual questions*. Cambridge (Mass), MIT Press.

Miller, G. (2005). 'What are the Biological Basis of Consciousness?' *Science* 309(July): 79.

Nagel, T. (1974). 'What is it like to be a Bat?' *Philosophical Review* 4: 435–450.

Noe, A. (2003). 'Perception and Causation: the puzzle unraveled.' *Analysis* 63(2): 93–100.

Noe, A. (2004). *Action in Perception*. Cambridge (Mass), MIT Press.

O' Regan, K. and A. Noe (2001). 'A sensorimotor account of visual perception and consciousness.' *Behavioral and Brain Sciences* 24(5).

Place, U.T. (1956). 'Is consciousness a brain process?' *British Journal of Psychology* 47: 44–50.

Rees, G., G. Kreiman, et al. (2002). 'Neural Correlates of Consciousness in Humans.' *Nature Reviews* 3: 261–270.

Ridley, M. (2004). *Nature via nurture*. Great Britain, Harper.

Rockwell, T. (2005). *Neither ghost nor brain*. Cambridge (Mass), MIT Press.

Rowlands, M. (2003). *Externalism. Putting Mind and World Back Together Again*. Chesham, Acumen Publishing Limited.

Sanz, R. (2005). *Design and Implementation of an Artificial Conscious Machine*. IWAC2005, Agrigento.

Searle, J.R. (1980). 'Minds, Brains, and Programs.' *Behavioral and Brain Sciences* 1: 417–424.

Sutherland, S. (1989). *Dictionary of Psychology*. London, MacMillan.

Sutton, R.S. and A.G. Barto (1998). *Reinforcement Learning*. Cambridge (Mass), MIT Press.

Tonneau, F. (2004). 'Consciousness Outside the Head.' *Behavior and Philosophy* 32: 97–123.

Whitehead, A.N. (1927/1978). *Process and Reality*. London, Free Press.

Domenico Parisi

# *Mental Robotics*

What is consciousness? From the point of view of science, this is the wrong question to ask. If we ask ourselves what is consciousness we are led to think that there is some entity called consciousness which has the following properties: it is one single entity, it is an entity with well defined boundaries that separate it from other entities, it is something that an organism either has or does not have, it is an entity with fixed characteristics. Real entities have the opposite properties: in each class there is always internal variation, they are never entirely different from other related entities, they have degrees, they change all the time, they evolve, develop, disappear. It is language, i.e., the sheer existence of a word such as 'consciousness', that induces us to ask the wrong question 'What is consciousness?' This is a philosophical question, not a scientific question. Philosophers are restricted to working with language but scientists need to go beyond language and observe, measure, and analyze reality itself. Instead of asking 'What is consciousness?' what we should do is look at the variety of phenomena to which we apply, rather confusedly, the word 'consciousness', and try to separately describe and explain each of these phenomena.

What are the phenomena of 'consciousness'? Some organisms, in particular human beings, in addition to behaviour and physical interactions with the external environment, have mental images, rememberings, thoughts, they make predictions and plans, they dream and have hallucinations, they may be aware or not aware of what they are responding to, they can have a sense of self and of self agency, they can have different levels of alertness and wakefulness. These are the phenomena that need to be analyzed and explained. Some of these phenomena constitute what is called mental life. What is mental life? Mental life is the self-generation of one's sensory-motor experiences. Sensory-motor experiences are normally caused by sensory input originating in the external environment or within the organism's own body. But some organisms have nervous systems that are able to self-generate their sensory-motor experiences. Self-generated sensory experiences are internal states that are similar to the internal states that are normally caused by external inputs but that occur in the absence of external inputs. How can we explain mental life?

One way to analyze and explain the behaviour of organisms is to construct artificial organisms that behave like real organisms, i.e., robots. If we are able to construct robots which behave like real organisms, we can claim that the principles followed in constructing the robots are the same principles that underlie the behaviour of real organisms. Current robots are very simple, and they reproduce the behaviour of very simple organisms. In particular they do not reproduce the mental life of more complex organisms such as humans. Mental robotics, i.e., the construction of embodied and situated agents that can be said to be aware, to have mental images, to remember, to think, to predict and to plan, is one of the directions that robotics will have to take in future if we want to move from today's humanoid robots to robots that can more legitimately be said to be human. Current humanoid robots are human in a very superficial sense: they have an external morphology which more or less resemble human morphology, they have bipedalism, they 'understand' and 'speak' a language in the very restricted sense of current automatic language understanding and synthesis systems, they generate and recognize 'emotional expressions' without actually feeling those emotions. Future human robots will have to have properties that current humanoid robots completely lack. One particularly important property is mental life.

### 1. Mental Life Defined

We assume that our robot's behaviour is controlled by an artificial neural network which is a simplified model of the human brain. As the brain is made up of neurons and synapses between neurons, so neural networks are made up of units and unidirectional connections between units. At any given time each unit has a quantitative activation level which corresponds to the rate with which a neuron 'fires' nervous impulses. A unit's activation level influences the activation level of other connected units, and the influence is modulated by the quantitative weight of the connection linking the two units, which corresponds to the number of synaptic sites on the post-synaptic neuron, and by the excitatory or inhibitory nature of the connection, which corresponds to the particular type of neurotransmitter that mediates the influence.

What does the neural network that controls the behaviour of a robot without mental life, i.e., of a purely reactive robot, look like? The robot's neural network has three types of units. Some units encode in their current pattern of activation some event or process which is taking place in the external environment. (For simplicity we consider only inputs from the environment that lies outside the robot's body. In real organisms inputs to the organism's brain can also arrive from within the organism's body. For the need to develop an 'internal robotics', especially if one wants to account for the motivational/emotional aspects of behaviour, cf. Parisi, 2004.) These are the sensory units. The sensory units send their connections to one or more successive layers of internal units, and the pattern of activation of the sensory units will cause patterns of activation in these internal units. The internal units send their connections to the third type of units, the motor units, causing a pattern of activation in the motor units. The pattern of activation of the motor units encodes a movement of some part of the robot's body —legs, arms, hands, face, eyes, phono-articulatory organs— with which the robot responds to the sensory input. Figure 1 shows the neural network of a purely reactive robot.

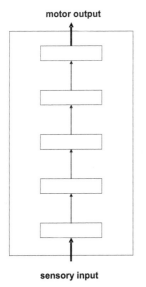

motor output

sensory input

**Figure 1. The neural network of a purely reactive robot.** Boxes represent sets of units (neurons). Arrows represent connections (synapses) between units.

We have called this robot purely reactive because its entire behaviour is a reaction to the input arriving from the external environment and the robot is under the complete control of the external environment. A simple animal such as an insect can be simulated by a purely reactive robot. However, there are other organisms, in particular humans, that cannot be simulated by purely reactive robots because they can be autonomous from the

external environment and because, in addition to physically interacting with the external environment, they can have a purely internal mental life.

Let us try to identify what might be the basic mechanism underlying mental life. As we have said, in purely reactive robots the activation patterns in the internal units are caused by the activation pattern
in the sensory units, which in turn is caused by an event in the external environment. Let us call an activation pattern in one layer of a
neural network's internal units an internal representation. Internal
representations are sensory-motor representations, that is, they
include information from both the sensory input and the motor output with which the organism responds to the sensory input. Different sensory inputs tend to evoke similar internal representations if
they are responded to with the same action, while similar sensory
inputs tend to evoke different internal representations if they are
responded to with different actions (Di Ferdinando and Parisi,
2004). Furthermore, internal representations may include proprioceptive sensory information originating in the movements with
which the organism responds to the input. It is possible that internal
representations in layers of internal units that are nearer to the
sensory input contain more sensory information whereas internal
representations nearer to the motor output contain more motor
information. However, in general all internal representations tend to
be sensory-motor because sensory input may be important to decide
what to do but what is really critical for survival is how the organism
responds to the sensory input, not the sensory input in itself.

In purely reactive robots, internal representations are caused by
sensory input from the external environment. In addition to internal
representations caused by external input, robots with mental life
may have internal representations similar to those caused by external sensory input but that are not caused by external sensory input.
These internal representations are caused not by external events but
by events that take place inside the neural network, that is, by other
units of the neural network. They are self-generated. Mental life is
the self-generation of internal representations.

If an internal representation is self-generated inside a neural network, what happens to the input that arrives from the external environment? Because of the connections linking the sensory units to the
internal units the external input will tend to cause its own internal
representation. So the question is: Which internal representation is
further processed by the neural network and controls the organism's

behaviour? The self-generated internal representation or the internal representation which is caused by the external input? In some circumstances the problem is solved because there is no input from the external environment. This happens when one is sleeping and mental life is manifested as dreams. But when the organism is awake input is always arriving from the external environment. Therefore, we hypothesize that what causes the self-generated internal representation also inhibits the further processing of the input from the external environment (Figure 2).

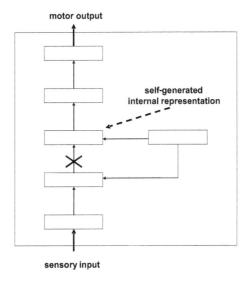

Figure 2. The neural network of a robot with mental life. The units that produce the self-generated internal representation also inhibit the further processing of the input from the external environment.

In the next sections we will discuss how this general model can be applied to some of the manifestations of mental life. We will also try to indicate why it might be advantageous for an organism to have a mental life. We assume that mental life is an adaptation. Organisms that have mental life tend to be more adapted, i.e., to have greater survival and reproductive chances, than organisms without mental life. This should not imply pan-adaptivism, however. Many potentially adaptive traits of organisms only evolve because the organisms are pre-adapted to them, and would not evolve otherwise; other traits are adaptively neutral but they evolve simply because they accompany adaptive traits; still other traits may evolve for purely chance reasons (Gould, 2002). However, for heuristic purposes it may still be useful to ask what are the adaptive function(s) of specific traits.

## 2. Manifestations of Mental Life

*2.1 Awareness*

A purely reactive robot responds to the sensory input from the external environment but is not aware of this input. Awareness in one of the manifestations of mental life. What is awareness? Awareness is the re-creation of an internal representation. Internal representations are fleeting events. They exist for a very short time and are quickly replaced by new internal representations caused by new inputs or by internal processes. Awareness is the re-creation of an existing internal representation and the simultaneous inhibition of other internal representations which would otherwise replace the existing internal representation (Figure 3). An organism can re-create not only internal representations caused by external inputs but also self-generated internal representations. Notice that an organism is not necessarily aware of its self-generated internal representations. To be aware of any internal representation, either caused by an external input or self-generated, the internal representation must be continuously re-created for some length of time.

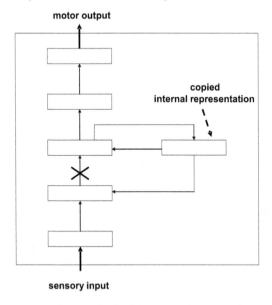

**Figure 3.** A neural network which is aware of its internal representations. Sensory input causes an internal representation which is copied and re-created while other internal representations are inhibited.

What good is for an organism to be aware of something? What a robot which is capable of re-creating its internal representations can do that a robot without this capacity cannot do? Awareness may play a role similar to selective attention. Organisms live in environments which at any given time send to their sensory organs a multitude of different inputs and each of these inputs would require a different response. For both physical and neural reasons in most cases the organism can respond to only one of these inputs at a time. This requires a mechanism for inhibiting all the inputs except the single input to which the organism will respond. This mechanism is selective attention.

Motivational states function as selective attention mechanisms. Imagine a robot which lives in an environment with both food and water. At any given time the robot's sensors encode both the location of the nearest food and the location of the nearest water. However, since food and water tend to be in different locations, the robot can either approach food or approach water but not both at the same time. To survive and reproduce the robot needs to both eat and drink. The problem is solved by including in the robot's neural network an additional set of units, called motivational units, which can encode one of two activation patterns: hunger and thirst. Which activation state in encoded at any given time is determined by the robot's current bodily state, which in turn depends on how much food and how much water the robot has ingested recently. The motivational units send their connections to the network's internal units and, by influencing the network's internal representations, they determine how the neural network responds to the input. Using a genetic algorithm it is possible evolve the connection weights of neural networks that exhibit the following behaviour: when the activation pattern in the motivational units is hunger, the robot ignores water and responds to food by approaching and eating food; when the activation pattern in the motivational units is thirst, the robot ignores food and approaches and drinks water (Cecconi and Parisi, 1993).

Awareness can be interpreted as an internal selective attention mechanism. By continually re-creating an internal representation and at the same time inhibiting all other internal representations that might displace the initial internal representation, awareness may enable an organism to continue to respond to the initial internal representation. This may be useful if the internal representation has to be more thoroughly analyzed and the response to the internal repre-

sentation requires time, or if one has to respond to the internal representation by self-generating other internal representations, and in
other ways.

## 2.2 Mental images, recollections, inventions, dreams, hallucinations

A mental image is the most typical phenomenon of mental life. A
mental image is an internal representation which is self-generated
inside a neural network, instead of being produced by some sensory
input from the external environment. The organism 'sees' or 'hears'
or 'feels' something but the inputs from the external environment or
from its own body that normally cause the seeing, the hearing, or the
feeling, are absent.

Mental images can be caused by a variety of processes. They can
be spontaneous, that is, without a recognizable cause, or they may be
caused by some well identified external input as, for example, when
I ask you to imagine Rome's Coliseum. They can be recognized as
having been experienced in a more or less well identified past, and in
this case they are rememberings or recollections. They can be created
by putting together in novel ways different parts of past internal representations, and in this case they are imaginations or inventions.
They can occur when one is asleep, and these are dreams, or when
one is awake, and they may be confused with reality, and these are
hallucinations.

Mental images can be useful in a variety of ways. This appears to
be obvious for recollections and inventions. But mental images may
also be useful, for example, as search images, that is, as prototypes to
be used when one is looking for an exemplar of the prototype. Even
reactive organisms are able to look for specific entities such as food
or a mate, adopting various strategies that increase the likelihood
that they will find food or mates. But explicitly knowing what one is
looking for can make the search behaviour more effective, where
explicitly knowing what one is looking for is to have a mental image
of what one is looking for. For example, using search images one can
look for something with very specific properties, or one can more
rapidly shift from looking for A to looking for B. Given the mental
image, what one is looking for is found when some entity in the environment matches the mental image. This presupposes an ability to
decide when two internal representations — the self-generated internal representation and the internal representation caused by the
external input — are the same or different, an ability which appears
to be more developed in humans or, more generally, in primates,

than in other animals. It is an interesting hypothesis that the ability to know when two internal representations are the same or different may have developed because it is an ability which is useful when one is looking for things on the basis of a mental image of what one is looking for.

## 2.3 Predictions

Predictions are self-generated internal representations that match the internal representation that will be caused by some future input from the external environment. The predictions that are of more interest here are predictions of future internal representations which depend on what the organism does, for example predicting that a glass will break if I let it fall on the ground or predicting the sound that I will hear when I will execute a planned movement of my phono-articulatory organs (Figure 4).

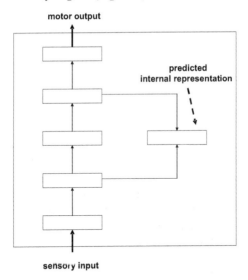

**Figure 4.** A neural network that predicts the internal representation that will result from the current internal representation and the physical execution of a planned movement in response to the current internal representation.

Learning to predict can be simulated using the backpropagation procedure. The self-generated internal representation, i.e., the prediction, is compared with the internal representation which is produced by the next sensory input from the environment when it will arrive, and the discrepancy between the two (error) is used to change the network's connection weights in such a way that, after a certain number of learning trials, the error goes to zero. The organism has learned to correctly predict its future internal representations.

What can an organism that can predict do that an organism unable to predict cannot do? As suggested by Clark and Grush (1999; see also Grush, 2004), being able to predict the next proprioceptive input from one's moving body can be important to move smoothly because the predicted input can be generated before the arrival of the actual input and one can respond to the predicted rather than to actual proprioceptive input. (For neural network models of this type of predictions, cf. Kawato, Furukawa and Suzuki, 1987; Wolpert and Ghahramani, 2004.) But being able to predict is a typical ability of humans, which underlies much of what makes human cognition different from the cognition of non-human animals. For example, predictions can replace missing inputs. Imagine a robot that has to reach a target by displacing itself in the environment. The robot receives sensory input from the target and it uses this information to approach the target. This is something that even a purely reactive robot can do. But imagine that while the robot is moving towards the target, an obstacle prevents the input from the target to reach the robot's sensors. A purely reactive robot would be helpless in these circumstances. Its behaviour would be completely, although temporarily, disrupted by the obstacle. In contrast, a predicting robot would continuously generate a correct prediction of the internal representation that will be caused by the next sensory input from the target. When, because of the obstacle, the sensory input from the target fails to arrive, the sudden discrepancy between the predicted internal representation (from the target) and the actual internal representation (from the obstacle) signals to the robot's neural network that something is wrong. The self-generated (predicted) internal representation inhibits the actual internal representation (from the obstacle), and the neural network responds to the predicted rather than to the actual internal representation, with no disruption. Using a combination of genetic and backpropagation algorithms, it is possible to develop the appropriate connection weights for neural networks that, in addition to the basic sensory-motor module, possess separate modules for (a) generating predicted internal representations, (b) judging whether the actual internal representation (which can be caused by either the target or an obstacle) matches or does not match the predicted internal representation, and (c) using this judgment to respond either to the actual internal representation (match) or to the predicted internal representation (mismatch). In environments containing obstacles robots controlled by these more complex neural networks exhibit significantly more efficient behaviour than simple reactive robots (Caligiore, Tria and Parisi, 2006).

Another way in which being able to make predictions can make behaviour more effective is the following. Imagine a robot which uses its arm to throw a stone in order to hit a prey. Stone can be of different weights and prey can be at different distances. The neural network underlying the robot's behaviour has input units encoding the weight of the current stone and the distance of the current prey, and output units encoding the force with which the stone is thrown by the robot's arm. The robot learns to predict if, given the current stone and the current distance of the prey, the force of the planned throwing action will allow the stone to actually hit the prey. If the prediction is Yes, the planned throwing action is physically executed. If it is No, the planned throwing action is not executed. This allows the robot to spare its energy by avoiding unsuccessful throwing actions. It is possible to evolve neural networks which, in addition to the sensory-motor module, include (a) one module for predicting if a planned throw will be a success or a failure, and (b) another module that uses this prediction to inhibit the throwing action if the action is a predicted failure. Since the physical act of throwing a stone consumes energy, robots with this more complex neural network are more energy-efficient than simpler robots with only a sensory-motor neural network (Caligiore, Tria and Parisi, 2006).

Being able to predict the internal representations that will be caused by future inputs can also be useful in order to learn by imitating other robots. Being able to predict can be a necessary pre-condition for learning by imitating others or at least a condition that results in more sophisticated imitation. One learns by imitating another individual because one compares the predicted effects of one's actions with the observed effects of the actions of the other individual, and uses the resulting discrepancy to modify the connection weights that cause the production of one's actions (Jordan and Rumelhart, 1992). This also can be simulated using the backpropagation procedure. After a certain number of learning trials the robot will be able to produce the same effects that are produced by the behaviour of another robot, and therefore, presumably, the same behaviour of the other robot.

The ability to predict may underlie another important ability, the ability to use and to construct technological artefacts. The use of artefacts presupposes the ability to predict what are the effects on the environment of one's actions when these actions are mediated by the artefact, while the construction of artefacts may require an ability to predict the effects of one's actions on, say, the shape of the artefact (e.g., in constructing a stone artefact).

The interest of this hypothesis that postulates the centrality of predicting for replacing missing inputs, for evaluating one's actions before actually executing them, for imitating others, and for using and constructing artefacts, is that all these behaviours and abilities are typically human. It is only necessary to assume that the tendency to learn to predict the consequences of one's actions is part of the human species-specific genotype in order to explain why humans are different from other animals in all these respects. It is probably the emergence of the human hands — a consequence of bipedalism — that has represented a critical adaptive pressure for developing an ability to predict the consequences of one's actions. Non-human animals have an extremely limited behavioural repertoire and they can produce a very small number of different effects in the environment with their actions. For them being able to predict the different consequences of their different actions is less important than for humans, who with their hands can cause an enormous variety of direct and indirect effects in the environment and therefore find it very useful to be able to predict these effects in order to choose what to do. (One should distinguish between predicting the specific consequences of one's actions — an ability which appears to be particularly developed in humans — with predicting the positive or negative reward value of future events, which may underlie much or all of animal learning.)

Another application of the prediction hypothesis is to explain some aspects of how human language is acquired by the child. Human language is learned from others and its development in the child goes through a well defined sequence of stages during the child's first year of life. In Stage 1 (first 3–4 months of life) the child produces all sorts of sounds so that he or she can learn to predict the acoustic consequences of his/her phono-articulatory movements. In Stage 2 (4–6 months) there is the emergence of babbling: the child is learning to imitate his/her own sounds (self-imitation). In Stage 3 (6–12 months) there is a tendency of the sounds produced by the child to resemble the sounds of the particular language spoken in the child's environment: the child is learning to imitate the sounds produced by others. In Stage 4 (from 1 year on) true language begins: the child is learning to produce the same sounds produced by another individual in the same circumstances, i.e., in response to the same objects and actions. The separate stages of this developmental process can be simulated (Floreano and Parisi, 1992) but the challenge of course is to evolve a developmental genotype that encodes the entire developmental sequence.

To give an account of language using the present framework is very important because language plays a crucial role in mental life, as we will see in the next Section.

### 2.4 Language and consciousness

A schematic neural network for a language-using robot is a network which includes two modules, which we will call sensory-motor module and linguistic module, respectively. The sensory-motor module maps all kinds of non-linguistic sensory inputs into the appropriate non-linguistic motor outputs. This is the module that allows the robot to reach for and manipulate objects with its

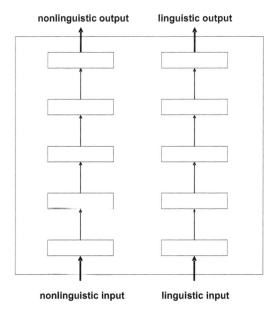

**Figure 5**. The sensory-motor module (left) and the linguistic module (right) remain separated from 0 to 12 months.

arms/hands, to displace itself in the environment, to move its head and eyes, etc. The other module is the linguistic module. The linguistic module also is a sensory-motor module but is a sensory-motor module which maps heard linguistic sounds into phono-articulatory movements that produce linguistic sounds. During the child's entire first year of life the two modules are either anatomically or functionally separated (Figure 5).

The child develops various sensory-motor abilities using its sensory-motor module and, as we have seen in the preceding section, learns to map heard sounds (either self-produced or produced by other individuals) into phono-articulatory movements that reproduce the same sounds using its linguistic module. At 1 year the two modules become connected and language proper begins. The child learns the appropriate connection weights for the connections linking the internal units of the sensory-motor module to the internal units of the linguistic module, and vice versa (Figure 6).

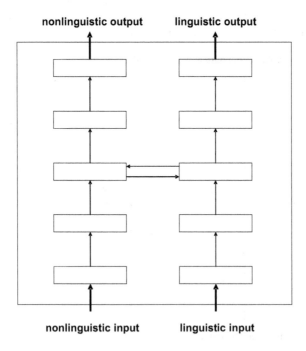

**Figure 6.** The sensory-motor module and the linguistic module become functionally connected at 1 year (beginning of true language).

Given the appropriate connection weights in the two directions, hearing a linguistic sound does not only evoke the internal representation of the sound in the linguistic module but this internal representation in turn evokes, in the sensory-motor module, the internal representation of the object or action which has been systematically paired, in the child's experience, with that sound. And the child responds with the appropriate action. This is language comprehension. Vice versa, seeing an object evokes the internal representation of the object in the sensory-motor module, which in turn may evoke in the linguistic module the internal representation of the linguistic sound systematically paired with that object. And the child may respond with the appropriate phono-articulatory movements. This is language production.

Given this model of language, language appears to be intrinsically linked with mental life. Of course, not all mental life is linguistic since mental images, recollections, and dreams can be purely visual or visuo-motor. However, unlike animal communications systems, human language appears to be based on the self-generation of internal representations: the self-generation of internal representations of objects or actions by the internal representation of sounds and the self-generation of internal representations of sounds by the internal representations of objects or actions. Furthermore, the two-way connections between the sensory-motor module and the linguistic module give rise to the recursive activation of one module by the other module, which is called thinking.

In section 3.1 we have discussed awareness but being aware of X should be distinguished from being conscious of X. (The use of the specific words 'awareness' and 'consciousness' to designate these two aspects of mental life is not important. What is important is to distinguish between the two aspects.) While being aware of X is a general capacity to re-generate internal representations and to block other internal representations, being conscious of X involves language. One is conscious of X if the internal representation of X evokes the internal representation of the linguistic sound which, in the robot's experience, is systematically experienced together with X.

To be (verbally) conscious of one's internal representations is crucial for higher level cognitive abilities such as reasoning and planning. For example, planning involves the serial prediction of the future consequences of one's actions. The organism predicts the consequences of a planned action and then, without physically executing the action, it predicts the consequences of another action in response to the predicted consequences of the first action, and so on for a certain number of actions and their consequences in succession. This is very difficult to do without being verbally conscious of one's actions and of their predicted consequences, that is, if one works directly with the internal representations of the actions and of their consequences. However, it becomes possible if one works with the self-generated linguistic descriptions of the actions and of their consequences. One reason is that the "space" of the linguistic module is smaller than the "space" of the sensory-motor module in the sense that there are fewer units and connections in the linguistic module than in the sensory-motor module. And it is very useful to be able to move in a smaller space rather than in a larger one if any activation pattern in the smaller space of sound representations can evoke the appropriate activation pattern in the larger space of sensory-motor representations (the meanings of those sounds).

An important property of the internal representations that are self-generated through language is their abstractness. We can define abstractness in neural terms in the following way. As already noted, different sensory inputs that are responded to with the same action tend to evoke similar internal representations, while similar sensory inputs that are responded to with different actions tend to evoke different internal representations. A pattern of activation of a set of units can be conceived as one point in the hyperspace corresponding to the set of units. This hyperspace has as many dimensions as the number of units in the set of units, and the point is positioned, in each dimension of the hyperspace, in a location that indicates the activation level of that particular unit. The internal representations evoked by sensory inputs that are responded to with the same action will form a cloud of points close to each other and distant from the points (internal representations) evoked by sensory inputs that are responded to with a different action. (Clouds of points can be interpreted as categories.) The internal representations that are self-generated through language are abstract in the sense that they tend to be points located centrally in a cloud of points. While specific objects and actions evoke different internal representations corresponding to specific points variously located in the appropriate cloud of points, if an organism experiences an object or an action together with the linguistic signal that designates them, or even more if it experiences the linguistic signal alone, the internal representation which is evoked in the sensory-motor module tends to be a point which is located centrally in the cloud of points and therefore abstracts from the specific properties of specific objects or actions (Mirolli and Parisi, 2005).

## 2.5 Self and self agency

The ability to predict the consequences of one's actions may underlie another important aspect of mental life: the sense of self and the sense of self agency. Robots have a body and live in a physical environment, and by interacting with both the robot's body and the external environment their neural network creates a world populated by various sorts of distinct entities. One of these entities is the organism's own body or, in more mental terms, the organism's self.

The self emerges from three processes. The first process is the recognition of one's body as a special component of the physical world. If the organism touches a physical object with its hand, its neural network will predict a tactile sensory input from its hand resulting from contact of the hand with the object. However, if the organism touches its own body, the neural network will predict both a tactile sensory input from the hand and another sensory input from the part of the body which has been touched by the hand. Furthermore, the neural network will predict the proprioceptive input resulting from the body's movements, a sensory input which cannot possibly arrive from the external environment. This is the first process that results in the emergence of the self.

The second process that causes the emergence of a sense of self from the neural network's interactions with both the body and the external environment concerns the self as agent. By being able to predict the consequences of its own actions the robot recognizes that some events happen for independent causes but other events happen because of its own actions. This has been shown in experiments in which participants press one of two buttons and the pressing of each button is regularly followed by one of two different sounds. Subsequently, the participants press one button and they are asked if they are the causes (authors) of the sound that follows. They say Yes if the appropriate (i.e., predicted) sound follows the two actions and with the normal time interval, but they say No if the wrong sound follows an action or there is some inappropriate temporal delay between action and sound (Sato and Yasuda, 2005). This seems to imply that human beings have a sense of being the causal agents of events if they have learned to predict these events as resulting from their actions.

The third process at the origin of a sense of self consists in becoming aware of the private character of one's mental life. A robot may notice that, given some internal representation (caused by input from the external environment), it is able to predict the behaviour of other robots, whereas given other internal representations (self-generated in its own nervous system) it is impossible to predict the behaviour of other robots. The first class of internal representations constitute the public, shared world of objects, whereas the second class of internal representations constitute the robot's private world, its self. (The private world also includes internal representations caused by input from within one's body. Cf. Parisi, 2004.)

### 3. Where are Self-Generated Internal Representations in the Real Brain?

Are the internal units that encode self-generated internal representations the same units that encode internal representations caused by sensory input? The answer to this question is not clear. Restricting our consideration to visual mental images, the model described in this chapter shares Kosslyn's position (Kosslyn, 1980; 1994) that visual mental images are like visual images caused by external visual input and are not symbolic or linguistic, as claimed by Pylyshyn (2002). However, while Kosslyn's research tends to support the view that the same neural substrate underlies both externally generated and self-generated visual images (Kosslyn, 2005), other researchers suggest that the internal units that encode self-generated visual internal representations (mental images) may include the secondary visual areas of the occipital cortex and areas in the parietal and frontal cortex, whereas the internal units that encode the internal representations caused by external sensory input include not only the above areas but also the retina and the primary visual cortex. Another type of evidence is that during REM sleep, when dreams are more common, the secondary but not the primary visual cortex appears to be active. Furthermore, in congenitally blind people, during dreaming, the secondary, but not the primary, visual cortex is active, and this might be explained by a recruitment of secondary, but not primary, visual cortex by motor function in congenitally blind people (Bertolo et al., 2003; Lopes da Silva, 2003).

## 4. Conclusions

Mental life includes a variety of different phenomena that we should be able to reproduce in robots if we want to construct human, not simply humanoid, robots. The phenomena of mental life are especially difficult to study because they are directly accessible to only one individual, and science is more at ease with phenomena that everyone can observe and measure. The reason why mental phenomena are private while behavioural phenomena are public is not mysterious. What causes mental internal representations in an individual's brain are events and processes inside the individual's brain which, for purely physical reasons, cannot cause similar internal representations in the brain of another individual. On the other hand, ordinary internal representations are ultimately caused by events and processes in the external environment which can cause more or less the same internal representations in the brain of many different individuals.

We have proposed a general neural model of mental life as the self-generation of internal representations in the neural network controlling a robot's behaviour. These self-generated internal representations are similar to the internal representations normally caused by external inputs but are generated in absence of external input, and they inhibit external input in order to take control of the robot's behaviour, including the repeated self-generation of a succession of internal representations. The self-generation of internal representations explains a number of phenomena of mental life, including awareness, mental images, rememberings, predictions, thoughts, dreams, and verbal consciousness. These are all different phenomena, caused by different processes and abilities, and one should not think that an organism which exhibits one of these phenomena will necessarily also exhibit all of them. Furthermore, self-generated internal representations can occur in different subsets of a neural network's internal units, for example in internal units nearer to the sensory interface or in internal units nearer to the motor interface with the external environment. However, it may be useful to explore the unifying hypothesis that a single basic process underlies all mental phenomena: the self-generation of internal representations. An important research task is to identify the adaptive advantages of each of these different manifestations of mental life and to construct neural network models that control the behaviour of robots exhibiting the different phenomena of mental life.

Let us conclude this chapter by indicating how mental robotics relates to other approaches in robotics and, more generally, cognitive science. Mental robotics is part of an approach to robotics that models the control system of robots using neural networks. Robots with mental life are robots whose neural network is able to self-generate its internal representations. Therefore, mental robotics is rather distant from other approaches to robotics that model the control system of robots using rules, symbols, or behaviours (behaviour-based robotics; cf. Arkin, 1998). On the other hand, mental robotics is also different from what Clark and Grush (1999) call cognitive robotics. Cognitive robotics is based on a notion of cognition that restricts cognition to higher level cognition, and more specifically to some of the phenomena which are part of mental life, that is, thinking and reasoning. In contrast to cognitive robotics, we believe that constructing robots to study the behaviour and mental life of organisms is especially useful because it does not isolate 'cognition' from organisms' more basic sensory-motor interactions with the physical environment. In our sense of internal representations, all neural networks, even those of purely reactive organisms, have internal representations since internal representations are activation patterns in some set of a neural network's internal units. The internal representations of mental life are identical to all other internal representations except that they are self-generated inside a neural networks and are not caused by external input. In any case, mental life, in our sense, includes much more than cognitive robotics' 'cognition': it includes awareness, as distinct from consciousness (cf. Section 4.1), dreams, hallucinations and, more generally, mental life phenomena that are outside rational control.

## References

Arkin, C. *Behavior-Based Robotics*. Cambridge, Mass., MIT Press, 1998.

Bertolo, H. et al (2003) Visual dream content, graphical representations, and EEG alpha activity in congenitally blind subjects. *Cognition and Brain Research*, 15, 277–284.

Caligiore, D., Tria, M. and Parisi, D. Adaptive advantages of the ability to make predictions. In Nolfi, S. et al (eds.) *From Animals to Animats 9*. New York, Springer, 2006.

Cecconi, F. and Parisi, D. Neural networks with motivational units In J.-A.Meyer, H.L. Roitblat, and S.W. Wilson (eds.), *From Animals to Animats 2: Proceedings of the 2nd International Conference on Simulation of Adaptive Behavior*. Cambridge, Mass., MIT Press, 1993, pp. 346–355.

Clark, A. and Grush, R. Towards a cognitive robotics. *Adaptive Behavior*, 1999, 7, 5–16.

Di Ferdinando, A. and Parisi, D. Internal representations of sensory input reflect the motor output with which organisms respond to the input. In A. Carsetti (ed.), *Seeing and Thinking*. New York, Kluwer, 2004.

Gould, S.J. *The Structure of Evolutionary Theory*. Cambridge, Mass., Belknap, 2002.

Grush, R. The emulation theory of representation: motor control, imagery, and perception. *Behavioral and Brain Science*, 2004, 27, 377–442.

Jordan, M.I. and Rumelhart, D.E. Forward models: supervised learning with a distal teacher. *Cognitive Science*, 1992, 16, 307–354.

Kawato, M. Furukawa, K., and Suzuki, R. A hierarchical neural network model for the control and learning of voluntary movements. *Biological Cybernetics*, 1987, 57, 169–185.

Kosslyn, S.M. *Image and Mind*. Cambridge, Mass., Harvard University Press, 1980.

Kosslyn, S.M. *Image and Brain: the Resolution of the Imagery Debate*. Cambridge, Mass., MIT Press, 1994.

Kosslyn, S.M. Mental images and the brain. *Cognitive Neuropsychology*, 2005, 22, 333–347.

Lopes Da Silva, F.H. Visual dreams in the congenitally blind. *Trends in Cognitive Science*, 2003, 7, 328–330.

Mirolli, M and Parisi, D. Language as an aid to categorization: A neural network model of early language acquisition. In A. Cangelosi, G. Bugmann, and R. Borisyuk (eds.) *Modelling Language, Cognition, and Action*. Singapore, World Scientific, 2005, pp. 97–106.

Parisi, D. *Internal robotics*. Connection Science, 2004.

Parisi, D. and Floreano, D. Prediction and imitation of linguistic sounds by neural networks. In A. Paoloni (ed.), *Proceedings of the 1st Workshop on Neural Networks and Speech Processing*. Rome, Fondazione Bordoni, 1992, pp. 50–61.

Pylyshyn, Z.N. Mental imagery: in search of a theory. *Behavioral and Brain Sciences*, 2002, 25, 157–238.

Sato, A. and Yasuda, A. Illusion of self-agency. Discrepancy between the predicted and the actual sensory consequences of actions modulates the sense of self-agency, but not the sense of self-ownership. *Cognition*, 2005, 94, 241–255.

Wolpert, D.M. and Ghahramani, Z. Computational motor control. In Gazzaniga, M.S. (ed.) *The Cognitive Neurosciences III*. Cambridge, Mass., MIT Press, 2004, 485–494.

Alberto Faro & Daniela Giordano

# An Account of Consciousness from the Quantum Field & Synergetics Theory Perspectives

The theory of synergetics developed by Haken (1983; 2004) which is at the core of the accounts of cognition based on dynamic systems, such as the ones proposed by Thelen (1998) and Kelso (1999), is an important step to explain flexible behaviors. According to this theory, different behaviors, or order states,[1] can be activated in a given context. The prevailing order state is determined by the values of the control variables,[2] or affordances in Gibson's terms (Gibson, 1979), in the current context and it is influenced by how many times the subject has experienced the current situation and on her/his perceptual characteristics. Synergetics seems more suitable to explain unconscious or weakly conscious processes (as these intervening in automated skills), since it does not deal with consciousness, i.e., it does not clarify how mind intervenes when the perceived context is different from the one assumed by the subject, and it is necessary to modify/adapt the affordances and related control variables in place.

[1]  An order state is a sequence of actions in which the subject has more or less the same goal and motive, as for example shopping, having a breakfast, driving and so on.
[2]  The control variables are the variables that allow the order states to evolve correctly.

In order to explain *consciousness* intended as the process of observing ourselves to adapt,[3] mainly by learning, to the environment, the authors have put forward the hypothesis that the brain is founded on two cognitive spaces (Faro & Giordano, 2004):

- the activity space (called Wn space) consisting of all the activity patterns organized within a narrative framework, i.e., the Story Telling Theory (STT) proposed by the authors in (Faro & Giordano 1996).

- the ontological space (called On space) consisting of all the ontologies emerging from the classes obtained by classifying the Wn patterns on the basis of their similarities (Faro & Giordano 1998).

The activity space is enough to explain how the mind manages unconscious or weakly conscious processes. This can be obtained by a suitable monitoring of the conditions that may cause the activity patterns to go wrong. In (Faro & Giordano, 2004), the authors have shown that the activity patterns expressed in STT terms are equivalent to the order states governed by the synergetics theory and have demonstrated also that both STT and synergetics theory may be useful for the analysis of unconscious or weakly conscious processes depending on if the study is done within a narrative semi-formal framework or needs a formal mathematical support.

In Faro & Giordano (1998; 2004) the authors have clearly advanced the hypothesis that learning/creativity featuring consciousness in the above sense cannot be explained by the only above activity space, but that this needs the joint working of the two mentioned cognitive spaces. In particular, the authors suggested that the problem at hand, the external representations, verbal descriptions and the value system in place address the attention of a subject towards some area of the $O^n$ space containing $W^n$ patterns that have some analogy with the present situation (e.g., goal, motives, actors or objects involved). A new pattern is created *consciously*, perhaps genetically by cross-over and mutation of the relevant existing patterns. Cross-over may take into account either the feature bundle or the prototype of the classes to which the relevant patterns belong to (i.e., knowledge schema). Consciousness is explicated also in the process of restructuring the classification space (framing and reframing) to facilitate the creation of new patterns. This theory of

---

[3]  By 'adapting' we intend the process of restructuring ourselves and the environment.

consciousness dealing with the subject ability of consciously creating activity patterns for adapting to external conditions, has been called by the authors Framing and Reframing Theory (FRT) in honor of the 'frame theory' (Goffman, 1974) which has highly influenced their work.

A weakness of FRT is the absence of a biological/physical basis of the assumed activity patterns organization in the brain. Namely, as Edelman puts it (1992): 'the effort of many works from linguistics (e.g., Lakoff, Langacker) philosophy (e.g., Putnam) and psychology (e.g., Rosh, Barsalou) are important, but without biology they remain insufficient ... We must incorporate biology into our theory of knowledge and language'. Therefore, relevant FRT open problems are: where and how the brain memorizes the behavior patterns of the activity $W^n$ space?, where and how the brain memorizes the behavior patterns classification of the activity On space?, where and how the mentioned activity pattern and ontological spaces interact to sustain both the conscious processes involved in the creative and adaptive behaviors and the unconscious processes featuring the behavior of skilled people?

The paper aims at answering to these problems by extending the quantum brain model (QBM) proposed by Ricciardi and Umezawa (1967) within the Quantum Field Theory (QFT), enriched by the hypothesis elaborated by Vitiello (1995; 2001) who depicts the brain as a dissipative quantum system (DQBM) to avoid memory overprinting. The proposed extension consists in further empowering the quantum model of the brain by adding a control mechanism based on FRT that is more powerful than the one assumed by the QBM, by which the mind gets the most relevant memory patterns for supporting problem solving activities depending on the task at hand. This brain model, denoted in the following as FMQB (Framing Model of the Quantum Brain), is presented in section 2 where its biophysical structure is tentatively proposed. In particular, section 2 first gives some hints about STT and FRT, then it illustrates how consciousness is explicated in learning and creativity within the FMQB framework. Section 3 claims that the Synergetics Brain Model (SBM) is a form of simplified version of FMQB. SBM may become very useful to structure an environment able to support human behaviors on the basis of few control variables. Moreover, in this section a methodology is outlined to identify the synergetics control variables starting from FMQB depending on the task at hand. In section 4 we further extend FMQB to try to escape the holistic degeneration of

QBM, DQBM and FMQB too that depict humans as monads which view other humans like a part of their environment immersed in a different world. To this aim a distributed version of FMQB is proposed that gives importance to the social experience and to our attitude to support social rituals and culture at least for creating the illusion that people share the same world, being this necessary to jointly perform tasks and problem solving.

## 2. FRT and Quantum Brain Model

### 2.1. Generalities of Story Telling and Framing and Reframing Theories (STT and FRT)

Regardless of how objects are represented by or in the brain (starting from or in cooperation with external signals, drawings or sketches), the key problem is how we make sense of them. Recognizing objects, actions and properties (in the following called objects for simplicity) usually refers to our ability of seeing and understanding, by our perceptual-processing machinery, stable psychological units, e.g., the basic level concepts introduced in Lakoff (1987): as dogs and cats, running and eating, hot and cold, black and white and so on. The reason is that these units appear as a whole in the physical experience that functions as a basic framing for them. However, if our understanding remained at this level, it would have little sense for action, e.g., it would be useful for avoiding stumbling on a dog but not for avoiding undesirable dog reactions. In order to give a more comprehensive meaning to objects and actions we agree with Goffman that identification of the scenario that suitably frames the current situation is needed, since framing reality is the main mechanism to give meaning to objects.

Now the main problem is to identify these scenarios. To solve this problem we recall the Story Telling Theory (STT), introduced by the authors in Faro & Giordano (1996), that proposes a narrative framing of the human activities by means of a partial ordering of episodes. An episode consists of a sequence of actions from the point of view of the episode character; usually it develops according to the Source-Path-Goal cognitive model we learned from our bodily experience (Lakoff, 1987). Considering together the episodes that allow one of the characters involved to reach her/his goal (or some termination condition) we obtain a new narrative framing called story. Here, both episodes and stories are called 'scenes' and are defined by dimensions such as:

- what (goal or the condition that causes the scene to eventually terminate),
- why (motivation),
- who (characters),
- when/where (localization in time and space),
- how (activity consisting of concurrent sequences of actions performed by the scene characters),
- what can go wrong (obstacles),
- exception handling (recovering activity).

The main contribution of STT is the one of proposing a framing in space and time of the human activity according to a narrative scheme that, as Bruner suggests (Bruner,1991), is likely a constitutive principle of the human mind. Also, the STT memory trajectories generalize the ones proposed by Thelen, since these latter develop on only the What-Where ($W^2$) plane, whereas the former ones, i.e., the *STT patterns* expressed in terms of episodes and stories, develop in an activity space called $W^n$ since it is characterized by the mentioned several categories.

Other important results of STT are as follows:

- the possibility of framing reality by using few categories suggests to us that the mind has an active role in selecting only some of the available inputs to sustain the current activity. The importance of this point is illustrated in section 3;

- the presence of a category i.e., what can go wrong, related to the activity breakdown is very useful to identify the control variables that may allow us to conclude the episode successfully or with a minimal goal degradation. The importance of this point is illustrated in section 4 devoted to how support humans to best control their activity within the synergetics framework.

- STT is at the basis of the situated action calculus (Faro & Giordano, 1997) that aims at minimizing action breakdowns by supporting us in finding the better action to be performed at a certain instant for a given scene although the scene will be completely known only after the action has been done.

STT was widely used by the authors to memorize design specifications in a manner that was assumed to be close to how the human mind stores the information to facilitate design understanding in a community of young designers. To support creativity of the designers the STT has been powered by a classification mechanism of the design specifications so that the designers may easily retrieve and reuse previous specifications relevant for the problem at hand. To demonstrate the compatibility of this reusing mechanism with the cognitive nature of the mind, the authors have developed the Framing and Reframing Theory (FRT).

FRT assumes that activity patterns (e.g., activity episodes, design specifications, and so on) are classified by an unsupervised mechanism in an n-dimensional setting, called ontological space $O^n$. This classification should reflect the regularities existing among patterns. In Faro & Giordano (1998), the authors have shown that a powerful way for identifying these regularities is to use the influence links existing between the patterns, where a link is a measure of something shared by the patterns, e.g., a measure of their similarity or better a measure of how much the subject evaluates that a pattern has been influenced during the creation process by other already existing patterns. A pattern may belong to different classes. Moreover, being possible to increase and decrease the strength of the inter-pattern links, it is possible to reframe the original space On thus obtaining a reclassification based on the modified links that may let new classes to emerge. The use of a design environment endowed by STT and FRT has been shown to improve the quality of the artifacts produced by a community of designers.

## 2.2. STT/FRT biophysical structure inspired by QBM

QBM has the alleged merit of having envisaged a memory structure implemented by a quantum field characterized by the non locality features requested by the modern neurological findings. But where is the memory in the brain?

Three networks exist in the brain, i.e., the neural network, the dendrite network and the protein network, that could be candidates for implementing QBM. As claimed by Jibu and Yasue (1995; 2004), neural networks seem more suitable for interfacing stimulus signals with the other parts of the body (i.e., other brain networks, sense organs and so on).[4] Jibu and Yasue show also that, although the collective behaviors of the dendrites and of the filamentous strings of proteins at microscopic level may be assumed to be controlled by a

---

[4]   Modern studies, e.g., Takahashi and Jibu (2004), are reconsidering the possibility that the quantum memory may be implemented by neural networks as pointed out in the following of this section.

quantum macroscopic wave, also such networks seem more suitable to transfer impulses (e.g., the ones received from the neuronal structure) to another global structure able to store this information: they behave as Josephson bio-junctions, i.e., as a superconducting electric medium, that integrates the impulses coming from the neurons into a quantum wave whose energy quanta are transferred without loss to the quantum memory.

Considering that the three brain networks do not seem suitable to host the quantum memory, Jibu and Yasue (1995; 2004) claimed that more likely the structure envisaged by QBM is given by the water that is around the neurons, the dendrites and the protein strings. In particular it is given by the states of minimum energy of the quantum field that controls the dipoles of the myriads of water molecules contained in the brain. Such field, called cortical field by Umezawa, operates over water domains of about 50 microns. Let us note that in the quantum field theory the coherence length of a field, i.e., its size, is inversely proportional to the difference between the lowest energy level and the first excited state: the size of 50 microns is obtained by computing such difference for the water dipoles. In the domains where the cortical field is at its energy minimum (also called vacuum state) all the dipoles have the same orientation. Thus we have infinite vacua for each water domain and infinite domains that may be used to store the sensorial inputs into a stable brain coding system as shown in figure 1).

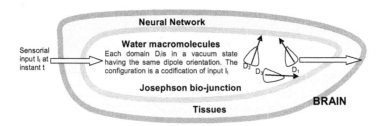

**Figure 1:** A set of vacuum states (vacua) codifying a sensorial input by water macromolecules domains according to the Jibu and Yasue assumptions.

The main shortcomings of QBM are:

- the problem of memory overprinting. Indeed, when a new input arrives, the brain passes from a set of vacuum states to another set of vacuum states. The new vacuum states depend on the received input and on the previous ones, but these latter are no more accessible.
- the lack of an accurate model of the brain-environment interactions. Indeed, the model assumes that the sensorial inputs are transferred as energy quanta to the cortical field, but it is not clear how accurately these quanta may represent the input. Moreover, the action of these energy quanta is the one of producing a photon beam that excites the cortical field, thus giving rise to excited corticons. The energy decay of such corticons towards the lowest energy level determines, on its turn, the passage of each water domain from a vacuum to another vacuum state and the emission of photons that may excite the corticons of other domains or may go through the Josephson bio-junction from the memory to the neural tissues. Does the 'learned' reaction-adaptation to the environment encoded in this new state include the modifications produced on the neural tissues by this latter photon beam? Does the former photon beam encode the sensorial input?

The dissipative quantum brain model (DQBM) proposed in Vitiello (1995) has the merit of giving a first convincing response to these problems. This has been obtained by modeling the brain-environment as a quantum closed system consisting of two coupled subsystems both residing in the quantum memory: one, let say A~ (to be pronounced as A tilde), represents the codification of the received environment stimuli, whereas the other, let say A, represents the codification of the information perceived by the self in correspondence to these stimuli, i.e., A~ 'acts as the address of the information to be recalled' which is coded on A. Let us note that in DQBM, the memory is not necessarily implemented in the brain water. Indeed, a neural implementation of the memory is being investigated (e.g., Takahashi and Jibu, 2004): it arises from considering the neurons as spinors. In such embodiment of QBM, the input is not stored by water macromolecules characterized by coherent dipole directions, but by suitable configurations of neuron regions characterized by the spin variable aligned.

According to DBQM, any sensorial input activates a vacuum state A~ in the brain consisting of a set of N~ domains of water dipoles having certain directions. Such vacuum state on its turn activates a double vacuum state A, consisting of a set of N domains of water dipoles having the same directions of the state A~, and being N = N~. By the coupling between A and A~, DQBM models how a subject feels the presence of the environmental stimuli. In DQBM 'a huge number of sequentially recorded information data may coexist without destructive interference'; the overprinting problem is then solved 'since infinitely many vacua are independently accessible in the sequential recording process'.

Although DQBM has the merit of having solved the memory over-printing problem and having proposed an elegant picture of the brain-environment interactions, some problems remain still open such as the following ones:

- it is not completely clear the role, if any, of the subject in selecting the inputs or her/his modifications to accommodate the current situation.

- it is not clear how the subject behaves in presence of an input that does not trigger any experience useful for managing the current situation, i.e., pattern learning is not considered in DBQM.

Concerning the first point, we observe that subjects are not contained in a surrounding environment, rather they are situated in contexts (Faro & Giordano, 1997). As a consequence, we interpret the coupling between A~ and A as the result of a tuning process in which the inputs received by the subject are structured and restructured according to her/his current order state until when the only inputs relevant for the subject order state are extracted from the overall input signal and, possibly, her/his order state is slightly changed to accommodate the so restructured input. However, this is not enough. In fact, the input selection at a certain instant does not depend only on the current 'photogram' (i.e., the available input at a given instant) but also on some other previous or subsequent ones as deeply discussed in Faro & Giordano (1997). For this reason, we advance the hypothesis of the existence of a vibrational variable that gives rise to a quantum field able to codify the context that may influence each photogram. Differently to the cortical quantum field and related corticons that bring together in space the inputs belonging to a photogram, we advance the hypothesis of an ordering quantum field and related *orderons* that bring together in time the photograms belonging to some meaningful context. In narrative terms, relevant contexts are: episodes and stories.

This allows us also to advance an hypothesis about the biophysical structure of the mentioned activity $W^n$ space. In fact, by the hypothesized orderon particles it is possible to fix together the photograms of any activity $W^n$ trajectory: each trajectory being framed by an ordering field and coded by a set of domains. Therefore, the first of the hypotheses advanced about the brain structure in Faro & Giordano (2004) has to be conveniently rephrased as follows:

*Hypothesis I*: the mind supports activity by using a set of cooperating neural networks or water macromolecules subjected to two quantum vibrational fields (i.e., the mentioned cortical and ordering fields) that allow the subjects to execute the steps of a procedure represented by a trajectory in the $W^n$ space depending on the steps previously performed and on the planned ones. To decrease the load of remembering these trajectories, the mind makes wide use of order state and control variables (this will be widely discussed in the next section within the Synergetics framework).

The tuning process by which self and environment are coupled is a first level of consciousness since it requests only few adjustments to give rise to a photogram by accommodating the slight difference between A and A~, i.e., between how the self is assuming to be situated in a given photogram and how the self sees itself behaving in the same photogram looking at itself in the mirror A~. More generally a multitude of mirrors are available for the self, perhaps 100,000 mirrors following Pirandello's suggestion (Pirandello, 1926), depending on how various relevant scenes S, i.e., episodes or stories, may influence the self.

However, if there is a great difference between A and A~ or S and S~, especially if the input is not able to recall any suitable memory photogram or scene, then a conscious learning activity has to be activated to find the photogram or the scene compatible with the input and the self. For example this happens if the subject is interpreting a complex painting, or she/he would like to play tennis and the environment does not support this request, or if the environment is provided with a swimming pool and the subject does know how to swim. A way to solve this problem is to reuse similar examples gained by her/his own experience or created by conventions, theories, and so on. These considerations do not change the second hypothesis about the brain structure the with respect to one advanced in Faro & Giordano (2004). Thus such hypothesis remains unchanged as follows:

*Hypothesis II*: the mind is founded on two spaces: the activity space ($W^n$ space) consisting of all the activity patterns coded in mind and the ontological space ($O^n$ space) consisting of all the ontologies emerging from the classes obtained by suitably classifying these patterns (episodes, stories in STT terms). The scenes of each class are similar between them and can be reused to find the right actions for the right scene..

In principle, the classification of similar scenes could be obtained by i) a suitable coding system as suggested by Pessa and Vitiello (2004), or ii) hypothesizing another quantum field devoted to this aim analogously to the one assumed for fixing together the photograms of a scene, or iii) assuming the existence of some unsupervised neural classifiers as suggested in Faro & Giordano (2004).

The coding system should be organized by storing similar scenes by close trajectories in the brain in such a way that spreading activation may activate a set of similar trajectories. For the existence of a clustering quantum filed, it is necessary to assume the existence of another vibrational symmetry governed by the Schrödinger equation. Due to the limited size of the quantum fields, also in this case similar scenes should be stored in a way that each scene is spatially close to the similar ones. The biological motivation for the existence of unsupervised neural classifiers in the brain has been widely discussed in literature especially after Kohonen has proposed his celebrated SOM algorithm (Kohonen, 1995). Also in this case, similar things should occupy close areas in the brain.

From the above analysis it is easy to understand that to have a classification in an n-dimensional setting the scenes should be stored as domains dispersed on the brain in such a way that they may belong to different classes, and classes should occupy various regions of the brain in order to allow that classes stored on close regions refer to similar classes. To allow the brain to classify the patterns in different ways (e.g., at least according to one of the three possibilities mentioned), the hypothesis III of Faro & Giordano (2004) is reformulated as follows:

*Hypothesis III*: the mind classifies the activity patterns by a group of neural networks according to the regularities possessed by the input (i.e., A~ or S~ in DQBM terms). This can be obtained by a neural network that has the influence matrix I (whose general element Irs represents how much a pattern r has been influenced by pattern s) as input, and an unsupervised classification of the patterns into some classes as output obtained by a Kohonen-like algorithm (Faro & Giordano, 1998). Other classification mechanisms could be adopted by the brain. For example a classification based on a clustering quantum field could be suitable if the classification has to obey also to the subject volition, whereas a classification based on energy functionals governing the memory trajectories in such a way that similar trajectories are stored in close brain locations does seem viable because it could become very complex at the increasing of the classes and of the scenes.

Let us note that the neural classification obtainable by using the influence links between the patterns and the one based on the input regularities are considered more or less as synonyms. In fact, two patterns, let say $P_1$ and $P_2$, should occupy the same position in the ontological space if they are fully interchangeable, i.e., if $S_1\sim$ is very similar to $S_2\sim$. On the other hand, because of their fully interchangeability the influence link between them should have the maximum value, i.e., $I_{12} = 1$. Roughly, we can say that less the influence link, greater the difference between $S_1\sim$ and $S_2\sim$, thus $I_{12} = 0$ means that $S_1\sim$ completely differs from $S_2\sim$.

The existence of the above neural classifier supports the possibility that $A\sim$ or $S\sim$ should be preprocessed by a suitable neural (or coding or quantum) system in such a way of activating respectively the probes $A_1\sim$, $A_2\sim$, . . . , $A_n\sim$ to recall similar photograms $A_1A_1\sim$, $A_2A_2\sim$,... $A_nA_n\sim$ in case one would like to interpret a photogram, or the probes $S_1\sim$, $S_2\sim$,... $S_n\sim$ to recall similar scenes $S_1S_1\sim$, $S_2S_2\sim$,... $S_nS_n\sim$ in case one would like to interpret/implement an episode or a story. This is expressed by the following hypothesis IV–a that remains practically unchanged with respect to the one proposed in Faro & Giordano (2004):

*Hypothesis IV-a*: the problem at hand and some external representation (e.g, formula or sketching) address the attention towards some area of the On space containing patterns that have some analogy with the present situation (e.g., goal, motives, actors or objects involved).

This hypothesis is illustrated in figure 2 where the neural classifier addresses the input towards a region suitable for it. The nodes shown in figure 2 do not exist in the reality: they represent the existence of scenes $SS\sim$ the subject has already experimented in the past. Such scenes may be activated (thus becoming available for the subject) by sending to the quantum level the set of signals pertaining to the overall addressed region including the signals $S\sim$ related to the known scenes. Let us note that it seems natural to think that the size of this region will be increased gradually until the signals injected to the quantum level give rise to some positive coupling corresponding to existence of some known scene. It is important to point out that this implies that subjects are able to recognize that they do not have the experience relevant for managing the current situation, i.e., one of the hallmarks of consciousness is that subjects are able to know of not knowing.

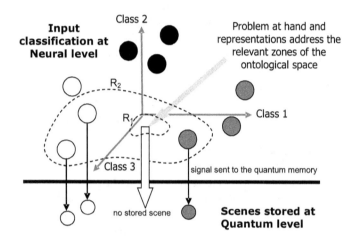

**Figure 2**: Regions of the input classification space addressed by the problem at hand. The addressed region may increase, e.g., from $R_1$ to $R_2$, if the signals sent to the quantum level does not recall any known scene.

After this activation phase, the subject is able to manage the unknown input by reusing known similar scenes, i.e., the ones activated by the previous hypothesis. Reuse implies to mix a part, possibly adjusted, of one scene with the parts, possibly adjusted too, of the others. This is expressed by the following hypothesis IV–b of Faro & Giordano (2004):

*Hypothesis IV–b*: A new pattern is created consciously, perhaps genetically by cross-over and mutation of the relevant existing patterns. Cross-over may take into account either the feature bundle or the prototype of the classes to which the relevant patterns belong to (i.e., knowledge schema). Some new orderons are created from this genetic process so that the new pattern is stored autonomously in the brain, whereas the input corresponding to the new pattern will be automatically classified as assumed by the above hypothesis III.

Fig. 3 illustrates the process of generating a newborn scene. As an example the creation of a new scene is stored at quantum level by reusing actions coming from three of the four scenes belonging to the region activated by the input. The codification of the state of the ordering quantum field fixing the photograms of the newborn scene has to be such of guaranteeing the coupling with the original input, possibly slightly modified, related to the initially unknown scene. Let us note that since reusing does not take into account the scenes in an homogeneous way, neither the available scenes are homogenously distributed over the region, the newborn scene may correspond to an input slightly different, let say $S\sim_{tf}$, from the original one, let say $S\sim_{ti}$. In such cases we say that the input have been restructured by the subject.

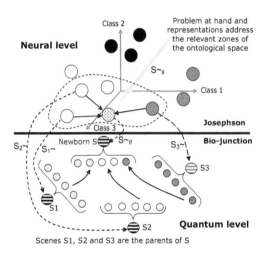

Figure 3: Creation of a new scene S within the FMQB framework

Moreover, it is useful to point out that in figure 3 we assume that the quantum memory is implemented by the collective behavior of the electric dipoles of the water macromolecules surrounding neurons and dendrites. Therefore the signals from the self organizing neural maps and the quantum memory have to go through the Josephson bio-junction. If this is not the case, i.e., if the neural level

*Artificial Consciousness*

does not behave as an interface between stimuli and other parts of the body, but as a myriads of spinors governed by the Schrödinger equation, then also the quantum memory could be implemented by collective behaviors at neural level and the signals from the neural classifiers to the neural memory are internal to the neural sphere. In this case the role of the Josephson bio-junction and of the water in the brain is for further study.

### 3. Controlling Activity by Synergetic Affordances

To show how STT and FRT may help the finding of the control variables that allow the episodes or stories to terminate successfully, we represent in terms of $W^2$ trajectory an episode dealing with a trip with a sailing boat. The sequence of the order states of the skipper are shown in the Tab.1, where also what can go wrong is pointed out for each order state. Let us note that each order state corresponds to a $W^2$ sub-trajectory.

**Table 1:** Order states (related with what can go wrong and control variables) of a skipper in the episode concerning a trip with a sailing boat

|   | Order States | What can go wrong | Control Variables |
|---|---|---|---|
| 1 | Exiting from the port | Colliding with other boats | Distance from the other boats and boat velocity |
| 2 | Sailing until the swimming area | Reaching another area | Compass and wind direction |
| 3 | Stopping the boat at the swimming area and anchor | Colliding with other boats | Distance from the other boats and depth of the water |
| 4 | Swimming | Allergic reactions etc. | Cleanliness of water |
| 5 | Starting the boat and take off anchor | Colliding with other boats | Distance from the other boats and depth of the anchor |
| 6 | Sailing until the port | Reaching another area | Compass and wind direction |
| 7 | Entering into the port | Colliding with other boats | Distance from the other boats and boat velocity |

By a simple inspection of Table 1 it is easy to understand that a good methodology for identifying the control variables is the one of identifying what are the variables that may avoid the abort or the goal degradation of the episode. These variables are likely the control variables envisaged by synergetics. As an example the control variables indicated in the third column are easily derivable from the 'what can go wrong' column.

After having identified these control variables, the main goal of the designers is the one of implementing the affordances that facilitate the management of these variables, whereas the goal of the user, i.e., the skipper in the mentioned example, is the one of constantly taking under observation these variables during the episode evolution. Figure 4 shows how the first three sub-trajectories develop in the What-Where plan. This confirms that not the overall input coming from the environment is necessary to govern the sailing boat and that the coupling between the skipper order state and the environment may be limited to only the few mentioned control variables.

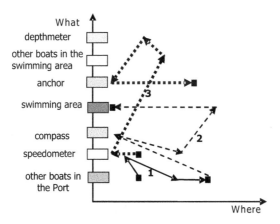

**Figure 4**: Representation of the first three order states of the 'trip with a sailing boat' in the What-Where plan. Let us note that What is related to objects (i.e., to the Who category of STT). The Where axis gives a measure of the distances of the objects (i.e., other boats, compass, swimming area, and anchor) from the skipper, whereas it gives a measure of speed and depth in correspondence to speedometer and depthmeter.

At this point it is useful to recall that synergetics has proposed a mathematical model to describe the controller behavior by the following V function (Kelso, 1999):

$$V(x) = k\,x - x2 / 2 + x4 / 4$$

where x denotes the set of possible order states and k is the control parameter. Usually k depends on the sensorial inputs and on the memory, e.g., in case we have to decide how to climb the stairs, k is as follows (Haselager et alii, 2003):

$$k = R/L + (N_{climb} - N_{clamb})\,S$$

where R is the scaling riser length, L is the leg length, whereas $N_{climb}$ and $N_{clamb}$ are, respectively, the number of times we have more or less recently climbed the stairs by bipedal climbing and by four legged clambering, and S depends on the perceptual characteristics of the observer. Experimentally it has been found that R/L = 0.88 is the value at which the subject passes from bipedal climbing to four legs clambering.

Knowing the mathematical model of the controller for each order state may be useful if we would like to facilitate or to avoid the transition from one order state to another one depending on the current goal. Figure 5 shows by a graphics the ranges of values that the control variables should have so that the sub-trajectories 1 and 3 can be performed successfully depending on the skipper expertise.

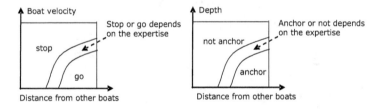

**Figure 5**: Order states 1 and 3 and corresponding ranges of values of the control variables

By providing an artificial device with the controlling functions for each order state we could obtain an efficient automated pilot able of adapting the boat behavior to moderate changes of the environmental conditions. However, if the situation differs greatly from the one assumed by the automated pilot, it is necessary a sort of creativity for managing the current situation. As an example, if the weather changes suddenly during the sailing, it would be necessary to take some decision to change the order state into one compatible with this new situation. An experienced skipper may found rapidly from her/his experience the right behavior according to the hypothesis IV–a, i.e., the one of going far away from the rocks and waiting for better weather conditions. Some chance to solve the situation could have also a novice if in her/his experience there is some episode relevant for the problem at hand, as for example the one of having swim in a rough sea. In fact also in this case it is necessary to control carefully the distance from the rocks. Thus the novice could take the same decision of the experienced skipper following the hypothesis IV–b.

Of course, also an artificial device, provided with a computer program, could drive the boat successfully as the mentioned expert and novice skippers may do. However, whereas the skippers may solve the problem by their consciousness in action, the artificial device reaches this aim by executing a program where input and behavior are clearly separated so impeding that any conscious act may enter into the play. This will be more clear by the considerations that are exposed in the next section.

## 4. Monadology and Society

The hypothesis that any memory photogram is stored in the brain by the coupling of two subsystems (i.e., the self and the environment) is at the core of DQBM. More or less a similar assumption has been done by the authors in their theory of mind (i.e., STT/FRT). In particular STT/FRT assumes that the meaning of any action is related to a context which on its turns includes this action. In STT/FRT the self has not a passive role but has her/his volition since she/he tries to execute successfully episodes and stories. For this reason STT/FRT resembles more close to the quantum monadology (Nakagomi, 2004), where consciousness is related to the process of correlating the *self* part with the other part depending on her/his volition. Consciousness emerges in achieving the coupling and disappears when the coupling is reached. In this latter case the self is experimenting the presence of the environment (Globus, 2003).

According to this point of view, the Rauschenberg's painting belonging to the series 'Mirrors of the Mind' shown in fig.6 may be interpreted as a representation of the conscious process the mind follows to achieve the self-other matching if the two circles are viewed as if they are evolving towards a state in which one mirrors the other, whereas the painting could be interpreted as a representation of how the mind perceives/feels the presence of the environment if the circles are viewed as if they have reached the state of mirroring one the other, e.g., being one the reversed copy of the other.

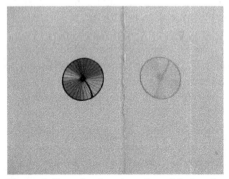

**Figure 6**: Rauschenberg's serigraph belonging
to the 'Mirrors of the Mind' series (1975)

All the mentioned approaches share the idea that the brain states derive from the symmetry breaking of some quantum variable. Stable states are achieved when a private part belonging to the subject matches another part related to the external world in which the subject is situated. Consciousness is *now* and it is in the continuous achievement of such self-other coupling driven by volition. Recently this symmetry breaking at quantum level has been proposed to be a way of implementing the breaking of a more general symmetry, i.e., the time symmetry (Primas, 2003), where there should be the general root of consciousness. Primas claims that consciousness is in our sense of the nowness arising from correlating mind and matter, the first subjected to the tensed time (where concepts such as before, now and after hold), the second consists of temporal ordering of events subjected to tenseless time. Let us note that, with respect to this idea, the way STT/FRT describes consciousness as the process of accommodating an action in a scene where the action is situated implies the time root of consciousness, although the full sense of now is not reached in the moment the action is done but it is appreciated at the end of the significant scene to which it belongs to.

Either at quantum or at the more abstract time level, consciousness of the living systems is in between two parts: one private which is inaccessible to the other living systems, the other conventional/public which allow such systems to live in the environment. However, this monadic nature may be counterbalanced by using conventions, rituals, values and so on in order to reach the coordination between living systems needed to give rise to efficient forms of organizations. This is why we have advanced in Faro & Giordano (2004) the hypothesis that takes into account the subjects tension towards a social life. This hypothesis is rephrased as follows:

*Hypothesis V*: the external representations (enriched by oral and written commentaries aiming at creating a value system) mediate the communication of the patterns among people in order to create conventions and rituals that are at the basis of a social life.

Of course social organizations of living systems do not guarantee that participating people share the same world, but only that the world of any system is compatible with the ones of the others. In other words, two persons may act coordinately even if one is in a scene and the other in another one, i.e., although they are in two different parallel scenes, at condition that these scenes are compatible between them. This has been already observed by the authors in Faro & Giordano (1997).

## 5. Concluding Remarks

Is it possible to construct an artificial conscious system according to the lines exposed in section 2? Can be the researches on consciousness exposed on section 3 productive for people, e.g., for creating better human-human and human-machine interfaces? Are the considerations done on the section 4 useful for creating effective/efficient societies, e.g., community of practice? When these questions will be answered?

Of course the answers, if any, to such questions either positively or negatively are left to future works. For the moment we could be satisfied that at the core of the proposed picture of the living systems based on STT/FRT endowed by quantum brain and synergetics theories and justified also by taking into account the time-entaglement model between mind and matter (Primas, 2003), people have their dignity (privacy is respected) and are free (entanglement with the world is mainly driven by volition/intentionality), although the trade-off is a human condition full of doubts. In fact we not only don't know the scenes where the other people are, but also the current scene where we operate is unknown to us, i.e., the scene becomes clear a-posteriori when a scene assumed for the action (i.e., as a resource for acting) is taken as the real one if nothing went wrong.

*Acknowledgments*

We would like to thank prof. Antonio Chella, prof. Salvatore Gaglio and prof. Riccardo Manzotti together with the Accademia di Studi Mediterranei of Agrigento for having offered the opportunity to us to contribute to the stimulating first Workshop on Artificial Consciousness.

## References

Bruner, J. (1991): *Acts of meaning*. Cambridge, MA Harvard University Press

Edelman G.M. (1992): *Bright air, brilliant fire (on the matter of the mind)*. Harper Collins Publishers.

Faro A. and Giordano D. (1996): Story telling reasoning to learn information systems design. *Proc. of the EuroAIED Conference on Artificial Intelligence in education*, Brna P., Paiva A. and Self J. Editors, Lisbon.

Faro A. and Giordano D. (1997): *Towards a situated action calculus for modeling interactions*. People and Computers XII, Springer.

Faro A. and Giordano D. (1998): Concept formation from design cases. *Knowledge Based Systems Journal N.7–8* Elsevier.

Faro A. and Giordano D. (2004): The role of the internal patterns and the external representations in sustaining creative processes. *Computing, Philosophy and Cognition* Magnani L. and Dossena R. (eds.), *Texts in Philosophy N.4*, King's College Publications London

Gibson J.J. (1979): *The ecological approach to visual perception*. Boston, Houghton-Mifflin.

Goffman E. (1974): *Frame analysis: An essay on the organization of experience*. London, Harper and Row

Globus G. (2003): *Quantum closures and disclosures*. John Benjamins Publishing Company

Haken H. (1983): *Advanced Synergetics*. Springer Verlag.

Haken H. (2004): *Synergetics*. Springer Verlag.

Haselager W.F.G., Bongers R.M., Van Rooij I. (2003): *Cognitive science, representations and dynamical systems theory. The dynamical systems approach to cognition*, Tschacher W., Dauwalder J.P. Eds, World Scientific.

Jibu M. and Yasue K. (1995): *Quantum brain dynamics and consciousness*. John Benjamins Publishing Company

Kelso J.A.S. (1999): *Dynamic Patterns*. MIT Press.

Kohonen T. (1995): *Self organizing maps*. Springer

Lakoff G. (1987): *Women, fire and dangerous things (what categories reveal about the mind)*. The Chicago University Press.

Nakagomi T. (2004): Quantum Monadology and consciousness. *Brain and Being*, Gordon G., Vitiello G. and Pribam K.H. (eds), John Benjamins Publishing Company

Pessa, E. and Vitiello, G. (2004). Quantum noise, entanglement and chaos in the Quantum Field Theory of Mind/Brain states. *Mind and Matter*, 1: 59–79.

Pirandello L. (1926): *Uno, nessuno centomila*. e.g. Garzanti Libri 2003

Primas H. (2003): 'Time-Entanglement between Mind and Matter', *Mind and Matter* 1 (2003), 81–120.

Ricciardi L.M. & Umezawa H. (1967): *Brain and physics of many body problems.* Kybernetic, 4, 44–48.

Takahashi Y. and Jubu M. (2004): Brain and quantum field theory. *Brain and Being,* Gordon G., Vitiello G. and Pribam K.H. (eds), John Benjamins Publishing Company

Thelen E. and Smith L. (1998): *A dynamic systems approach to the development of cognition and action.* MIT Press

Vitiello G. (1995): Dissipation and memory capacity in quantum brain model. *Int. J. Mod. Phys.* 9, 973–989.

Vitiello G. (2001): *My double unveiled.* John Benjamins Publishing Company

Pietro Morasso

# The Crucial Role of Haptic Perception

## Consciousness as the Emergent Property of the Interaction Between Brain Body and Environment

That consciousness cannot be a purely mental phenomenon, in robots as well in living organisms, has become the common wisdom in recent years among roboticists, neuroscientists, and a new wave of philosophers. The idea, as was concisely and effectively formulated by Chiel and Beer (1997), is that 'the brain has a body'. This means that sensors and actuators, action and perception cannot be disregarded when addressing cognitive topics and in fact are center-pieces of any plausible theory of the mind. Everybody agrees with that but agreement becomes less sharp when researchers attempt to perform one step ahead and outline possible embodiment schemes of cognition.

Many scientists take inspiration from philosophy and this implies, on one side, the intellectual comfort of highly structured thinking, but, on the other, the *curse of arbitrariness* of any top-down attempt of boxing empiric reality into a unitary framework. So one may be tempted by a purely phenomenological approach which is apparently solid but suffers a complementary curse, the *curse of dimensionality*. After all, some kind of meta-knowledge is necessary in order to escape somehow from the double web of infinite conflicting theories or infinite unrelated facts. I suggest that some help may come from literature: novelists and poets do not address cognitive problems per se but are obviously interested in specific, highly personalized problems of human cognition and behaviour and sometimes use very pregnant metaphors which may be of help for cognitive scientists. Moreover, while avoiding the fog of universal theories, they never forget that a good page of literature conquers its reader when it is specific and universal at the same time.

In this introduction I include a small collection of examples that, perhaps unknowingly for the authors, touch upon very deep questions of embodied cognition and consciousness. The collection is somehow random but I think it is sufficient to make the point, leaving a more systematic search to some PhD student in search of a theme. Let us consider first a passage from José Saramago (La caverna, 2001) that concerns the knowledge and the cognition of a skilled artisan, like a potter:

> For hours and hours ... the potter made and destroyed small statues of nurses and mandarins ... In truth, only a few people are aware of the existence of a *small brain in each finger of the hand*, somewhere between one phalanx and another. The other organ that we call brain, that we get when we are born, that we bring around in the skull and that carries us in such a way that we carry it, never succeeded to produce anything else than vague intentions, generic, diffuse, and mostly poorly varied, as concerns what hands and fingers are supposed to do ... Consider that when we are born, fingers do not yet have a brain, which is formed little by little as time goes by and with the aid of what the eyes see. The help of the eyes is important, as much as the help of what they see. This is why what the fingers could ever do best was just to *reveal the hidden truth*. What in the brain could be perceived as infused, magic or supernatural knowledge, whatever we mean with supernatural, magic, and infused, is in fact something that was originally discovered and learned by the fingers. For the brain in the head to know what is the stone, it was necessary that well before the fingers could touch it, sense the roughness, weight, density, it was necessary that they were injured.

The knowledge is captured by the 'small brain in each finger' that allows the potter to reveal the truth hidden in the raw matter. The deep concept is that the hand (and the fingers) is not merely a complicated piece of biomechanics but is itself a cognitive organ without which the 'brain in the skull' is a helpless producer of 'vague, generic, diffuse, and poorly varied intentions'.

In a passage from *Atonement* (2002) Ian McEwan depicts in a mastery way the magic discovery by a young girl of the true herself — her soul maybe? — in the simple act of flexing a finger:

... she raised one hand, flexing her fingers, and wondered, as it already happened to her in other occasions, how she took possession of that kind of fleshy spider vice at her own complete service. Did it have a gleam of own life? She flexed a finger and extended it back. The mystery was sealed in what came before the movement, the instant that separates stillness and motion, when the intention reaches its effect. It was as the break up of a wave. If she succeeded to stay on top of the crest, she thought, she might have discovered which part of her was responsible of the phenomenon. She brought the index finger near her face and started fixating it, giving the order to move ... and when finally it did, the gesture seemed to originate from the finger itself, not from some unknown point in her mind. When did it know it was supposed to move? When did she move it? It was impossible to be caught by surprise. Only the before and the after existed. There was no sign of seam, junction line, yet she knew that beyond the smooth tissue that lined her there was the true herself – her soul maybe? – which had the power to stop pretending and give the final order.

Again, the awareness of the power to move is suggested to originate from the body, not the brain. The intrinsic physical content of this knowledge, also in relation with the visual component of it, is present in both previous passages but is more evident (and dramatic) in this quote from Pier Paolo Pasolini (Una vita violenta, 1959):

Also the other ... started to stick stamps of glances over Tommaso here and there all over his body.

The link between seeing, moving (the hand as in calligraphy or drawing/painting), touching and knowing is also one of the leading themes of 'My name is red' (1998) by Orhan Pamuk. It appears that the best painters, after years and years of practice, are those who in the end become blind and at that moment the hand, not the eye, becomes the absolute master of the perfect drawing. This is summarized in the following short quote about blindness and memory:

Remembering is knowing what we see. Knowing is remembering what we see. Seeing is knowing without remembering. This means that painting is remembering the dark.

In any case it is not only the conscious state of the mind that appears to be dominated by physical and material experiences: also the unconscious part of the mind is likely to operate in a similar way, as is suggested by Stanley Kubrick, in an interview by Michel Ciment (1980) related to his 'A Clockwork Orange' movie (1971):

> At the symbolic and oniric level, Alex represents the uncon-
> scious. The unconscious has no conscience. In his unconscious
> each of us rapes and kills.

But perhaps it is a poet (Juan Ramon Jimenez) that in his poem 'Butterfly of light' best captures the essence:

> … what remains in my hand is only the shape of its flight …

and the same idea was put in marble by Antonio Canova in his statue
Amore e Psiche (figure 1).

Without ever mentioning it, many of the quotations above refer
indeed to haptic perception or haptics, in general. The word comes
from the ancient Greek, in particular the verb απτεσθαι(to
touch/grasp) and the corresponding adjective, απτικος. It was used
frequently by Aristotle and it is related to the sense of touch but it is
not limited to tactile perception because it is has an integral and perhaps predominat active/motor component. It is the earliest
sensorimotor channel to develop in the foetus.

**Figure 1**: Amore e Psiche (Antonio Canova).

## 1. The Orphan Brain: The Phantom Limb Illusion

The intimate relationship between the brain and the body and the importance of this relationship for the maintenance of the sense of the self is well evident in different pathological conditions, such as the phantom limb syndrome, in which the brain is *orphan* of part of the body.

A phantom limb is the sensation that an amputated or missing limb is still attached to the body and is moving appropriately with other body parts. There is an elaborate folklore surrounding it. For example, consider Admiral Nelson who lost his right arm during an unsuccessful attack on Santa Cruz de Tenerife: he experienced compelling phantom limb pains, including the sensation of fingers digging into his phantom palm and interpreted it as a 'direct proof of the existence of the soul'. In some cases, the people's representations of their limbs don't actually match what they should be. Some people with phantom limbs find that the limb will gesticulate as they talk. Many people find that sitting on their hands can seriously impede their ability for verbal description. Most of us still gesture when speaking to someone on the telephone. Given the way that the hands and arms are represented on the motor cortex and language centers, this is not surprising. Some people find that their phantom limb feels and behaves as though it is still there, others find that it begins to take on a life of its own, and doesn't obey their commands.

The first clinical description of phantom limbs was provided by Silas Weir Mitchell in 1872 (see Melzack, 1992 for a review). In general, it is possible to learn a lot about the question of how the self constructs a body image and becomes conscious about it by studying patients with phantom limbs. Until recently, the dominant theory was that phantom limbs were caused by irritation in the severed nerve endings (called 'neuromas'). When a limb is amputated, many severed nerve endings are terminated at the remaining stump. These nerve endings can become inflamed, and were thought to send anomalous signals to the brain. However T. Pons (1991) showed that the brain can reorganize if sensory input is cut off and from this a team of researchers lead by V. S. Ramachandran demonstrated that phantom limb sensations can be explained in terms of a *remapping hypothesis* that determines the cross-wiring in the somatosenory cortex (Ramachandran & Blakeslee, 1998; Ramachandran & Hirstein, 1998). Moreover, it appears that these effects are based more on the unmasking of pre-existing connections than on sprouting of new connections.

In a sense, the phantom limb syndrome can be regarded as a kind of sensorimotor illusion in which the patient *projects* to the outside world what is instead a process in the brain. However, this is not limited to pathological conditions: on the contrary it appears to be a general and powerful tendency of the brain. Consider the use of a tool that requires some kind of sensorimotor skill to handle, for example a screwdriver or a surgical scalpel; after a sufficient practice one often begins to *feel* the tip of the screwdriver as part of his body that, in a sense, finalizes all its resources to carry out the task. In a more formal way, it is possible to study sensorimotor illusions in normal people that share the same background with the phantom limb syndrome. Consider the *Phantom nose illusion*, which has been evoked in two different experimental situations:

1)    In one experiment, Lackner (1988) asked his subject to sit blindfolded at a table, with his arm flexed at the elbow, holding the tip of his own nose. The experimenter applied a vibrator to the tendon of the biceps: the subject not only felt that his elbow joint was extended (a classical result in the literature on the tonic vibration reflex) but also that his nose had actually *lengthened*. Lackner invoked Helmholtzian *unconscious inference* as an explanation for this conscious illusion.

2)    In another experiment, Ramachandran & Hirstein (1997) asked his subject to sit in a chair blindfolded, with an accomplice sitting in front of him, facing the same direction. The experimenter stood near the subject; with his left hand took hold of the subject's left index finger and used it to tap and stroke the nose of the accomplice repeatedly and randomly, while at the same time, using his right hand, he tapped and stroked the subject's nose in precisely the same manner, and in perfect synchrony. After a few seconds of this procedure, the subject develops the uncanny illusion that his nose has either been dislocated, or has been stretched out. The interpretation of the authors was that the brain is probably using a *Bayesian logic* in fusing multimodal sensorimotor information and, in this particular experimental situation, the most probable interpretation is not the correct one.

Both experiments demonstrate the striking plasticity or malleability of our body image and the correspond conscious experiences, in spite of its apparent solidity and feeling of permanence.

Another striking instance of a displaced body part can be demonstrated by using a dummy rubber hand (Botvinick & Cohen, 1998). The dummy hand is placed in front of a vertical partition on a table. The subject places his hand behind the partition so he cannot see it. The experimenter now uses his left hand to stroke the dummy hand while at the same time using his right hand to stroke the subject's real hand (hidden from view) in perfect synchrony. The subject soon begins to experience the sensations as arising from the dummy hand.

It is even possible to *project* tactile sensations onto inanimate objects such as tables or shoes that do not resemble body parts (Ramachandran & Hirstein, 1998). The subject is asked to place his right hand below a table surface (or behind a vertical screen) so that he cannot see it. The experimenter then uses his right hand to randomly stroke and tap the subject's right hand (under the table or behind the screen) and uses his left hand to simultaneously stroke and tap a shoe placed on the table in perfect synchrony. After 10–30 seconds, the subject is likely (in about 50% of the cases) to start developing the uncanny illusion that the sensations are now coming from the shoe and that the shoe is now part of his body (Ramachandran et al., 1998).

## 2. The Emotional Content of the Conscious Body Image: The Capgras Syndrome

The disorder called Capgras delusion (from his discoverer Joseph Capgras) is a rare neurological syndrome in which the patient comes to regard close acquaintances, typically either his parents, children, spouse, or siblings, as 'impostors'; in other words he/she might claim that the person 'looks like' or is even 'identical' to his/her mother, but is not the real person. Although frequently seen in psychotic states, more than a third of the documented cases have occurred in conjunction with traumatic brain lesions (Capgras & Reboul-Lachaux 1923), suggesting that the syndrome has an organic basis. The remarkable thing about these patients is that they are relatively intact in other respects, such as cognitive functions, memory and sensorimotor competence.

Disregarding the purely psychological explanations of this syndrome, e.g. in Freudian terms, a more plausible explanation was put forward by Hirstein & Ramachandran (1997) who reasoned that the messages from the temporal lobes where body images are formed are usually transmitted to the limbic system, which is composed of clusters of cells concerned mainly with the perception, experience and expression of emotions. The 'gateway' to the limbic system is the amygdala. Thus, the visual centres of the brain in the temporal lobes send their information to the amygdala, which assesses the emotional significance of the incoming visual input and then transmits this to other limbic structures where these emotions are 'experienced'. Is it possible that in these patients there had been a disconnection between the face area of the temporal lobes and the amygdala, while leaving relatively intact the two brain regions. As a result of this, the patient can recognize people's faces (this is what makes the syndrome different from prosopagnosia) but when he looks at his mother even though he realizes that what he sees resembles his mother, he does not experience the appropriate warmth that the mother's face should convey, and this mismatch is interpreted as evidence of a fake mother. An indirect experimental support to this hypothesis was obtained by Hirstein & Ramachandran (1997) by comparing skin resistance records when these patients were presented images of their mother vs. images of unknown people. It is know indeed that when a normal person looks at something emotionally salient, like his mother, this message is transmitted from the visual centres of the brain to the amygdala, where the emotional significance of this visual event is detected. The message goes to the limbic system and then to the hypothalamus and from there to the autonomic nervous system that controls noradrenergic activity, inducing a number of changes (such as increased sweating, heart rate, and blood pressure) that can be detected by measuring skin resistance. The patients analysed by Hirstein & Ramachandran (1997) did not exhibit any change in their recordings of skin resistance, in contrast with normal control subjects.

### 3. Plasticity and Functional Recovery in Neurological Patients

The experiments on referred sensations in phantom limbs are important because open a window on the fundamental plasticity of the human brain. In particular, they suggest that, contrary to the static picture of brain maps provided by neuroanatomists, the brain topography is extremely labile. Even in the adult brain, massive reorganization can occur over extremely short periods, and referred sensations can therefore be used as a 'markers' for plasticity in the adult human brain. This kind of fundamental plasticity, which explains many of the aspects of the phantom limb syndrome, can be the starting point for designing new approaches to the rehabilitation of neurological patients such as stroke survivors affected by a hemiparetic syndrome: in the phantom limb syndrome the brain is orphan of part of the body and in the hemiparetic syndrome part of the body is orphan of part of the brain. The conventional wisdom about those patients is that there is little ground for functional recovery a few months after the ictus, when they become chronic.

The hemiparesis is the result of damage to the efferent pyramidal fibres in the internal capsule, but in the first few days after a stroke, oedema and diaschesis may contribute to the paralysis. Is it conceivable that during this period the negative feedback from the paralysed limb leads to a form of *learned paralysis* analogous to that seen in the phantom limb syndrome, so that despite resolution of the swelling the paralysis remains. The affected limb, in spite of intact muscle actuators and proprioceptive sensors, becomes paralysed in part for the destruction of some brain tissue, in part for the fact that in absence of purposive movement the brain does not receive organized kinaesthetic information and thus is deprived of functional haptic patterns. The consequence is a kind of functional amputation which has two aspects: 1) the limb assumes a standard, non-functional pathological posture; 2) the limb tends to be ignored by the patient and thus is functionally cut-off from the conscious body schema that guides purposive behaviour.

The considerations above are very important to guide the design of novel approaches to neuro-rehabilitation that are based on two basic concepts: 1) even the brain of the hemiparetic adult patient has a tremendous reserve of neural plasticity; 2) what matters is not so much the recovery of movement per se but the recovery of the conscious body schema that is the inner source of movement and skill. I briefly summarize some of them although this is a rapidly moving field of applied research.

One idea is to facilitate recovery using interactive protocols and devices in which both limbs (the unaffected and the paretic one) are called into action.

One idea is coming again from the study of phantom limbs in amputated patients. It happens to some patients that they feel their phantom as paralysed and this is usually associated with a discomfort and/or pain. This is probably related to the specific post-trauma history of the patient in which indeed he/she was constrained in different ways, reducing his mobility and therefore inducing the brain to freeze the internal representation of the limb in a sort of learned

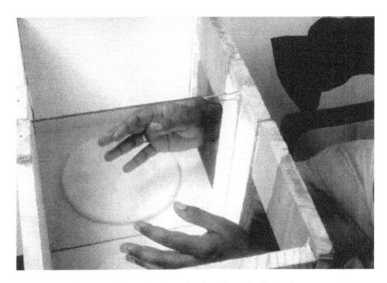

**Figure 2**: The mirror box. A mirror is placed vertically in the centre of a box whose top and front surfaces have been removed. The patient places his normal hand on one side and looks into the mirror. From Ramachandran & Hirstein (1998) The perception of phantom limbs: the D.O. Hebb lecture, Brain, 9, 1603–30.

paralysis of the phantom. Ramachandran & Hirstein (1998) designed a device for inducing the brain of these patients to unlearn the frozen posture: it consists of a simple box (figure 2) with a vertical mirror and two holes through which the patient inserts the good arm and the phantom arm. The patient views his normal hand and its mirror image, thus creating the illusion of two hands. He is then asked to perform mirror-symmetric movements with both arms and the mirror box will send the brain positive visual feedback that the phantom arm is indeed moving. This procedure was reported by Ramachandran & Hirstein (1998) to solve the phantom limb paralysis of many patients. From this came the idea of applying a similar approach with hemiparetic patients (Altschuler et al., 1999, Satian et al., 2000) providing the brain with positive visual feedback by means of the good arm that operates as a sort of master.

The master-slave concept is also used in other approaches based on robot therapy. Lum et al. (1993) developed the mirror-image motion enabler (MIME), consisting of a robot moving the affected arm on the basis of motor commands generated by the non-affected

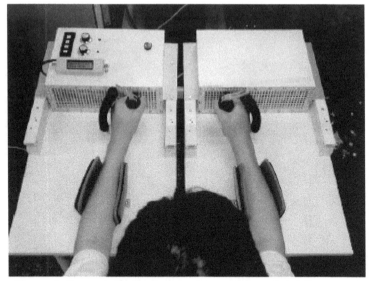

**Figure 3**: Computer-assisted arm trainer; patient with left hemiparesis practices a repetitive bilateral pronation and supination movement of the forearm. From Hesse S, Schulte-Tigges G, Konrad M, Bardeleben A, Werner C (2003) Robot-assisted arm trainer for passive and active wrist movements in hemiparetic subjects. *Arch Phys Med Rehabil*, 84, 915–20.

arm, via a 6-axis digitizer: the master arm commanded the mirror image movement of the robot, thus enabling the subject to practice bimanual shoulder and elbow movements. A similar approach was adopted by Hesse et al. (2003) for the wrist movements by using a computer-assisted arm trainer (figure 3).

Although robots are frequently considered as purely motion devices, they can be designed as haptic devices, exhibiting the tunable compliance typical of coordinated human movements. Two examples of haptic robots that have been applied in neurorehabilitation with positive results are MIT-Manus (Krebs et al., 1999) and Braccio di Ferro (Casadio et al., 2006). Different from the standard industrial robots, which are position controlled and therefore are very stiff when interacting with the outside world, haptic robots like Braccio di Ferro (figure 4) are impedance controlled. This means that what is commanded is neither the desired position of the end-effector $x$ nor the applied force $F$ but the relation among the two, i.e. the mechanical impedance of the robot as felt by the subject, which in general is a function of $x$ and its time deriva-

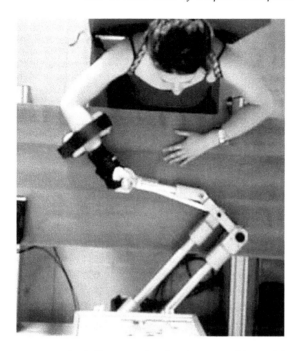

**Figure 4**.
The haptic robot Braccio di Ferro

tives: $F = F(x, \dot{x}, \ddot{x})$. Accordingly, the control law of the motors of the robot is expressed by the following equation:

$$T_m = J(q)^T \cdot F(x, \dot{x}, \ddot{x})$$

where $T_m$ is the vector of motor torques and $J$ is the Jacobian matrix of the robot. By designing the function $F = F(x, \dot{x}, \ddot{x})$ in an appropriate way it is possible to emulate, in very vivid terms, the haptic properties of different kinds of objects or manual interactions with a person, therefore providing to the patients a very realistic and rich proprioceptive feedback.

The experience gained with this kind of device in the rehabilitation of hemiparetic patients is that by using different combinations of assistive and resistive feedback the patients not only improve in their ability to generate active movements (both in terms of force and range of motion) but also in the reconstruction of a body image of the affected limb.

The field is still open to more effective integration of bilateral coordination, visual and proprioceptive feedback. A very important side-effect of this research will also be in terms of a better understanding of the mechanism of for the acquisition, maintenance and plastic adaptation of the brain-body representation of the self.

We may also wonder if the methods developed for the analysis and treatment of purely bodily pathologies, such as hemiparesis and other neuromotor syndromes, are appropriate for approaching mainly cognitive pathologies, such as the Alzheimer disease. After all, as the old saying goes: *Mens sana in corpore sano*.

### 4. The Importance of Haptic Perception

As previously suggested, adaptive behavior is an emergent property of the interaction of the brain, the body and the environment and this implies a continuous exchange of signals/energy between the nervous system, the body and the environment (figure 5). In this process motor neuronal input is shaped by the biophysics of the sensory organs and the motor neuronal output is transformed by the biomechanics of the body, thus creating, at the same time, constraints and affordances that become an integral part of purposive, conscious behaviour. In the phylogenetic development we may identify different design approaches that at the same time relate to the *hardware* of the body and the *software* of the functional capabilities. Consider, for example, the alternative between hydrostatic skeletons (tentacles, tongues, trunks) and hard skeletons: the former solution emphasizes reach-ability whereas the latter is better as regards fine force control.

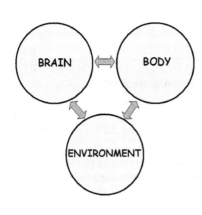

In all cases, the harmonic interaction between the brain, the body and the environment is mediated by what can be labelled in a general sense as *haptic perception*: this implies a complex coupled dynamics between the brain regions, the biomechanis of the musculo-skeletal system, the biophysics of the different sensory channels, and the physics of the environment. Haptic perception is related to touch but it cannot be

**Figure 5.**

reduced to touch. It is active, not passive. It fuses tactile information, kinesthetic information, force information, sense of effort, sensorimotor expectations, etc. Haptic experiences are the essence of most activities of daily life such as palpating, weighing, pushing, hitting, cutting, caressing, grasping, etc. One of the earliest pre-natal experiences, thumb sucking, is clearly a haptic experience: see fig. 6. This is an experience in which the competence of multi-joint coordination is matched with the tactile exploration of the body, the haptic pleasure of this exploration, thus fostering the formation of the conscious representation of the self.

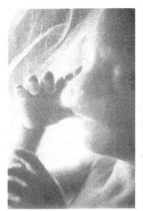 

**Figure 6**: Pre-natal and    post-natal haptic experiences

After birth, the haptic pre-natal experience of thumb sucking is smoothly translated into the corresponding post-natal experience of breast-sucking, which is greatly enriched by the visual and the auditory feedback arousing from the mother-child interaction. Obviously this is the quintessential sexual experience and is certainly full of meaning that life begins with a sexual act between a man and a woman and the formation of the self of the new-born is consolidated through a different but equally strong sexual relationship between the mother and the child. In some cultures less sexuophobic than ours, like Tantra, the central role of sex in human life is recognized and is attributed a mystic value.

The western culture is certainly diplopic from this point of view. Sex is marginalized and criminalized, on one side, and commercially exploited, on the other. The official wisdom is that sex is a strictly private matter whose only socially acknowledged purpose is reproduction. However, in this attitude one may perceive a fundamental contradiction, in addition to its obvious hypocritical flavour: the reason is that this occurs in a culture that also considers humanism as a founding pillar and sees the sexual drive as an animalistic, sub-human experience. In fact, it is typical of most animal species, with the exception of bonobos and a few others, to finalize sex only to reproduction in very limited periods of time. On the contrary, a distinguishing human tract is to be able to completely uncouple sex from reproduction and use it as an expression of human interaction. It is up to ethics and aesthetics to finalize this fundamental element of human knowledge towards truth, good, and beauty.

### 5. The Neural Substrate of Conscious Experience

According to William James, the neural substrate of consciousness is the whole brain, because the stream of consciousness is highly integrated and unified. It is a fact that consciousness/awareness is not on/off but is graded and this implicitly defines a sort of 'consciousness space' with a fuzzy boundaries between conscious and unconscious states. On the other hand, adaptive behavior, that qualifies human and machine intelligence, obviously requires a sufficient degree of awareness. As adaptive behaviour is not a pure property of the brain but an emergent property of the brain, body, environment interaction, so is consciousness, which then cannot be reduced to a purely mental phenomenon.

On the other hand, as the biomechanics of the motor apparatus and the biophysics of the sensory organs constrain and shape the brain-body-environment interaction, so the biophysics of neurons, synapses, and glia constrain and shape the ways in which conscious experience can emerge and articulate itself. This points to the importance of theoretical neuroanatomy, which in fact is a flourishing domain of neuroscience research, for outlining the range of possibilities.

Sporns et al. (2002) proposed a quantitative measure of neural complexity $C(X)$, which expresses the interplay between functional segregation and functional integration: the extent to which small subsets of a system are functionally segregated while large subsets are functionally integrated. Indeed, integration and differentiation are general properties of conscious experience. Substantial evidence indicates that the integration of distributed neuronal populations through reentrant interactions is required for conscious experience. Related to this is the Human Connectome Project (Tononi, 2005), in analogy with the well known Human Genome Project. In order to have an idea of the size of the project, we should consider that the *human genome* is composed of approximately $3\times10^9$ base pairs, containing around 20,000–30,000 genes; the *human connectome* is much larger ($10^{11}$ neurons with $10^{15}$ connections). Consider also that 1 µl of cortical tissue contains on average $10^5$ neurons, $10^9$ synapses, and 4 km of axons.

In technical terms, the connectome can be represented as the union of a binary connection matrix and connection-specific physiological data, i.e. it is a structural description that combines connection topology and biophysics. A general rule is that as connectivity increases so does the relative proportion of *cerebral white matter* in the brain. In fact, the relative contribution of white matter has increased throughout phylogeny to such an extent that its volume and metabolic requirements may present a limitation to further increases in connectional complexity. In any case, the enormous complexity of the human connectome does not allow an analysis at a single scale. Tononi suggests to use three different scales in a coordinated way: micro/meso/macro. The central hypothesis of this research is that the pattern of elements and connections as captured in the connectome places specific constraints on brain dynamics, thus shaping the operations and processes of human cognition. In turn, recording the activity of the human brain in combination with the structural model provided by the connectome will help to discern causal interactions in large-scale brain networks.

As a matter of fact, if we consider phylogenetic development we see that, early in the game of life, evolution has set the basic biophysical properties of axons and dendrites and this is associated with the relative stability of the genetic code through phyla. As evolution proceeded, it was forced to introduce in the process some optimisation criteria, as the complexity of the organisms increased. Chklovskii et al. (2002) investigated this problem and suggested two aspects of the optimization process:

- Minimization of the conduction delays in axons, the passive cable attenuation in dendrites, and the length of 'wire' used to construct circuits;
- Maximizaton of the density of synapses.

On the basis of such criteria, Chklovskii et al. (2002) carried out a formal optimization, consistent with the biophysical properties of axons and dendrites, yielding an overall figure of 3/5 as the optimal relative fraction of volume occupied by wiring. They compared it with the properties of different samples of brain tissue and found values that very closely approach that fraction.

From his studies on theoretical neuroanatomy, Tononi (2005) derived a theory of consciousness as the capacity of a system to integrate information. This claim is motivated by two key phenomenological properties of consciousness:

1) *differentiation* — the availability of a very large number of conscious experiences;

2) *integration* — the unity of each such experience.

The theory states that the quantity of consciousness available to a system can be measured as the amount $\Phi$ of causally *effective information* that can be integrated across the informational weakest link of a subset of elements. A complex is a subset of elements with $\Phi > 0$ that is not part of a subset of higher $\Phi$. The theory claims that the quality of consciousness is determined by the informational relationships among the elements of a complex. Each particular conscious experience is specified by the value, at any given time, of the variables mediating informational interactions among the elements of a complex. The supporting neurobiological observations include the following ones:

• The association of consciousness with certain neural systems rather than with others;

• The fact that neural processes underlying consciousness can influence or be influenced by neural processes that remain unconscious;

• The reduction of consciousness during dreamless sleep and generalized seizures;

• The time requirements on neural interactions that support consciousness.

This theory has certain interesting implications about consciousness:

• It is graded;

• It is present in infants and animals;

• It should be possible to build conscious artifacts.

Another theory of consciousness, derived from the current knowledge of theoretical neuroanatomy and neuroscience, has been developed by J.P Changeux and colleagues (see Dehaene et al. 1998). The theory is based on the fact that there are two main computational spaces that underlie brain processes during effortful tasks (see figure 7):

- a set of specialized modules (perceptual, motor, memory, evaluative, attentional, …);
- a unique global workspace composed of distributed and heavily interconnected neurons with *long-range axons*.

Workspace neurons are mobilized in effortful tasks for which the specialized processors do not suffice and this implies the selective mobilization/suppression of specific processor neurons. During task performance workspace neurons become spontaneously coactivated, forming discrete though variable spatio-temporal patterns, modulated by vigilance/reward signals. In other words, the authors suggest a distributed architecture of neurons with long-distance connectivity that provides a *global workspace*, interconnecting multiple specialized brain areas in a coordinated, though variable manner, and whose intense mobilization might be associated with a subjective feeling of conscious effort .

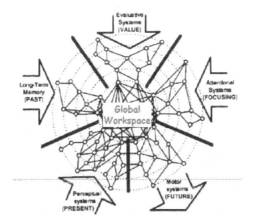

**Figure 7**: Schematic representation of the five main types of processors connected to the global workspace. From Dehaene S, Kerszberg M, Changeaux JP (1998) A neuronal model of global workspace in effortful cognitive tasks. *Proc. Natl. Acad. Sci. USA*, 95, 14529–14534.

## 6. Concluding Remarks

In the previous sections I explained in which sense I think that haptic perception is a basic channel for the emergence and maintenance of natural consciousness. It is not the site of consciousness per se, as amygdala is not the site of emotion. But without this channel, no conscious experience can occur.

To which extent is this relevant for advanced robot design and cognitive robotics? Is consciousness of any importance for robots? Clearly, this is a (vexing) question that pertains to the general class of questions about the technical/technological merit of imitating/emulating nature and/or biology in the design of artefacts. The pros and cons have been debated at length.

However, if we decide that robot consciousness is necessary for both robot-human interaction and for the robot itself, then we are forced to admit that

- it cannot be infused from the outside in terms of a software/hardware module, but is an emergent property of the interaction between brain, body, and environment;

- it is graded, highly flexible and adaptable, not rigidly digital or 'genetically' predetermined.

On the other hand, it is possible and probably advisable to introduce from the outside or to pre-programme 'genetically' a set of 'emotional drives' that help the technological organism to shape its behaviour, by being attracted towards some patterns/situations and repulsed by others. This is also the basis for a mechanism of attention and memory, which focuses the limited computational resources of the robot brain in one direction or another. However, consciousness is something else: as emergent property of the brain-body-environment interaction, it requires that these subsystems are 'matched' in order to 'resonate' and what comes out of this sensorimotor resonance is strongly specific and thus is a highly individual experience. While emotional drives are stereotyped, states of consciousness are strongly personal and largely unpredictable. This is where haptic perception comes in: it allows the system to resonate, thus linking drives with goals and, ultimately, allowing the individual to carry out the planned tasks.

Consider, for example, the drive for food, which is one of the fundamental drives in all the animal kingdom. In most cases, it triggers a genetically pre-determined behaviour such as picking up a fruit from a plant of hunting a prey. In some case, however, the food is unreachable or it runs away too fast: this is what pushed humans, among other species, to invent tools and/or weapons to overcome the barrier, the obstacle or whatever. However, tool making is not exclusively human: some primates do it as well as a pair of birds: the woodpecker and, most notably, the New Caledonian crow (Kenward et al., 2005).

**Figure 8**: Tool use by a naïve New Caledonian crow. a, A hand-raised juvenile uses a twig to retrieve meat from an artificial crevice. b, Close-up of a tool made from a Pandanus leaf (from the Royal Botanic Garden, Kew, London). From Kenward B, Weir AA, Rutz C, Kacelnik A (2005) Behavioural ecology: tool manufacture by naive juvenile crows. *Nature*, 433, 121.

Figure 8 shows how the crow, after having attempted unsuccessfully to fetch the food byte from an artificial crevice, selects and bends a Pandanus leaf (typical of its habitat) in such a way to fit the constraint posed by the crevice. All of this is obviously carried out through haptic interaction, which allows the crow to understand the affordances/limitations of its body, to evaluate the appropriateness of the tool material, to shape it according to the need, and finally to catch the food. This is not a purely trial and error process. After the naïve individual has learned in one case how to satisfy its drive, it will become conscious of it and then become 'creative' in new occasions, for example by using exotic material (for a Caledonia crow) such as iron wire. Other apparently similar species would starve to death in that situation, failing to become aware of the affordances provided by extending the body with an apparently neutral tool: no consciousness, no ability to learn and generalize, less ability to survive. The claim is that, without a well sophisticated haptic perception system, consciousness cannot emerge. The human hand, with its opponent thumb and the support of the well articulated structure of the arm, is the best haptic device. It is not optimised/specialized for any specific goal except for tool making and handling. Apparently, also the Caledonian crows followed a similar evolutionary line but obviously a good haptic beak is no match to the human hand.

An additional advantage of the conscious experiences, made possible by a suitable haptic system, is to free the individual from the slavery of emotional drives: such drives indeed orient behavior in a useful way but in some cases determine dead-end situations from which an intelligent/conscious organism is suppose to escape. The competence acquired in practicing tool making and tool using is what you need in order to escape from the many unpredictable cul de sac that may occur in the lifetime of an individual: as in playing chess, be prepared to delay reward, test the opponent, build a good defense tool, and push your attack in the soft spot of the opponent.

## Acknowledgement

This work was supported by EU FP6 Project GNOSYS.

## References

Altschuler E, Wisdom S, Stone L, Foster C, Ramachandran VS (1999) Rehabilitation of hemiparesis after stroke with a mirror. *Lancet*, 353, 2035–6.

Botvinick M, Cohen J (1998) Rubber hands feel touch that eyes see. *Nature*, 391, 756.

Capgras J, Reboul-Lachaux J (1923) L'illusion des 'sosies' dans un délire systématise chronique. *Bull. Soc. Clinique Med. Mentale*, 2, 6–16.

Casadio M, Morasso P, Sanguineti V, Arrichiello V (2006) Braccio di Ferro: a new haptic workstation for neuromotor rehabilitation. *Technol Health Care*, 14, 3, 123–42.

Chiel, H.J. and Beer, R.D. (1997) The brain has a body: Adaptive behavior emerges from interactions of nervous system, body and environment. *Trends in Neurosciences*, 20, 553-7.

Chklovskii DB, Schikorski T, Stevens CF (2002) Wiring optimization in cortical circuits. *Neuron*, 34, 341–7.

Dehaene S, Kerszberg M, Changeaux IP (1998) A neuronal model of global workspace in effortful cognitive tasks. *Proc. Natl. Acad. Sci. USA*, 95, 14529–34.

Hesse S, Schulte-Tigges G, Konrad M, Bardeleben A, Werner C (2003) Robot-assisted arm trainer for passive and active wrist movements in hemiparetic subjects. *Arch Phys Med Rehabil,* 84, 915–20.

Hirstein W, Ramachandran VS (1997) Capgras syndrome: a novel probe for understanding the neural representation of the identity and familiarity of persons. *Proc Biol Sci,* 264, 437–44.

Lackner JR (1988) Some proprioceptive influences on the perceptual representation of body shape and orientation, *Brain,* 111, 281-297.

Kenward B, Weir AA, Rutz C, Kacelnik A (2005) Behavioural ecology: tool manufacture by naive juvenile crows. *Nature,*433, 121.

Krebs HI, Hogan N, Volpe BT, Aisen ML, Edelstein L, Diels C (1999) Overview of clinical trials with MIT–MANUS: a robot-aided neuro-rehabilitation facility. *Technol Health Care,* 7, 419–23.

Lum PS, Reinkesmeyer DJ, Lehman SL (1993) Robotic assist devices for bimanual physical therapy: preliminary experiments. *IEEE Trans Rehabil Eng,* 1, 185–91.

Melzack, R. (1992) Phantom Limbs. *Scientific American,* no. April, pp. 120–126.

Pons TP, Garraghty PE, Ommaya AK, Kaas JH, Taub E, Mishkin M (1991) Massive cortical reorganization after sensory deafferentation in adult macaques, *Science,* 252, no. 5014, 1857–60.

Ramachandran VS, Blakeslee S (1998) *Phantoms in the brain: Probing the mysteries of the human mind.* William Morrow & Company.

Ramachandran VS, Hirstein W (1998) The perception of phantom limbs: The D.O. Hebb lecture. *Brain,* 9, 1603–30.

Sathian K, Greenspan AI, Wolf SL (2000) Doing it with mirrors; a case study of a novel approach to rehabilitation. *Neurorehabil Neural Repair,* 14, 73–6.

Sporns O,Tononi G, Edelman GM (2002) Theoretical neuroanatomy and the connectivity of the cerebral cortex. *Behav Brain Res,* 20, 69–74.

Tononi G (2004) Information integration theory of consciousness, *BMC Neuroscience,* 2, 5–42.

Tononi G (2005) The human connectome: a structural description of the human brain. *PLoS Computational Biology,* 1(4): e42.

Peter Farleigh

# The Ensemble and the Single Mind

## A Sceptical Inquiry

Mindful creatures appear to act and feel as one. Or at least I believe this to be true of one creature in particular — myself — even if I could be deluded about others around me. Some would say even in my *own* case I am deluded. Deceptions may be, but it is very hard to shake off what seems to be an undeniable fact that I am mindful, that I am conscious, and so are you. If I attend to a perception, if I make a decision, if I perform a process of 'making up my mind', it seems like it is a process involving the *whole* mind, or at least the whole of my *conscious* mind. If we regard the mind to be the sum activity of the brain, we know the brain is made of many things, and hence the mind is a sum of many smaller activities. Just as the living body is made of a vast dynamic ensemble of cells, the brain and central nervous system also form an ensemble of specialised cells — a dynamic network of neurons. And it seems this network not only has a physical aspect, but and we may say *strangely*, it can have a mental aspect as well.

It is here that we confront the 'explanatory gap' that is said to exist between our external or third-person knowledge of the physics of the body, and our internal or first-person knowledge of the phenomenology of the mind. No doubt it would be regarded as a great advance towards bridging the gap, if empirically we could locate and map the activity of the neural correlates of specific instances of conscious activity (the NCC). But while we may want to claim that we now have a pretty good knowledge of how neurons work individually, and even of how small networks perform, there is clearly a very long way to go before we understand how a brain-load of neurons work to produce a thinking, feeling, conscious mind.

Any conscious feeling I have appears to be extended in time. Any sensation, any feeling, takes a finite interval of time no matter how fleeting it may be. If I catch my finger in a door and reel back in agony with the sharp pain, the pain is felt for an extended time. It may vary in intensity, it may throb, but the feeling as a single feeling of pain, is experienced over some interval of time. We can imagine millions of neurons firing furiously in response—nerve cells in my finger and arm and then large networks of neurons in my brain. The feeling seems smooth, though in the case of pain it may be described as 'sharp'. Feelings seem to be without temporal parts, even though they are supported by or supervene on the action of a great swarm of neurons, each firing very quickly and repeatedly.

We can imagine too, that within the various waves of neuronal activity corresponding to the throbbing phases of the pain, the feeling arises or emerges in the activity of one network of neurons, but then as other networks are stimulated this initial feeling is somehow passed on to them. It is though the feeling flows and reverberates through the networks. Yet the signals between the neurons and between the networks are simply lower-level electro-chemical signals or molecular messengers. These signals are not something that is generally regarded in any way possessing a mental or experiential character; they are merely physico-chemical actions. Common intuitions generally do not lead us to regard those neurons firing in response to a painful situation to be *individually* conscious of the pain, even in some small or vague *proto*-conscious way. We tend to believe that consciousness is a property, or a feature of the activity of larger networks or of the whole brain, and not of the microscopic neuron in-and-of-itself. How these many things then become one, or act as one, is a key issue. In fact William James regarded 'the ancient problem of "the one and the many,"' as 'the most central of all philosophic problems' (James, 1907).

## Causal Roles and Neuronal Activity

Given these physicalist assumptions, it is natural then to ask; *what is the role of causation* and *what is the role of neuronal activity* in respect to the mental attributes that the aggregate displays? Is one role more important than the other? Is it the case that the key to understanding consciousness lies with the specific activity of the individual neurons and that the signals between them are merely *triggers* for this activity, or are the signals themselves more intimately part of the emergence of consciousness? If so, how are they? What makes a complex causal structure suddenly gain an inner mental life?

So far as we know conscious-generating structures exist only in the biological world, and this fact leads to a commonly held chauvinism in favour of biology. Rejecting this bias, we may ask: is it possible to build similar conscious-generating structures in a non-biological realm? And indeed this is the goal for many philosophers and neuroscientists. Alongside the theoretical and philosophical aims, there is a concomitant endeavour in many research departments to build a conscious machine from scratch. This might be in the form of a conscious computer sitting on a desk, or a conscious robot roaming a room, or even some sort of biological-mechanical hybrid. Thus in creating such a machine a successful theory could be proven, or a philosophical explanation fully legitimised. It is much more likely, and is in fact more the case, that the two approaches — philosophical analysis and technical synthesis — will go hand-in-hand as the overall inquiry into each aspect proceeds. As Igor Aleksander writes '… the conscious machine gives us some insight — possibly all the insight we need — into what it is that any organism, including the living brain, needs in order to generate a mind-like property for that organism' (Aleksander, 2000).

## Machine Consciousness and Functionalism

At the foundation of most artificial consciousness projects is a very strong commitment to a *functionalist* theory of mind. It is based on the strong belief in the thesis of multiple realisability, or a substance-neutral theory of mind (Kim, 1992), and therefore gives weight to the rejection of those theories of mind that tend toward a biological or neural chauvinism.

Functionalism, though, has fared badly with any attempt at an explanation of the phenomenal qualities which are regarded as a crucial, or even as *the* defining character of consciousness. Taken in terms of a *reductive* functionalism, the problem of explaining qualia has been fraught with problems, and calls by philosophers such as David Chalmers have been made to consider *non-reductive* versions of functionalism. This would allow one to keep both a commitment to a fully-fledged phenomenal consciousness, *and* argue for the possibility of a machine possessing such. While on one hand Chalmers does not want to lose sight of the essential phenomenal aspects of consciousness like qualia, on the other hand, as he holds to the standard mechanistic-functionalist approach of physicalism, he believes quite strongly that there is no reason to deny the possibility of a machine having a consciousness mind. He argues for this stand, even if it means being categorised as a kind of dualist or, if we like, a non-reductive materialist.

For the functionalist, *organisation* is a key aspect. This idea is a central issue for Edelman and Tononi when they state succinctly that 'consciousness arises from certain arrangements in the material order of the brain.' The key phrase here is 'certain arrangements,' for most arrangements produce nothing like consciousness at all. In fact the vast majority of arrangements or organisations of matter in the universe clearly will not generate even a hint of feeling, awareness or consciousness. Chalmers in harmony with this basic idea, naturally asks the obvious question:

> ... just what *kind* of organization gives rise to conscious experience? How simple can an organization be before experience vanishes? And how can we predict the specific character of an experience (not just its structure) from its physical basis? (Chalmers, 1996, pp. 276–7).

And elsewhere he addresses the concept of functional organisation:

> To clarify this, we must first clarify the notion of functional organization. This is best understood as the *abstract pattern of causal interaction* between the components of a system, and perhaps between these components and external inputs and outputs. A functional organization is determined by specifying (1) a number of abstract components, (2) for each component, a number of different possible states, and (3) a system of dependency relations, specifying how the states of each component depends on the previous states of all components and on inputs to the system, and how outputs from the system depend on previous component states. Beyond specifying their number and their dependency relations, the nature of the components and the states is left unspecified (Chalmers, 1995, pp. 309–328).

It is in preparing to answer this question that Chalmers proposes a rule that he calls the *Principle of Organizational Invariance*. He explains;

> According to this principle, what matters for the emergence of experience is not the specific physical makeup of the system, but the abstract pattern of causal interaction between its components (Chalmers, 1996, pp. 276–7).

And he explains this more formally:

> Call a property *P* an *organizational invariant* if it is invariant with respect to causal topology: that is, if any change to the system that preserves the causal topology preserves *P*.
> The sort of changes in question include:
>
> (a)   moving the system in space;
>
> (b)   stretching, distorting, expanding and contracting the system;
>
> (c)   replacing sufficiently small parts of the system with parts that perform the same local function (e.g. replacing a neuron with a silicon chip with the same I/O properties);
>
> (d)   replacing the causal links between parts of a system with other links that preserve the same pattern of dependencies (e.g., we might replace a mechanical link in a telephone exchange with an electrical link); and
>
> (e)   any other changes that do not alter the pattern of causal interaction among parts of the system (Chalmers 1993).

Another way to express Chalmers' principle, and to put it more matter-of-factly, is to say that given two systems, with identical causal structures, though not necessarily built of the same substrate; if one system is conscious, then the other will be identically conscious. So if we construct a computer that has exactly the same, sufficiently fine-grained causal structure as a conscious biological neural network, then that computer will be identically conscious. It will be conscious, even though the computer is constructed of silicon-based material, and the biological network is made of carbon-based ones.

In order to justify this principle, Chalmers appeals to the simple thought experiment where one is asked to consider replacing the brain cell-by-cell with a functionally equivalent silicon-based 'cell'. Will such an equivalent (silicon) brain be conscious? Chalmers argues that it would be. But this in many ways is a hard argument to counter, for of course it is more likely you would come to this conclusion if in the beginning you hold to the assumptions, first, that functionalism is true, and second, that it is possible to very accurately make a functional isomorph of the biological cell. That is if a single neuron can be treated as a little functional unit, then without positing any mysterious extras, the functionalist analysis would equally apply to any aggregated collection of neurons of any magnitude.

We could then ask; are our *a priori* assumptions correct in this analysis? Can we really come to a full knowledge of the function of a living cell in the same way that we fully know the operation of say, an electronic NAND gate, the most universal logical element of a computer? The scientific world is not about to draw a line under the topic of cell biology and say there is no more work to be done here, for we know it all. Journals of cell biology are not about to cease publication and conferences cancelled. The study of the single cell and neuron goes on. Yet we have no journals or conferences dedicated to the theory of the NAND gate — we know all there is to know about their operation. If we didn't, we would not be so successful in designing and building computers.

It is time to pick apart the concept of what we mean by functional organisation, and inevitably this means picking apart some of our mechanistic conceptions and biases.

## Functionalism as Mechanism

Functionalism and the emphasis here on organisational structure, is an analysis that is hardly different from the traditional notions of *mechanism*, which took dynamic systems to be reducible to their material parts and their motion. These parts are assumed to be independent substances in the sense of 'requiring nothing else for their existence', and so the relations between them are *accidental* to their being, and are therefore only ever *external* (Russell, 1911). That is, their relations are not in any way constitutive of the existence of the parts. They can include various abstract, geometric and logical relations. This leads us to another way of expressing what the Principle of Organizational Invariance is saying: that is the two systems, brain and machine, are functionally equivalent because their *patterns of external relations* are equivalent. Or as Alfred North Whitehead expressed it: 'one set of external relations is as good any other set of external relations' (Whitehead, 1926, p. 157).

Complex mechanical systems can only ever be regarded as mere aggregates of their substantial parts — big machines are made of smaller machines. The operational events and processes of these mechanical systems are also incidental to the nature and being of their parts and their aggregate structures. Matter and structure are therefore ontologically prior to any process that the system may engage in. Causation is inevitably regarded as *efficient* or *transeunt* — the 'billiard-ball' style causation and its variations in classical physics. And here 'transeunt' refers to that sort of causation involving the action of one thing on another as an external cause of change (Johnson, 1924). It is an action that 'goes across' from cause to effect, and even if those events are contiguous as Hume conjectured, it nevertheless allows for the possibility of causal *intervention, substitution* and *pre-emption* (Ganeri, 1996).

To give an example of causal substitution in a purely mechanical system we can look at a simple illustration which will also serve as an intuition pump for our main thought experiment to follow.

## The Dissociated Ensemble

### Hume in Mexico

Popular at sporting events with large numbers of spectators is the 'Mexican Wave'. One spectator decides to quickly take to his feet, raising his arms in the air, then as quickly sits down again. His immediate neighbour decides to do the same thing, and so the process is continued on down the line of cheering sporting fans. It's a phenomenon that has become familiar to us all since its conception at the 1986 World Cup in Mexico and more lately has even been worthy of a study published in *Nature* (Farkas, Helbing, Vicsek, 2002).

Let us take this illustration of a human chain reaction as an example of a simple causal chain. Imagine a number of people seated in a row. Each is given the simple instruction that when they see the person to their right stand up and sit down, they should do the same. Of course there will be a slight delayed reaction between each participant but that is an essential aspect. The person on the end with no right-hand neighbour is the first to start the process. The wave can only begin when she chooses to stand up and sit down, and when she does so it sends a 'message' along the line as each person completes their move thus creating the wave. We may like to say that the wave 'emerges' from the total process.

Now imagine if we break the causal chain at each link along the line. We can do this by taking each of our subjects and providing them with a blindfold that stops them from seeing their neighbours and they are not so close as to be touching anyone, either. So now they have no idea whether their neighbour has made a move or not. But we provide each of them with a preset clock connected to a mechanical device that taps them on the foot. Each person is told to stand up and sit down only when they feel a tap. We arrange things so that each clock is timed to tap at a preset interval—a time that was equivalent to the delay each person would have experienced in the original arrangement.

With the clocks all correctly set, the Mexican wave can again occur, but here we are 'staging' it without any of the participants relying on a causal connection existing between them and their neighbour. There is a limitation of course, as there is no flexibility in this system for it no longer relies on the first person having a choice as to when to make the first move. Nevertheless for a fixed time frame set by the clocks, the wave will occur without any observable difference in the character of original wave. The two systems will, given certain limits, provide the same action or produce the same phenomena though they have different causal structures — one system has its parts connected in a causal chain, and the other has each part operating as a separate but 'well-timed' individual. It is as if the staged version is connected in a causal chain but in fact each 'cause' has been substituted by the clocks. Cause and effect between the players, in one sense is there in appearance, but not with any real connection. They are only virtual causes. We could therefore consider this version as a kind of *Humean* Mexican Wave, for we can be sceptical about whether there is any real connection between events, or whether they are mere regularities.

What then is the important thing that gives us the 'wave'; is it the causal connections, or the individual activity of the participants? Clearly in our case here, if the participants move up and down with the right timing then the wave will appear, and so we can say that it is the activities of the unit components — the participants — that are more important than the causal connections between them. Can we expect the same conclusions about that particular causal network we call the brain?

*Our Thought Experiment:*

Consider the entire human nervous system. In a very simple sense, the nerve cells in this system can be treated as nodes in an enormous causal matrix, which starts with a stimulus and ends in a response. In receiving signals from other neurons or nerve cells, a single neuron is thought to weigh up each input signal as either contributing to a *stimulus* response, or as can be the case, contributing to the *inhibition* of a response. The neuron then either 'fires' or doesn't fire in response to its inputs — inputs which may also include feedback from its own output. If anything is 'carried along' in this process, from stimulus to response, we now most often talk in terms of *information* transmission. It is almost a cliché, but the brain is very often regarded as an *information processor*, and many of its aspects and functions are commonly couched in informational and computational terms.

If I were to catch my finger in a door, some sort of 'information' is generated in the nerves of my finger and carried through the nervous system to my brain and then onto the motor-neuron system terminating in various physical responses such as calling out in agony, avoiding the danger and in nursing a throbbing finger. But information can come in many forms and sometimes it can be misinformation — sometimes we can be deluded.

*Sensory Substitution*

Let us examine the situation which we may term *sensory substitution*. This is what we find in Descartes' famous story of the malicious deceiving demon and the brain-in-a-vat thought experiments. Take an example where your finger is pricked with a pin, and where naturally you'd be feeling a sharp sensation as a result. Consider the case if we were to cut the nerve fibre somewhere at the base of your finger so that your finger at its tip becomes numb to any feeling. Jabbing your finger now would not elicit any feeling for clearly the signals are not getting to the brain. But now imagine if we had some sort of electro-chemical stimulating device that could be fed into the severed (proximal) nerve with an artificial signal. This signal we choose to be an exact copy of the output signal from the other more distal nerve cell — an exact copy that is, of a signal produced in this neuron by the pricking of the finger with a pin.

To restate this, suppose a nerve cell $A$ is at the tip of the finger and receives the jab, it responds by sending a nerve signal down the line. Now say if we have severed the connection between cell $X$ and cell $Y$ at the base of the finger, and there would normally be an output signal $x_o$ from $X$ into $Y$, but particularly let's say that this signal will have a certain character related to the signal of the stimulus, say $j$ for jab. So let us call the output signal from $X$ that normally goes into $Y$ in this case $x_{oj}$. In severing the connection between cell $X$ and cell $Y$ we are letting the output $(x_{oj})$ from $X$ just dangle in the air going nowhere. And where it was connected to $Y$ we are now inputting an artificial signal into $Y$ and this signal is an exact copy of $x_{oj}$.

So every time the artificial stimulator sends a pulse you will feel as though your finger has just been jabbed with a pin. We could time it so that we do in fact jab your finger with a pin at the same moment as sending a pulse from our stimulator. In this case you *see* your finger being pricked with a pin, and *feel* it being pricked with the pin at the same time, even though your nerves have been severed. The sensory input has been pre-empted by the stimulating device.

Of course it should be noted that there is no *flexibility* in this system — no plasticity, we might say. If your finger is stroked by a feather while the stimulator is pulsed you will still feel as though your finger has still been pricked by a pin. We had the similar limitation with our Humean Mexican Wave, but for a specific setup and timings we can reproduce the original effect. We could resort to a more elaborate thought experiment involving one of Descartes' demons to overcome these limitations, but this is not to distract us here. The point of this thought experiment at this stage is to note that there is nothing in particular that is special about the sensory inputs to our system from the world, for they can be pre-empted or substituted by some other means. The whole brain-in-a-vat scenario is based on the concept of sensory substitution, and Descartes' demon is a pre-emptive demon.

A similar and very clear example also is to imagine a robot that uses a video camera to navigate its way around a room. The light coming into the camera is shone on a CCD matrix where it is converted to digital signals, and from there on within the workings of the robot, these digital signals remain as digital signals even if they become highly transformed. At the very end of their journey through the system they may be converted to motor controls which enable the robot to operate within the world, but for the most part the information is encoded as digital signals.

The input signals could of course be substituted. Our robot needs not to live in a real world; it could easily exist in a virtual world. That is, its video input signals could be provided directly by another computer programmed to have a virtual reality model of the room. Similarly the motorised or physical output of the robot could be replaced by simply sending signals to the virtual reality computer, which in turn interprets them as appropriate movements of the robot in its virtual world. Thus all the messy mechanical bits of the robot can be avoided leaving only its computer 'brain' plugged into the virtual reality computer. We can then of course get rid of the two computers, and reduce the whole system to a single computer that runs both the appropriate virtual robot software, *and* the virtual environment software.

This fairly obvious idea of modelling a robot and its environment completely in software caused something of a storm once when Marvin Minsky rather impolitely imposed it on the MIT robotics group led by Rodney Brooks (Freedman 1994). Brooks, the leading roboticist, of course had to defend his livelihood. Yet his main argument rested on the claim that it is harder to model reality in software than to make a robot to operate in the real environment. In principle this does not undermine the argument that sufficiently advanced software could replace the whole system. And for all the sophisticated hardware that exists, inputs inevitably become digital signals whatever produces them. If a robot looks at a tree then there is no particular 'treeness' in the signals that enter the robot's computer brain. Similarly there is no 'treeness' in the neuronal firings in our visual system when we see a tree. Signals are signals, and these signals can be pre-empted by any other system that can mimic the particular organisation of those signals. No matter how much we are in favour of saying the crucial aspect of consciousness is embodiment — an embodied computer, or our embodied brain — there will always be a boundary between what the robot senses and the representations it has in its memory and the world, and similarly what we sense of the world and what goes on in our brain. This boundary can also be bridged by all manner of pre-emptive stimuli — a virtual reality system, hallucinatory drugs, probes in the brain, and so on.

Sensory substitution means of course that representations or symbols can never be truly 'grounded' which is a goal urged by many (Harnard, 1990), and it could be argued that it was Descartes and his malicious demon who demonstrated this fact centuries ago — though for reasons to support his substance-dualism. Of course his dualist legacy remains in the background of our thinking and language. Even to talk in terms of 'embodiment' can sometimes mean a careless descent back into crypto-dualistic thinking. One can sometimes get the impression that it is as though there are all these potential minds floating around like lost spirits and we come across them all the time — they are called computers — but if only they could find the appropriate (robotic) body to be embodied in, then and only then, shall they become true minds with qualitative feelings, beliefs and desires and so on. But let us return to our thought experiment.

### Gradual to Complete Dissociation

We can now take our nerve-cutting and sensory substitution exercise further. Of course we could do the same operation where instead of cutting the nerves at the finger, we could cut the neural fibre say near the shoulder or at the base of the spine, but we would get the same result.

The total neural system—the peripheral nervous system plus the CNS—has a slightly different causal structure in the severed case as compared with the original complete version, but hardly different, as it is just one cut. Both systems give rise to the conscious awareness and the feeling of being jabbed in the finger with a pin. This difference is clearly nothing to get too excited about as we regard the real seat of consciousness to be in the brain, and so far we are only tampering with its input signals. But it is fairly obvious we can take this method and apply it to *every* nerve cell in the body and *every* neuron in the brain and then examine the systems in each case.

Therefore let us imagine taking apart someone's *entire* neural system for just a second or two. Keep all the neurons or nerve cells in their physical place, but cut all the connections between them. Leave every neuronal output dangling but connect every input to an artificial neural stimulator that injects the signal that each neuron would normally receive under the conditions of feeling a stabbing pain in the finger—just for a second or two. Imagine if neuron N93756 in the brain fires in some way in response to the pricking of a finger and has, in this case, received a signal 'squiggle-squiggle' say, on its input synapse S7564, and a signal 'squoggle-squoggle'[1] on synapse S2745. Then in the disconnected case, for this same interval of time, we have a little stimulator sending a squiggle-squiggle to S7564 and another artificial signal generator sending a squoggle-squoggle to S2745. All of these signals of course are timed to be sent with the appropriate synchronisation to mimic the timing of the signals in the natural system.

**Question:** Does the *completely dissociated* brain feel the pain associated with the pricking of a finger? If not, does it lose its consciousness or its sensation gradually as each neuron is progressively disconnected, or does it lose it suddenly at one crucial point in the operation?

## The Dissociated Chunk version

Before looking at where this thought experiment leads us, we can also consider a variation on the idea where we simply take a chunk out of the brain—say that chunk out of the region of the brain that normally 'lights up' when the person receives a jab in the finger. Again the method is to leave the outputs from the neural networks at

---

[1]   I've liberally borrowed these highly technical terms from John Searle's description of the operation of his Chinese Room.

the cut dangling, but put artificial stimulators on the inputs at the cut. In this case we are not dissociating every neuron just cutting away a part of the brain and stimulating it artificially. So again, considering the moment that the person has their finger pricked, the signals going into the separated chunk are artificial versions of the signals coming out from the brain at the site of the cut. And the returning signals from the chunk to the brain? They again, are left dangling but another set of stimulators supply the appropriate input signals to the brain.

For this moment the brain operates as it did in its natural state only that a number of causal links have been broken and are substituted by artificial ones.

A similar arrangement could be made with a computer. Consider the situation where you have a CPU that operates in tandem with a floating-point co-processor. If we were to unplug the co-processor the system will not be able to run as usual, (though if it is clever enough and can detect there is no coprocessor there it could switch its operation to do those floating-point routines in software – but this is a side issue). So consider the case where you are operating this computer as normal – doing lots of very heavy mathematical computations. Then, unbeknown to you, two of Descartes' demons quickly hop inside and pull the coprocessor out for a little time. And equally as fast, one demon starts providing all the input signals sent from the CPU to the co-processor and the other demon provides the signals from the coprocessor back to the CPU. You have no idea this has happened, for the system functions as you would normally expect it to during that interval. There isn't much we can say about the computer situation for we are not asking about its feelings – unless of course we are making some bold claims that our particular computer with its coprocessor is in fact an artificially conscious system.

The question arises again and there are two obvious answers: either the person with the dissociated brain-chunk feels the pain or does not, *or* in this case may feel some aspect of the pain depending on what part of the brain is dissociated.

## Resolving the Dilemma

For the sake of simplicity in concluding let us just take the example of the completely dissociated case for analysis. We have then our two systems for comparison; one, the *natural system* of a completely connected and working brain and nervous system feeling the pain of a finger being pricked by a pin, and the other, the *completely dissociated system*, where every neuron is disconnected from every other during the moment of the pricking of the finger, and each is stimulated by its own little set of artificial pulses on its inputs. What then are the arguments for and against the dissociated system possessing conscious feeling, and in this case a conscious feeling of pain?

*Option One – The Intuitive Answer:*
*The dissociated system feels no pain.*

It is hard to *imagine* that a whole host of disconnected neurons could be conscious, even though they may be buzzing with activity and even if that action is like the action they would normally have if they were in the naturally connected state. It just *intuitively* seems like there would be no consciousness there, no *feeling* of the pain. What would we think if we dispersed these neurons throughout the universe, each with their set of artificial stimulators connected to their inputs? Let us imagine we have a neuron buzzing away on every planet that exists through out the cosmos. Every neuron dispersed into the vast emptiness but each neuron independently firing away, yet still in sync with the overall timing. Would it mean that there is a feeling mind operating in an extremely diffuse sense? It would imply that such a thing might be found already. Imagine if we were able to select an active neuron from the brain each and every person on earth, and say the aggregate activity of all of these disparate neurons forms yet another neuronal network – a global network that is *feeling* something, simply because these neurons, though unconnected, happen to be firing with the right timing.

In arguing against the functionalist approach, Ned Block (1981) proposed the situation where a billion Chinese people were all instructed to function like a brain just for an hour. He argued that the nation as a whole would not have the same qualitative experiences that a normal conscious brain would have, because *intuitively* it just didn't seem possible. But intuitions can sometimes be misleading, as Chalmers pointed out in countering Block's argument. Chalmers argued that a collection of billions of non-conscious neurons also on this intuitive account would not be conscious either, yet in a functioning brain such a collection is.

Block's Chinese nation still had some form of connection between the functional elements – everyone was given a two-way radio to send and receive instructions with others. In our dissociated case, Chalmers would have to agree that the dissociated brain is *not* conscious, but not for intuitive reasons. He would argue it is because the causal structure is not the same as brain in its usual, highly connected state, and causal structure is the key notion in his approach. But if every cause can be pre-empted why, apart from the plasticity aspect, is this an argument against attributing consciousness to a swarm of individual actions? What is so special — what is so *mentally* special — about cause in this case? If one billiard ball hits another ball it is a purely physical event, and there is not the slightest mental aspect to it. If one neuron was to fire and in this firing causes another neuron to fire, what is so mentally special about that causal connection, as it too is open to causal substitution or pre-emption?

If we are to argue for the functionalist approach, and argue for functional organisation and causal structure as the key to understanding consciousness, then we need to say what is so mentally special about efficient and transeunt causes. These causes are physical causes that transmit or give rise to physical effects. If we were to ask what character does an effect inherit from its cause, we can only reply by talking about the physical character of both events. We would have to extend our notion of causal inheritance if we want to include mental character, but the analysis of the system from the beginning offers no scope for this.

If we lived in an earlier era, in a culture committed to beliefs in pneuma or animal spirits, then we may consider consciousness to be like some sort of juice, or some ghostly matter that is squeezed along the neural connections. May be this essence would change its character as it travelled through more and more connections. It would extend our simple notions of causal inheritance but not in the way we would want to accept today. Such a belief would most likely commit us to highlighting the importance of casual connections as the vehicle for consciousness, but we have long given up on a substance dualism of this type.

If nothing more can be said about causation, or rather if nothing more can be said about the type of causal analysis we traditionally apply to these problems, then some form of eliminativism may be the only answer. If we cannot say why causal structure is the important thing, not just for some physical aspects, but for the mental aspects of a complex system, then we would have to admit to an ignorance in our understanding of cause, or be forced to conclude that there is no mind in any situation to speak of. That is, not only is there no feeling of pain in the dissociated system, but consciousness is a myth in a natural system in any case. But beware, there is no room here for a half-baked eliminativism, which most versions of the doctrine inevitably turn out to be. A pure and absolute form of eliminativism would be the only option. There is room to say that a certain machine gives the *illusion* of being conscious, for this illusion is being interpreted by a human observer. But is it a case of the pot calling the kettle black to then say the human observer has an illusionary consciousness also? There is no room to say my *own* consciousness is an illusion, for we have then to explain the illusion, and explain why I am *conscious of* my own consciousness being an illusion. The illusion argument just becomes an infinite regress.

It would be hard to find any mental aspect attached to a simple computational process. Two or more computational processes taken together would also lack anything of the sort. With a reductive form of functionalism we at best are able to write a computer program that may *appear* to be intelligent, may *appear* to hold a conversation, and may pass a couple of Turing Tests, but this of course says nothing about the reality of meaning and the actuality of raw feels. It is just like the fact that computers appear to do simple arithmetic, but of course they don't *understand* simple arithmetic. If we start the analysis with mechanistic assumptions with the emphasis on functional organisation, then eliminativism—and eliminativism in its most extreme form—is the most consistent outcome. It is the logical conclusion of the whole reductionist scheme. There is no mind-body problem it is just a body-body problem. The explanatory gap is the gap between explanations applied to simple bodies as opposed to those applying to highly complex bodies.

But here, many are uncomfortable. Something seems to have got lost in the process. This conclusion seems extreme—it just doesn't *feel* right, for it is *feelings* that have disappeared.

*Option Two — The Counterintuitive Answer:*
*The dissociated system feels the pain*

So let us look at some arguments that may indeed *support* the idea that this unconnected ensemble of neurons, taken as a whole, feels the pain.

Apart from the obvious difference in their causal connections, the natural system and the dissociated one are in other ways quite similar. Let us ignore the case where the neurons are spread out and dispersed all across the universe, but instead are maintained in their usual position in the brain. So each disconnected neuron is physically sitting in its usual place, and each fires with the same timing and with the same characteristic 'waveform' as it did before. In active natural brains we know that neurons produce weak electromagnetic fields — measured as electroencephalograms (EEG) and magnetoencephalograms (MEG). This is because each neuron is a little EM dipole and in detecting and measuring the EEGs and MEGs of the system we are measuring the aggregate electromagnetic fields.

Now in the dissociated brain, with each neuron buzzing away just as it did in the natural case, we would expect the resulting electromagnetic fields to be the same. (We have of course constructed our little artificial stimulators with shielding so they do not contribute any extraneous EM fields themselves.) So *physically* there are many characteristics that are the same in both cases, we just need remember that the flexibility or plasticity is not present in the dissociated case as it is in the natural case. We could remind ourselves also of the Mexican Wave illustration too — the physical features with respect to the wave were the same in both cases. We concluded that it was more the activity of each of the participants that was the important thing for creating the Mexican Wave, while the causal connections were important for the plasticity of the system.

We may speculate then, that just as there are physical characteristics that are common to both systems, the mental characteristics may also follow suit. There are certain commonly proposed solutions to the mind-body problem may be candidates here. For instance if we argue for a representationalist theory of mind, we can easily find the same representations in the dissociated case as we do in the natural case. If network 'N62834' in the visual system is activated in a certain way when the subject sees their grandmother, and so is part of the representation of that perception, then it remains a representation in both the connected and dissociated cases. Even if it is argued that such representations are too direct, and that our chosen network is part of virtual machine supporting rather more indirect representations, the argument would still apply. Some researchers argue that we should be looking for virtual machine consciousness rather than machine consciousness — see for instance Sloman and Chrisley (2003) — but our thought experiment and its questions in conclusion can still be asked with respect to these systems also.

If we want to talk about consciousness being more specifically a matter of information processing, then information states, too, could be found equivalently in both systems. The two theories, representational and informational, are of course one and the same if we are promoting a computational view of the mind. In general if we adhere to the principle that the brain is the hardware and the mind is the software, then we may easily lean toward the idea that the dissociated brain feels the pain just as the natural one would.

But, and we may be again relying on an argument from intuition; *where* are the qualia? Where do the raw feels sit? — if that is a reasonable question. To take up this option we are inevitably forced to admit a kind of non-reductive functionalism. Is it the case that each neuron has a little bit of consciousness — an elemental bit of qualia — that somehow is compounded or aggregated so that the system as a whole feels the jab-in-the-finger pain? This 'as-a-whole' argument reminds one of the systems reply to Searle's Chinese Room — where it was claimed that while the person in the room might not understand Chinese, the room as a whole would understand Chinese. It is an equally strange response, for what parts of the room are important to understanding? Where do we draw the boundary on what is within the whole and what is not? Are 'wholes' merely that because they are conventionally so; that they are simply named as such? And how does each piece of the Chinese Room contribute to the room's ability to understand? For someone outside the room observing what is happening may come to the conclusion that the room understands Chinese because it simply *behaves* that way, but the important question is what is really going on as seen from the inside. Our fragmented brain might look like it is performing as it normally would, and it still has the same EEGs and MEGs as before, but the important question is; what is that brain *really* feeling? This could be taken as a variation of the zombie argument — the brain seems to be operating normally but is anyone home?

The question of causal inheritance arises again if we could take a simple panpsychic view. Let us speculate that each little neuron has a tiny, tiny bit of conscious which contributes to the consciousness of the whole, much like the fact that each neuron is a tiny, tiny electromagnetic dipole that contributes to the EEG and MEG signals of the whole brain. But then how would these little bits of consciousness combine together unless they were in some way like fields, akin to electromagnetic fields? As consciousness is to do with an inner life, how would a host of little inner lives form a coordinated ensemble that has a greater inner life in itself, if there was no way of connecting these inner lives together? William James saw this point long ago illustrating it with a nice thought experiment:

> Take a sentence of a dozen words, and take twelve men and tell to each one word. Then stand the men in a row or jam them in a

bunch, and let each think of his word as intently as he will;
nowhere will there be a consciousness of the whole sentence
(James, 1890, p. 160).

Of course we *may* argue that our dissociated brain feels the pain as it
takes only one cell to do the feeling. James's argument need not come
into play, but this is to revive the 'grandmother cell' theory, where a '
'grandmother cell' is a hypothetical neuron that responds only to a
highly complex, specific, and meaningful stimulus, such as the
image of one's grandmother' (Gross, 2002). Such a theory then
requires us to say how consciousness arises in a single neuron. But
our task to answer the overall mind-body question is merely shifted
to a lower physical or biological level and would no doubt remain
unsolved.

## Conclusion

I have deliberately not sided with one answer or other to the thought
experiment in order to highlight the dilemma. I have found opinions
of others to be quite divided in response to this problem, and this
was much to my surprise. I was able to gauge some of these
responses first when I presented this as a short talk to a conference
audience at the United Nations University in Tokyo in May 1999,
and then as a poster at a Tucson conference in April 2000, but most
from private conversations with philosophical colleagues.

There are, I realise, many additions and variations that can be
made with the experiment. For brevity I have only looked at whether
the dissociated brain felt the pain or not, and did not consider the
case that it may only partially feel it, or posses a different feeling all
together. I did not consider in detail the question as to whether consciousness dimmed as neurons were being gradually dissociated, or
whether a loss of consciousness occurred all of a sudden at one 'tip-
ping point'.

I have not considered regarding neurons themselves as tiny little
networks, so that the brain is a network of networks and so on. Again
the question would be whether the neuron as a causal network is the
important thing for its support for the consciousness of the whole
mind, or whether it is the activity of certain sub-cellular parts.

My main aim in presenting this thought experiment is to highlight
the different and opposing conclusions to a problem that begins
with certain simple mechanistic and functionalistic assumptions.

Either we say there is no mind in the dissociative case, but we then
have to say what is so special about our traditional notions of physi-

cal cause, or there again we could simply embrace eliminativism. Or, we say that mind is still present in the dissociative case, but we then have to say how the many become one, or avoid that problem by simply embracing a dualist alternative.

If we are want to avoid becoming either eliminativists or dualists, then the only option is to seriously question our initial assumptions about the nature of matter, structure and cause.[2]

## References

Aleksander, Igor (2000) *How to Build a Mind* London: Weidenfeld & Nicholson.

Block, N. (1981). 'Troubles with Functionalism'. In (Block, ed.) *Readings in the Philosophy of Psychology*, Volume 1. Cambridge, MA: Harvard University Press.

Chalmers, David J. (1993) A *Computational Foundation for the Study of Cognition*. http://cogprints.org/319/00/computation.html

Chalmers, David J. (1995) 'Absent Qualia, Fading Qualia, Dancing Qualia,' in Metzinger, Thomas, Eds. *Conscious Experience*, chapter 15, pp. 309–328. Schoningh/Imprint Academic.

Chalmers, David J. (1996) *The Conscious Mind* Oxford: Oxford University Press.

Edelman, Gerald M. and Giulio Tononi (2000) *A Universe of Consciousness: How Matter Becomes Imagination*. New York: Basic Books.

Farkas, I and D. Helbing, T. Vicsek, (2002), 'Mexican waves in an excitable medium.' *Nature* 419, 131–132. Also see http://angel.elte.hu/ wave/

Freedman, David H. (1994) 'Bringing Up RoboBaby,' *Wired*, Issue 2.12, Dec. 1994 p 78.

Ganeri, Jonardon, Paul Noordhof, and Murali Ramachandran. (1996) 'Counterfactuals and Preemptive Causation' *Analysis* 56(4): 219–225.

Gross C. G. 'Genealogy of the 'grandmother cell'' *Neuroscientist* 2002 Oct;8 (5):512–8.

Harnard, S. (1990), 'The symbol grounding problem.' *Physica D*, 42:335–346, 1990.

James, William (1890) *Principles of Psychology*.

James, William (1907) *Pragmatism* New York: Longmans, Green.

Johnson, W. E. (1924) *Logic*: Part III, Cambridge University Press.

Kim, J. (1992) 'Multiple realization and the metaphysics of reduction.' *Philosophy and Phenomenological Research* 52:1–26.

Maudlin, Tim (1989) 'Computation and Consciousness', *Journal of Philosophy* 86, pp. 407–432.

Rorty, Richard (1967) 'Relations, Internal and External.' in *The Encyclopedia of Philosophy* (v. 7) ed. Paul Edwards, Macmillan and Free Press, pp. 125–133.

---

[2]   I would like to thank Riccardo Manzotti and Tim Bayne for their very helpful comments and suggestions.

Russell, Bertrand, (1911) 'The Basis of Realism' *The Journal of Philosophy, Psychology and Scientific Methods*, Vol. 8, No. 6 (Mar., 1911), pp. 158–161.

Searle, John R. (1980) 'Minds, Brains, and Programs' *The Behavioral and Brain Sciences*, vol. 3.

Searle, John R. (1992). *The Rediscovery of the Mind.* Cambridge, MA: MIT Press.

Sloman, A. and Chrisley, R. (2003) 'Virtual machines and consciousness'. *Journal of Consciousness Studies* **10**:4–5, pp. 133–172.

Whitehead, Alfred North (1926) *Science and the Modern World* Cambridge University Press.

# Index

Note. Both British and American spelling have been used in this volume, but have not been distinguished in the index.

www.ingramcontent.com/pod-product-compliance
Lightning Source LLC
Chambersburg PA
CBHW071105050326
40690CB00008B/1125